D0882552

Prelude to Genocide

PRELUDE TO GENOCIDE

Nazi Ideology and the Struggle for Power

Simon Taylor

ST. MARTIN'S PRESS
New York

© 1985 by Simon Taylor

All rights reserved. For information, write:
St. Martin's Press, Inc., 175 Fifth Avenue, New York, NY 10010
Printed in Great Britain

First published in the United States of America in 1985

ISBN 0-312-63636-9

Library of Congress Cataloging in Publication Data

Taylor, Simon.
    Prelude to genocide.

    Bibliography: p.
    Includes index.
    1. National socialism. 2. Nationalsozialistische
Deutsche Arbeiter-Partei—History. 3. Germany—Politics
and government—1933-1945.   I. Title.
DD256.5.T285 1985   320.5′33   85-10854
ISBN 0-312-63636-9

Contents

Contents

IV. Ideology and Genocide

Plates between pp. 116 and 117

Glossary and abbreviations

AdV	Alldeutscher Verband – Pan German League.
BVP	Bayerische Volkspartei – Bavarian People's Party.
DAF	Deutsche Arbeitsfront – German Labour Front.
DAP	Deutsche Arbeiter Partei – German Workers' Party.
DNVP	Deutschnationale Volkspartei – German National People's Party.
DVP	Deutsche Volkspartei – German People's Party.
DZA	Deutsches Zentralarchiv, Potsdam.
Gau (Gauleiter)	Regional unit of administration of NSDAP (regional leader).
HA/GHH	Historisches Archiv der Gutehoffnungshütte, Oberhausen.
IfZ	Institut für Zeitgeschichte, Munich.
KPD	Kommunistische Partei Deutschlands – German Communist Party.
Landbund	Farmers' Association
Landvolk	'Rural-people': radical peasant protest movement.
Mittelstand (Mittelstandler)	'Middle-estate' or middle class (member of the Mittelstand).
NSBO	Nationalsozialistische Betriebszellenorganisation – National Socialist Factory Cell Organisation.
NSDAP	Nationalsozialistische Deutsche Arbeiterpartei – National Socialist German Workers' Party (Nazi Party).

NS-Hago	Nationalsozialistische Handwerks-, Handels- und Gewerbe-Organisation.
OSAF	Oberster SA-Führer.
RdI	Reichsverband der deutschen Industrie – Confederation of German Industry.
Reichsbanner	Republican para-military organisation.
Reichsnährstand	Reich Food Estate.
SA	Sturmabteilungen – Storm-troops.
SPD	Sozialdemokratische Partei Deutschlands – German Social Democratic Party.
SS	Schutzstaffeln – Protection Squads.
Stahlhelm	Nationalist ex-soldiers league.
Völkischer Beobachter	Major Nazi newspaper.

Acknowledgments

I am pleased to acknowledge the financial assistance that I have received from a number of institutions in carrying out the research for this book. The Social Science Research Council not only financed my postgraduate studies between 1974 and 1977, but has also been generous in providing funds for part of the research that I have carried out in the Federal Republic of Germany. The Department of Sociology at Liverpool University has also suppported this research. I am grateful too for financial support from the British Academy, especially for their sponsorship of my research in the German Democratic Republic, where I was received as a guest of the Academy of Sciences.

It is also a pleasure to thank the staff of the Bayerisches Hauptstaatsarchiv and the Institut für Zeitgeschichte in Munich, the Bundesarchiv in Koblenz and the Deutsches Zentralarchiv in Potsdam for the invaluable assistance that they gave me.

Finally, I would like to thank Nicos Kokosalakis and Gideon Ben-Tovim of the Department of Sociology at Liverpool University, for their help and guidance over a number of years, and Lydia Mertins for her efforts in preparing the final manuscript of this book. But my greatest debt is to my wife, Rhiannon. She has been translator, interpreter and language teacher attached to this project, and recently played a major role in the arrival of our son Stephen, who has enlivened many a late-night hour when I have been working on the final stages of this book.

S.T.

Introduction

My initial intention was to limit this book to an analysis of the development of Nazi ideology from the founding of the NSDAP (as the German Workers' Party) in 1919 to the Nazi seizure of power in 1933. However, the very nature of this task has forced me to make a wider appraisal of the significance of ideology for the historical development of German fascism. The title of the book: *Prelude to Genocide: Nazi Ideology and the Struggle for Power,* therefore identifies three separate but inter-related questions.

First, what was the ideology of German fascism during the Kampfzeit (the 'period of struggle' from 1919 to 1933)? Secondly, did the *political struggle* for power determine and mould this ideology, and how did the seizure of power affect this process? And thirdly, to what extent was Nazi genocide – specifically the extermination of European Jewry – determined by the ideology of National Socialism as it evolved during the Kampfzeit? The structure of this book reflects the way in which I have sought to answer these three questions.

Part I is concerned mainly with the development of Nazi ideology. Chapter 1 examines the intellectual origins of German fascism in the Kaiser Reich and the social basis of National Socialism under Weimar. It draws together a number of historical threads to provide an introduction to Chapter 2, which reproduces an extensive selection of translated NSDAP propaganda posters and election leaflets, chosen to illustrate the evolution of Nazi ideology and the development of Nazi anti-Semitism between 1919 and 1933.

Part II examines the struggle for control of the NSDAP's ideological direction, and looks at how the party constructed its 'appeal' and consolidated its following. The role of the Nazi radicals and their influence upon the political ideology of National Socialism is discussed in Chapter 3. Chapter 4 analyses the links between the Nazi party and big business which made possible the seizure of power, and specifies how Hitler's accomodation with the demands of industrialists and the conservative establishment determined the NSDAP's interpretation of 'national socialism'. Chapter 5 analyses in detail the appeal of Nazi ideology for different sectors of German society, making frequent reference to the examples of Nazi propaganda given in Chapter 2. Chapter 5 also looks at how National Socialism exploited the weakness of Weimar democracy and endemic economic crisis to create a Nazi eschatology, which reduced social reality to a death-struggle between the competing forces of *Germantum* and *Judentum*: German and Jew.

Part III deals with the *rupture* between the ideology and the social basis of the NSDAP during the Kampfzeit, and the nature of the Nazi state in the aftermath of the seizure of power. Chapter 6 documents the betrayal of the NSDAP's Mittelstand-politik; Chapter 7 explores the significance of ritual and symbol for National Socialism, and examines the methods of ideological control developed by the Nazi state.

Finally Part IV assesses the importance of our analysis for a wider understanding of German fascism. Chapter 8 offers a critique of the role of ideology in the interpretation of German fascism; Chapter 9 analyses the 'genocidal logic' of Nazi ideology, and traces the origins of the Final Solution to the political racism developed by the NSDAP during the struggle for power.

This book is not meant simply as a contribution to academic historiography. I began the research for it ten years ago, by asking the simple question, 'How did it happen?' What provoked the massacre of six million human beings because they were Jewish? That is not an academic question, nor is genocide a thing of the past. Nazism and racism did not perish with Hitler and the Third Reich – they are still potent ideologies today.

As his books were burnt by the Nazis on 1 May 1933, the German dramatist Ernst Toller asked in despair:

> What has mankind learned from suffering and sacrifice, from catastrophe and despair ...

The answer today, as then, is 'Nothing'.

PART I

The Origins
and Development of
Nazi Ideology

CHAPTER ONE

From the Kaiser to the Fuhrer

According to Seymour Lipset, the archetypal voter who gave his support to the NSDAP in 1932 was

> a self-employed, Protestant member of the middle class, who lived either on a farm or in a small rural community, and who had previously voted for a party of the political centre or for a regional party which opposed the power and influence of large-scale industry and the trade unions.[1]

The notion that National Socialism was essentially a movement of the German middle classes or Mittelstand was advanced by a number of socialist commentators during the 1920s, empirically verified by Loomis and Beegle, Heberle, and Pratt immediately after the War, and has since been confirmed by Alexander Weber.[2] Later in this chapter we shall look in detail at the social composition of the Mittelstand during the Weimar era. First, however, we must trace the historical origins of the German Mittelstand in order to be able to understand the nature of National Socialism's appeal after 1918.

The formation of the German Mittelstand

During the Middle Ages the states which were later to form the German nation were among the most advanced in Europe. In a

[1] S.M. Lipset, 'Der Faschismus, die Linke, die Recht und die Mitte', in Ernst Nolte, *Theorien über den Faschismus*, Köln 1967, p.463.

[2] C. Loomis & J. Beegle, 'The spread of Nazism in rural areas', *American Sociological Review* 11 (1946), pp. 729ff. R. Heberle, *From Democracy to Nazism*, Louisiana 1945. S. Pratt, *The Social Basis of Nazism and Communism in Urban Germany*, MA thesis, Michigan State University 1948. A. Weber, *Soziale Merkmale der NSDAP-Wähler*, PhD thesis, Freiburg 1969.

number of regions, such as the Rhineland, northern Bavaria and the Hanseatic ports, a commercial mercantile class evolved which even in the late fifteenth century was attempting to shake off the ideological shackles of the church and challenge the political power of the feudal aristocracy. But the discovery of the New World and the opening of the sea routes to Africa and India switched the centre of European commercial activity from the North Sea and the Mediterranean to the states bordering the Atlantic Ocean, and led to the stagnation of the economy of central Europe.

In 1529 the German Peasant Wars (Bauernkrieg) ended with the defeat of the small farmers and artisans. The victorious nobility consolidated the power of agrarian feudalism and the church crushed the secular aspirations of the merchants. While in England and France a strong central power was imposing political unity upon a number of feudal principalities, the failure to attain a German nation-state perpetuated political instability in central Europe. During the seventeenth century the Thirty Years War (1618-1648) destroyed the economic infrastructure of many of the Germanic states and laid the countryside waste. The Westfälische Peace Agreement of 1648 merely prolonged their economic backwardness by splitting central Europe into some two thousand independent political units under the influence of 350 major principalities.

So compared with Britain and France, the German bourgeoisie was economically feeble and politically immature. Manufacture took place under licence from the feudal oligarchies and was in turn regulated by the artisan guilds. All aspects of production and distribution were rigorously controlled. In the larger states there were guilds of button-makers, stocking-makers and belt-makers who jealously guarded their trade: competition was forbidden by law. Each state levied its own taxes and imposed tolls upon imported goods, and although it filled the coffers of the aristocracy, this system effectively prevented the establishment of any national market. Thus the mercantile bourgeoisie remained economically and ideologically *petite*. Production was centred upon small semi-autarkic units, while the doctrine and practice of the absolute state suppressed the first stirrings of a democratic consciousness. Democracy, liberalism and the teachings of the enlightenment remained largely 'foreign' to the petite bourgeoisie's experience. Only in the larger, more economically advanced states, did any liberal intellectual strata emerge before the beginning of the nineteenth century.

Liberalism arrived in Germany in the form of the armies of the French Republic and Napoleon Bonaparte, and survived only until Napoleon's downfall. Under French patronage it enjoyed a brief flowering, but the stigma of national occupation proved a powerful psychological weapon in the hands of the traditional ruling classes. 'German' resistance gathered under the flag of the king of Prussia and national liberation finally came about through the force of Prussian arms. As a result of this, the feudal oligarchies successfully discredited the *ideals* of liberal democracy by associating its *practice* with the humiliation of French occupation. At the Vienna Congress of 1815 a weak confederation of German states was established, but it was held together solely by the mutual antagonism of Austria and Prussia. Indeed Germany was effectively 'recreated' in the image of the pre-revolutionary era, with the absolutist position of the monarchy re-established. Demands for democracy were rejected as indications of a 'destructive modern spirit', and increasingly the aristocracy responded to attacks upon its absolute authority with wide ranging censorship and, where necessary, vicious physical repression based upon military courts.

In the 1840s a wave of political unrest spread across the German states as the pressure for political reform fused with social conflicts set off by the first stages of industrialisation. In 1844 an uprising of impoverished handloom weavers was bloodily suppressed. Four years later the first attempts to create a liberal national assembly based upon a democratic constitution came to grief on the bayonets of the state militias and the Prussian army. The failure of the 1848 Revolution had a profound effect upon petit bourgeois thinking. For the first time the issues of liberalisation and unification became separated. As one 'revolutionary' activist who had taken part in the 1848 Revolution stated:

> Next to the question of achieving national unity, I am indifferent to whether despotism or constitutionalism, Junker or democrat [rules] if it is within a single German nation.[3]

---

[3] *Fragen an die deutsche Geschichte*, Stuggart 1974, p.65.

The power-house of German industrialisation was the state of Prussia, for despite its feudal political institutions the Prussian Kaiser instigated a liberal *economic* politik which satisfied many of the demands of the rising industrial bourgeoisie. With the accession of the arch-reactionary Bismarck to the chancellorship in 1862, however, it seemed as if a renewed confrontation between feudalism and mercantile liberalism was inevitable. But Bismarck successfully traded off the economic benefits of an expansionist foreign policy in return for the support of the bourgeoisie in holding back democracy and preventing the introduction of parliamentary government. In 1863 the (liberal) Progressive Party announced that it was in favour of a limited (property-based) franchise rather than universal suffrage; Bismarck had in effect driven a wedge between the petite bourgeoisie and the newly emerging proletariat. Working-class radicals left the arena of liberal politics and set out to found a class-conscious proletarian party, which later emerged in Ferdinand Lassalle's German Workers' League. This split among the forces opposing the absolute state in the nineteenth century was an event of major significance for the development of Germany in the twentieth century. For at the point when the German petite bourgeoisie began to demand a more fundamental role in the government of the state, a politically self-conscious proletariat with democratic and socialist aims was emerging as a force in German society.

Bismarck's repressive internal policies were balanced by notable foreign policy successes. Victory over Austria prepared the way for the reunification of Germany 'from above', under Prussian leadership. Finally, in 1871, with the German states unified by a popular and ultimately victorious war against France, the Second German Reich was called into being by the Prussian Kaiser at a splendid victory ceremony in Versailles.

This Kaiser-Reich was acclaimed as the achievement of the long awaited German nation-state. But set against the aims of the 1848 Revolution, which had attempted to achieve 'unity through freedom' and to create the foundations of a modern democratic state, the forging of a German nation through military might was a significant defeat for bourgeois liberalism. It was not the principle of parliamentary sovereignty that had been victorious but the Prussian model of 'rule over the parties'; it was not the petite bourgeoisie who had won influence, but the Prussian Junker landowners and their allies. Bismarck instituted a national dictatorship whose internal policies were directed primarily against the Catholic minority and the working-class majority. In this he gained the support of the 'national-liberals', who above all feared the 'red anarchy' of the Social Democratic Party, whose influence was growing in the wake of the 1873 economic recession.

But even this short-lived accord between national-liberalism and the absolute state broke down in 1879, when a second wave of political counter-revolution broke upon the new nation. Because of the demands of heavy industry and agriculture the policy of free trade was abolished in favour of state protectionism; it was a policy that hit the small producers hard, while tax increases cut back the purchasing power of the working class. Bismarck's response to popular unrest was to create a paternalist state which hid the iron fist of dictatorship in the velvet glove of 'social welfare'.

Even after the demise of Bismarck the ruling oligarchy attempted to continue his strategy of suppressing internal political conflict through foreign policy adventures. Under Kaiser Wilhelm II Germany tried to break out from the confines of Europe into a *Weltpolitik* – to create a colonial empire to rival that of the other major imperial powers.

But Germany arrived late at the feast; England, France and Russia had already carved up the world. In attempting to capture its own colonial markets Germany soon found itself isolated. The massive industrial capacity of the German Reich could not find sufficient outlets, and it was the attempt to overcome this economic and political contradiction that led to the drive for European hegemony and to the outbreak of the First World War.[4]

The intellectual origins of National Socialism

As Reinhard Kühnl has observed:

> The ideological elements which fascism was later to accentuate were already present in the Kaiser-Reich. Nationalism and racism, authoritarianism and militarism, were popularised through mass organisations such as Soldiers' Leagues, Colonial and Navy Clubs,

[4] For Germany's war aims, see Simon Taylor, *Germany 1918-1933, Revolution, Counter Revolution and the Rise of Hitler*, London 1983, p.3.

the Pan German League and the Gymnastic clubs, as well as by the school system.[5]

In fact it is possible to trace most of the ideological motifs of National Socialism to the ideas of the German Romantics and their disciples in the mid-nineteenth century. Their theories made an indelible impression upon a whole generation, and inspired in the *völkisch* movement a mode of conservative thought which proved to be a fertile seedbed for the growth of petit bourgeois radicalism in the twentieth century.[6]

Among the early formulators of what George Mosse has called the 'German Ideology' were Paul de Lagarde, Guido von List, Alfred Schuler and above all Julius Langbehn.[7] They were not so much original thinkers as synthesisers of popular beliefs and conservative doctrines. But their multifarious ideologies did have a common theme – how was the transformation of Germany from a neo-feudal collection of principalities to a nation-state to be achieved without an inevitable disintegration of 'traditional' culture? More pragmatically, how could the transition from a rural, agricultural artisan economy to a modern industrial state be achieved without the extinction of the archaic German Mittelstand?

From about the middle of the nineteenth century bourgeois and petit bourgeois intellectuals wrestled with the problems of the nation state and the consequences of German unification. In opposition to the principles of liberalism and rationalism the German Romantic Movement attempted to 'hold back' the social and political effects of industrial capitalism, while at the same time eulogising the notions of national unity and social cohesion. The Romantics looked back to a state of nature in which the social unit was characterised by personal inequality and patriarchal order – a 'golden age' which could be set against the modern disruptive machine age in which man's ties with the earth were dissolved and he lived in a state of spiritual poverty and social isolation.

[5] R. Kühnl, *Faschismustheorien*, Hamburg 1979, p.73.

[6] The word *Volk* (adjective *völkisch*) is a particularly Germanic concept, meaning not only a people but also a racial entity. It was believed that a transcendental 'essence' united the members of a Volk. This 'essence' may be variously defined as 'nature', 'blood', or mythos, but it was always linked to the concept of a common creativity which bound the individual to the culture and the heritage of his people.

[7] See G. Mosse, *The Crisis of German Ideology*, London 1966.

In his book *Rembrandt as an Educator*, Langbehn summarised the common aim of all Romantics as being to 'transform Germans into artists'. He claimed that the enriching power of nature was in conflict with the cultural aridity of the town and city, which threatened the purity of the soul with its insistence upon 'rationality' and 'materialism'. The central importance of the soul in Romantic ideology is accounted for by the fact that the 'cosmic life force is to be found in man's soul', and it was alienation from this cosmic life force that the Romantics feared most. Since the cosmic life force could only be liberated by man's interaction with nature, it was a short step to the romanticising of the German landscape and a revival of the Earth Cult. Of course, given the backward-looking ethic implicit in Romanticism, the glorification of the peasant was also a common theme, which Langbehn summoned up by suggesting that 'it is the peasant who actually owns a piece of land, and has a direct relationship with the centre of the earth. Through this he becomes master of the universe.'[8]

During the late nineteenth century occultism and spiritualism enjoyed something of a vogue throughout Europe, and in Germany the cult of Theosophy was particularly strong. Theosophy focused upon the inheritance of 'life-forces' and 'cosmic energy', which its supporters claimed were carried in the blood of a people (*Volk*) or tribe. For the Romantics this 'discovery' was of principal importance, because the loss of 'cosmic energy' could now be traced to the dissolution of tribal unity and the estrangement of man from his native soil. The hereditary leader or monarch was also a product of this 'blood-force', for the monarch not only represented the summit of the political hierarchy, but also 'embodied the essence of the tribe', thereby guaranteeing its social cohesion.

Langbehn did not confine himself to writing metaphysical monographs. He translated his ideas into a specific programme for the German Volk. He believed that it was essential to found an organic state which would recognise no difference of interest between Junker, bourgeoisie or proletariat. Instead the whole Volk would be bound together in a bond of common creativity and brotherhood. Yet Langbehn did not suppose that classes should be

---

[8] Julius Langbehn, *Rembrandt als Erzieher*, Leipzig 1900, p.178. 'The good farmer sits like a king in his court.'

abolished, for he considered inequality to be consistent with the 'state of nature'. 'Equality is death', he maintained, 'a corporate state is life'.[9] Published in 1900, Langbehn's programme represents the transition from Romantic ideology and the idealisation of the past to a politically motivated conservative doctrine. In turn the emphasis of German Romanticism turned from the 'idea' to the 'deed'.

The dawn of the new century seemed to galvanise the völkisch sects into activity – a struggle to the death with the forces of modernity seemed inevitable! In particular the need to transform theory into practice prompted a renewed outburst of activity among conservative thinkers, who now focused upon the value of 'struggle' in the process of 'creating artists'. Force thus became a legitimate weapon in the defence of the 'old ways' against the materialist onslaught. War and battle were lauded as the crucible of artistic creativity. Moreover the forces of modernity were identified and crystallised; the Jew, creature of urbanism and arid materialism, had infiltrated the German homeland, while Marxism and rationalism had taken hold of the proletarian masses in their stronghold of Berlin.

Another doctrine that völkisch thinkers considered to be in need of reinterpretation was Christianity. Paul de Lagarde 'discovered' that the course of Christianity was being plotted and controlled by a force unerringly hostile to the Aryan race. 'True Christianity' had apparently been subverted by the Jew Paul, and over time this Jewish-Christianity had joined forces with other poisonous ideologies in a conspiracy designed to subvert the natural racial purity of the German Volk. Lagarde claimed that the course of this conspiracy was outlined in the Protocols of the Elders of Zion. In his mind this 'plan for Jewish domination' (in fact the Protocols were a notorious anti-Semitic forgery) became associated with a Catholic-Jesuit conspiracy to undermine the nation.[10] In a similar vein Langbehn attempted to synthesise the images of warrior and Christ, suggesting that all Germans should take up their swords against their worldly enemies just as the Germanic bishops had done in the Middle Ages. But it was Houston Steward Chamberlain, an

[9] ibid., p.224.
[10] See Paul de Lagarde, 'Religion der Zukunft', *Deutsche Schriften*, Göttingen 1892, pp. 217ff.

eccentric Englishman, who provided the most lasting stereotype of the Aryan Christ struggling to free himself from the confines of rabbinical doctrine. And Chamberlain's work, *The Foundations of the Nineteenth Century* (published in 1899) was to become a standard text during the Third Reich.

In attempting to translate their philosophical and ideological notions into pragmatic policies the völkisch intellectuals were forced to rethink the elitist attitudes of the Romantics and to reject their anti-political image. But the task was inherently contradictory. A corporate *Volksstaat* might be attractive to the conservative petite bourgeoisie, but it would have little appeal for the upper classes and the imperial oligarchy. The alternative was some sort of accommodation with the working classes, but this would be culturally and politically unacceptable to most of the middle classes, for the spectre of socialism was never far behind the promise of democracy. Essentially the petite bourgeoisie was in a cleft stick. Too great an identification with the Kaiser-Reich left them in a predicament in which they were denied effective political power to protect their economic interests against the encroachment of modern industry and gradual rationalisation. But only the absolute state seemed to be capable of holding down the pressure of working-class organisation and thus protecting the petite bourgeoisie from political extinction through socialism.

The Youth Movement

Ernst Weymar's analysis of nineteenth-century school text-books demonstrates the degree to which völkisch thought had infiltrated and been consolidated within the educational establishment before 1914.[11] Secondary school-books eulogised the 'destiny of the Volk', often associating it with a resurgence of German imperialism. The trend towards modernity, whether in the sciences or the arts, was condemned as an indication of moral decay, while the 'spirit' of the Teuton during the Dark Ages was upheld as a model for future generations. The country boarding schools in particular played an early role in institutionalising many aspects of romantic and völkisch doctrine. These schools, founded at the end of the nineteenth

---

[11] Ernst Weymar, *Das Selbstverständnis der Deutschen*, Stuttgart 1961.

century by Hermann Lietz, were to train many of the leaders of the Wandervögel (wandering birds) before the war, and later of the Hitler Youth.

Lietz himself stressed that academic learning should take second place to the building of racial character which could be strengthened through 'contact with the landscape of the fatherland' and knowledge of Teutonic culture. Lietz believed that his system would eventually create an aristocracy of men who would turn back the tide of materialism and 'take up the fight against the dark instincts of the masses'. And although in terms of the traditional völkisch movement the country boarding schools failed to answer the needs of the moment, they helped trigger a revival of romanticism among young people in the early twentieth century, and in the process made the Wandervögel a household name.

The Wandervögel was initially a single organisation set up in 1901 by Karl Fischer at Steglitz. However, largely because of the institutionalisation of a strong Fuhrer (leadership) principle which Fischer encouraged, the movement fragmented into a plethora of groupings and regroupings, each with its own rigid hierarchy and each sharing to a lesser or greater degree the ideological characteristics which were the hallmark of the German Youth Movement.

From a handful of members in 1901 the Wandervögel grew to a movement of 15,000 by 1911 and perhaps some 25,000 by 1914. Excursions into the German countryside and an aura of nature mysticism were common to all groups, although, as George Mosse notes, it is difficult to assess when the movement became truly völkisch. Implicit in the whole organisation was a spirit of rebellion against what was perceived as the 'sterility' of comfortable bourgeois society, allied to a radical conservatism which romanticised the 'natural social bonds' of the past.

For the first time the völkisch movement saw its own elitist ideas given expression in a popular mass movement. The mobilisation of youth under strong 'natural' leadership appeared as an alternative both to the Marxist cadre principle (which gave too much prominence to ideological purity) and to liberal bourgeois notions of democracy.

Yet for all the excitement and fervour which the Wandervögel generated, the movement remained an essentially petit bourgeois

phenomenon. Upper-class youth preferred their elitist duelling clubs
and student fraternities, while proletarian youth organised almost
exclusively in Social Democrat-led organisations. Furthermore the
Wandervögel became embroiled in controversy over the principle of
admitting Jews to their activities. Naturally anti-Semitism was a
latent tendency in the völkisch Youth Movement, but Karl Fischer
for instance viewed the Jews as a separate but equal Volk who should
·organise on the basis of their 'innate' racial feelings. By 1914,
however, the Wandervögel displayed an anti-Semitism typical of the
völkisch movement, viewing the Jews as the embodiment of the
forces of modernity, and believing the 'collapse of German culture' to
be the result of a Semitic racial conspiracy.

So the most fundamental consequence of the late development of
the German state was the consolidation of profoundly reactionary
forms of political consciousness among the non-proletarian sectors of
imperial society. Whether it was the aristocratic absolutism of the
ruling class, or the conservative or völkisch doctrine of the
Mittelstand, the Kaiser-Reich was characterised by authoritarianism and a particularly rabid form of anti-socialism. Lukács has
identified the origins of this ideological tendency:

> ... underdeveloped as German capitalism was in the mid-nineteenth
> century, it was no longer confronted by formless social masses, as the
> French bourgeoisie had been before the great revolution ... indeed it
> was confronted by a modern, if still undeveloped proletariat. This
> difference is most apparent if we remember that in France, Gracchus
> Babeuf lead an uprising with conscious socialist aims some years *after*
> the execution of Robespierre, while in Germany the Silesian Weavers'
> uprising broke out four years *before* the 1848 Revolution. Further, that
> on the very eve of this (liberal) Revolution, the first perfected
> formulation of the ideology of the revolutionary proletariat appeared –
> the Communist Manifesto.[12]

So in Germany the emerging proletariat began its struggle for
political representation just as the progressive bourgeoisie was
beginning its own democratic-liberal assault upon the absolute state.
In England and France the bourgeoisie had already attained and
consolidated its own revolution and created a bourgeois democratic

---

[12] Georg Lukács, *Die Zerstörung der Vernunft*, Neuwied 1962, pp. 48ff.

state *before* being confronted with the political demands of a class-conscious proletariat.

Having failed to achieve 'unity through freedom', the German bourgeoisie had to accept 'unity before freedom' through the Prussianisation of the German states. And once unification had been achieved the petite bourgeoisie could carry through a liberal democratisation of the imperial state (even presuming it could be achieved) only at the risk of being overwhelmed by the growing power of the working classes and Social Democracy.

The absolute state held back the proletarian threat through a limitation of the franchise and a three-class voting system in Prussia; through the denial of parliamentary government and, where necessary, through direct physical repression. The absolute state also offered a degree of economic protection to the German Mittelstand – it organised the cartel system of production and distribution, and denied unfettered free competition. Such a system, however, was dependent upon an equilibrium between market expansion and productive expansion. Once the rate of economic reproduction *overtook* the possibilities of internal or colonial expansion, a contradiction would rapidly intensify which could have only two possible results. Either the market for German capitalism would have to be massively enlarged to take account of its reproductive capabilities, or else an internal *Konkurrenz Kampf* (competitive war) would wipe out the excess capacity within the economy. In such a case the Mittelstand – the peasants, the handicraft workers and the small businessmen – would be economically annihilated by the modern rational production methods of heavy industry and high finance.

Ironically it was the war-economy which first exposed the Mittelstand to the harrowing effects of economic rationalisation, for the failure of the German military to secure a speedy victory led to the institutionalisation of an economic system geared to armaments production at the expense of consumer goods.[13] As small businesses collapsed through shortages of markets and raw materials, and the production capacity of heavy industry increased two- or three-fold, a radicalisation of the German Mittelstand took place. Initially,

---

[13] For details of the effects of the war upon the German economy, see R. Kühnl, *Die deutsche Revolution 1918/1919. Quellen und Dokumente*, Köln 1979, pp. 33ff.

however, it was far from clear what political direction this radicalisation would take.

The Pan-German League (Alldeutscher Verband)

Among the various clubs and associations which did so much to popularise völkisch ideals was the Pan-German League. Although only one of a number of mass organisations patronised by the ruling elites of the Kaiser-Reich, the Pan-German League is of particular interest because it illustrates the lines of continuity which link the völkisch leagues of the imperial era to the growth of National Socialism after the First World War.

The Pan-German League was founded in 1890 and rapidly became one of the foremost advocates of an aggressive military imperialism based upon völkisch principles.[14] At first the League displayed the prejudices typical of the völkisch movement – a romantic view of the native landscape, hostility to modern industrial society, and a passion for rural peasant life. But this anti-modernist stance was compromised as funds flowed in from industrialists and aristocrats who were keen to support the League's expansionist policies with hard cash. In 1908 Heinrich Class emerged as the new leader of the Pan-Germans. Class was closely associated with the upper circles of German society, and his influence within the aristocracy and heavy industry was quite considerable. His grand air – he always dressed in top hat and frock coat, and behaved like a Prussian squire – proved especially attractive to the upward striving petite bourgeoisie.

In 1914 Class published a book entitled *If I were the Kaiser* in which he advocated the enforcement of a German dictatorship which would bring about an ideal society founded upon corporate völkisch principles. At the pinnacle of Class's hierarchy was a monarch who wielded absolute power in the name of the community. The only check upon the power of the sovereign was an advisory council, made up of an elite whose qualifications were based upon extensive land ownership and 'service to the state'. The aristocratic element, Class believed, was an essential 'organic-substance' upon which the

---

[14] For the history of the Pan-German League, see A. Kruck, *Geschichte des Alldeutschen Verbandes*, Wiesbaden 1954.

leadership of the Volksstaat must be grounded.

Class was less than forthright, however, when it came to discussing the role of modern industry within the Volksstaat. Here of course he faced the classic dilemma of the völkisch movement, which demanded the means of imperialism but feared the economic consequences of favouring large-scale industry and its baron owners. Class in effect evaded the issue by praising archetypal 'German' entrepreneurs such as Krupp and Kirdorf without endorsing the social developments which were inevitable by-products of modern capitalism. Class's scorn and hatred was reserved for modern finance capital, embodied in the new department stores and the banks, which he saw as agents of exploitation and the representation of a Semitic conspiracy to undermine the health of the Germanic race.

Yet Class's society remained starkly elitist, and it was only in 1917, having been panicked by the dire threat of proletarian revolution, that the Pan-German League attempted to translate its ideals into action by forming an alliance with the German Nationalist Party (DNVP). In effect this alliance sealed the destruction of the Pan-Germans as an effective völkisch movement, for they soon found themselves trapped within the confines of traditional German conservatism. Indeed this served only to illustrate the serious shortcomings of the völkisch movement generally, for it could never bridge the gap between ideological elitism and the political necessity of mobilising mass support.

During 1917 the munition workers' strike and the increasing pressure upon the German military dictatorship (both internally for political reform and externally from the allied armies) spawned a number of pre-fascist mass organisations under the patronage of heavy industry and the east Prussian landowners. Their purpose was to create for the first time a popular mass basis for authoritarian politics – a counter-weight to increasing demands for democratic reform and the growing power of the revolutionary left. Thus the Fatherland Party and the so-called '*Sammlung* (Meeting) Movement' are seen by Friedrich Meinecke as 'an exact prelude for the rise of Hitler'.[15] And the founding of the German Worker and White Collar Staff Party (DAAP) early in 1918, whose political agitation encompassed and fused together anti-Semitism, authoritarianism

---

[15] F. Meinecke, *Die deutsche Katastrophe*, 2nd ed., Wiesbaden 1946, p.50.

and nationalist-imperialism, is seen by Dirk Stegmann as:

> A clear illustration of the break with authoritarian conservatism, and
> the engagement of pre-fascist ideological concepts in order to mobilise
> allies at every opportunity for the retainment of the social, political and
> economic status quo.[16]

The military collapse of the German armies in the summer of 1918
and the crumbling of the imperial state brought Class and the
Pan-Germans to a point where they advocated an openly
manipulative, demagogic approach to the problem of capturing mass
support for reactionary ideals and holding back the wave of
revolution. In a policy note Class pleaded for a purposeful onslaught
against the Jews, who could be blamed for the military collapse and
'red anarchy'. For Class the Jewish question was not only 'a
scientific-political matter, but a practical demagogic issue', and he
blatantly outlined the manipulative function of anti-Semitism:

> ... only a short while ago our friend Lehmann wanted nothing to do
> with the anti-Semitic movement. Kirdorf ... who was once an
> outspoken defender (of the Jews) is now a rabid anti-Semite. So is
> everyone else in heavy industry. I believe that the army and the
> Prussian aristocracy are equally vehement in their views. But our
> whole people (Volk) must also be persuaded to join with us. Personally
> I would not shrink from any means [to achieve this aim], and I hold
> with the words of Heinrich von Kleist which we used against the
> French – 'Strike them dead, the world tribunal will never question
> your motives.'[17]

There are direct connections from both the Pan-German League
and the Fatherland Party to the German Workers' Party of Anton
Drexler and thus the NSDAP. In March 1918 Drexler founded the
'Free-Workers' Committee for a Just Peace' with the direct support
of the Fatherland Party. In November a 'workers' circle' was formed
with the support of the publisher Lehmann (a close friend of Class,
see above) which in January 1919 was officially inaugurated as the
German Workers' Party (DAP). With the sanction of the Bavarian

[16] D. Stegmann, 'Zum Verhältnis von Grossindustrie und Nationalsozialismus 1930-1933, in *Archiv für Sozialgeschichte* (1973), pp. 402-3.

[17] Deutsches Zentralarchiv, Potsdam, (DZA) file of Alldeutscher Verband (AdV) Nr. 121, also quoted by Stegmann, op. cit., p.403.

Reichswehr, Adolf Hitler joined the DAP in September 1919 and was instrumental in renaming the party the National Socialist German Workers' Party (NSDAP) early in 1920. In that year Hitler visited Heinrich Class and announced himself as an avid disciple. Even the NSDAP's Twenty-Five Point Party Programme published in February 1920 was in part directly lifted from Class's own pre-war programme.[18]

The Mittelstand during the Weimar Republic

As early as 1923 Clara Zetkin observed that fascism drew its support from 'the proletarianised or so-threatened small and middle bourgeoisie, the bureaucracy … and bourgeois intellectuals'.[19] Since then more exact sociological studies have demonstrated how the NSDAP drew its membership disproportionately from the Mittelstand, and how the middle classes voted *en masse* for the National Socialists after the onset of the Great Depression.[20]

The disintegration of the political centre and moderate right-wing parties after 1928 went hand in hand with the spectacular rise of the National Socialist Party. The liberal and centre parties' share of the vote fell from 38.7 per cent in 1928 to just 9.6 per cent in July 1932 (11.9 million votes to 3.5 million), while the NSDAP's share rose from 2.6 per cent to 37.4 per cent. Only the Catholic Centre Party (Zentrum) and the Bavarian People's Party (BVP) were able to maintain their position during this four-year period, largely because of the confessional basis of their support. At the same time working-class parties, the Social Democrats (SPD) and the Communists (KPD), although falling back slightly in their total percentage of the vote (reduced from about 40 per cent to 36 per cent) still gained one million votes. This in turn suggests that the NSDAP was able to attract support from traditionally non-voting sectors of the population, and to a large extent the support of first-time voters. (The percentage of voters rose from 75.6 per cent of the population in 1928 to 84 per cent in 1932.)

More exact figures showing the extent to which the NSDAP was a Mittelstand party have been compiled as follows:

[18] Werner Maser, *Die Frühgeschichte der NSDAP*, Frankfurt 1965, pp. 207ff.
[19] Cf. C. Zetkin, 'Der Kampf gegen den Faschismus', in E. Nolte, op. cit., p.91.
[20] See n.2 above for details.

Membership figures for the NSDAP before 1933

Social group	NSDAP (%)	Society (%)
workers	28.1	45.9
white-collar workers	25.6	12.0
self employed	20.7	9.0
civil servants	8.3	5.1
farmers	14.0	10.6
others	3.3	17.4

(from B. Vogel, *Wahlen in Deutschland*, Berlin 1971, p. 165)

And Tyrell, using statistics which relate to the composition of the party before December 1930, notes:

> these findings confirm previous findings; the small number of women in the party, the unrepresentatively high proportion of the middle-class strata, the rapid increase in agricultural support after 1928/9 and the low percentage of the working class.[21]

Two other characteristics should also be noted. First, of the approximately 270,000 'workers' who joined the NSDAP before 1933, some 50 per cent were unemployed. Moreover workers from large industrial conurbations such as the Rhineland, Berlin and Westphalia were proportionally under-represented in the party in comparison to those from regions of small industry such as Saxony and Thuringia.[22] Secondly, the NSDAP was a notably 'young' party, in that its members were generally under 40 in 1933. Thus of those who joined the party between 1930 and 1933, 43 per cent were between 18 and 30, and a further 27 per cent between 30 and 40. In the Reichstag elected after the September 1930 elections, the NSDAP returned the second largest delegation, of whom 60 per cent were under 40. The largest party, the Social Democrats, had only 10 per cent of their delegates under 40.

However we must be wary of any tendency to 'stylise' the Mittelstand *as a class*. Such a simplification not only ignores the structural complexity and indeed the heterogeneity of the German

---

[21] R. Kühnl, *Der deutsche Faschismus*, Köln 1975, p.98.
[22] See M. Broszat, *Der Staat Hitlers*, Munich 1969, p.52.

middle strata – it also risks accepting at face value the Nazi propaganda myth of the 'Third Estate'. For the German Mittelstand was *not* a class in any analytical sense; rather it was a jumble of archaic and modern social strata joined together by a consciousness which had its roots in the late Middle Ages. The social bonds which drew together the small peasant farmer, the shopkeeper, the technician and the civil servant were purely *ideological*, for their concrete economic and political demands were often quite contradictory. This point can be clearly illustrated if we take a more detailed look at the composition of the German Mittelstand.

Using data from Theodor Geiger's empirical study of the social stratification of the German people, published in 1932, Arthur Schweitzer has produced the following picture of the make-up of Weimar society:

> The capitalist class forms slightly less than 1 per cent of the population: the working class just over 50 per cent. The 'new' Mittelstand, made up of employees in industry and the civil service (technicians, scientists, etc.) make up about 17 per cent of society, and the 'old' Mittelstand, consisting of farmers, the self-employed, etc. form another 17 per cent. Finally the proletariode, namely those strata that have sunk to a precarious level of existence (the pauperised middle classes as well as the lumpen proletariat) form the final 13 per cent.[23]

Among the 'old Mittelstand' two particular characteristics can be discovered; first, a continuity of social consciousness which extends from the Kaiser-Reich to the post-war Weimar era almost unchanged; and secondly, an increasing awareness of social isolation brought about by the threat of economic pauperisation as a result of the war-economy, the revolutionary dislocation after 1918 and the hyper-inflation of 1923. Thus the very onrush of 'modernity' in the aftermath of the war provoked among the 'old Mittelstand' a renewed tendency to hark back to a mythical 'golden age', when the authority of the state supported their independent status and the operation of a free-market economy was checked by the power of the guilds and cartels.

On the political level the old Mittelstand found it difficult to discover a champion for their interests among the constellation of

[23] A. Schweitzer, *Die Nazifizierung des Mittelstandes*, Stuttgart 1970, pp. 4ff.

forces which vied for control of the state in the immediate post-war era. The patronage of the powerful Junkers, which under the Kaiser had guaranteed some measure of protection to the old Mittelstand, was almost worthless after 1918 as the authoritarian right lost influence to liberal reformist forces and was obliged to accept the social compromise of the Stinnes-Legien pact. The failure of the Kapp Putsch in 1919 merely underlined the incapacity of the old nationalist forces to regain power, symbolising the isolation of 'old Germany' in the new liberal democratic state.

Geiger himself noted how the old Mittelstand's consciousness was determined by geographical and social isolation. 'Home workers' accounted for a substantial percentage of the rural Mittelstand, many of whom combined an agricultural subsistence with 'taking in work' during the winter. Farms were small: about three-quarters of all German farmers worked an area of less than five hectares (about twelve acres), yet these farming units accounted for only one sixth of Germany's agricultural land. The mass of peasant-farmers identified particularly strongly with the norms of their locality, and contacts with the national economy were limited by a high degree of rural self-sufficiency. The farmer's semi-feudal consciousness was exemplified by Geiger's statement that he was 'less concerned with creating "more or better" than with keeping his individual possessions and property'.[24] Indeed we shall see that National Socialist propaganda successfully concentrated upon appealing to the farmer's sense of outrage at his loss of status and prestige, rather than simply offering solutions to his material plight.

But it was the crisis that broke in the agricultural sector after 1927 which really set in motion the process of alienation which Nazism readily exploited. Moreover the crisis affected indirectly the whole of the old Mittelstand as the shockwaves spread throughout rural society. This crisis was the precondition for the Nazi 'breakthrough' towards the end of the 1920s:

> Out of barely imaginable poverty and an archaic artisan and rural consciousness, a social type came into being under the Weimar republic, combining a conservative attitude with the wildest political radicalism.[25]

[24] T. Geiger, *Die Soziale Schichtung des deutschen Volkes*, Stuttgart 1932, p.87.
[25] ibid., p.91.

The new Mittelstand

During Kaiser-Reich the bureaucracy had been specifically fashioned as an instrument of authoritarian government, and the civil service displayed all the symptoms of 'association' with the mores and values of the imperial ruling class. Under the impact of the First World War, however, a radicalisation occurred, expressed in a short-lived blossoming of bourgeois liberalism at the time of the November Revolution. Indeed during the war a modern form of class consciousness began to assert itself in the publications of civil service associations, in which demands were articulated for a minimum wage and the institutionalisation of free collective bargaining.[26]

But the working-class parties failed to harness this radicalism to proletarian traditions or to the socialist movement in general, and within a short time a Mittelstand consciousness began to reassert itself both among the bureaucracy and indeed among the professional and scientific middle classes. The demand grew for the formation of Mittelstand organisations based upon corporate principles in opposition to the concept of a single white-collar union which could confront employer organisations as part of the trade-union movement. Inevitably such organisations saw themselves as distinct from the proletariat 'below', yet economically (if not culturally or socially) antagonistic to the capitalist 'above'. In the case of the civil service the consolidation of the Weimar Republic created a further ideological split, between the new 'party' civil service loyal to the Social Democracy and the old 'imperial' civil service which still cherished its pre-war image as a right-wing traditional elite.[27]

So although the 'new Mittelstand' was itself a product of the modernisation of German society, whose existence was not immediately under threat from more rational forms of production, the political demands of these strata still expressed themselves in a manner remarkably similar to that of the old Mittelstand.

[26] J. Kocka, 'Zur Problematik der deutschen Angestellten, 1914-1933', in Hans Mommsen *et al.*, *Industrielles System und politische Entwicklung in der Weimarer Republik*, Düsseldorf 1974, p.794.

[27] It should be noted that the German civil service included not only the administration but all state employees, whether bureaucrats, teachers or railway workers. Thus many of the new civil service owed their position to the strength of the SPD in working-class strongholds.

Conclusions

This chapter has encompassed a number of inter-related developments which are of fundamental importance for the development of German fascism. The late formation of the German state in the nineteenth century meant that the principles of democracy and liberalism failed to strike deep roots in the arid soil of the absolute state. The accident of history that juxtaposed the 1848 liberal revolution with the first stirrings of a proletarian political consciousness reinforced pre-existing archaic and reactionary tendencies among the German Mittelstand. Finally the Kaiser-Reich extended political patronage and offered some degree of economic protection to the 'old Mittelstand', and at the same time raised the spectre of 'revolution, expropriation and Marxism' as the consequences of democratisation or of slackening the iron grip of political dictatorship.

Under the impact of the war all sections of German society were politically radicalised. But the November 1918 revolution failed to achieve proletarian socialism. Instead, in the words of Arthur Rosenberg, it brought about 'a middle class revolution, won by the working classes, in a struggle with feudalism'. The failure of the November revolution lead to a situation of political stalemate, whereby the political institutions of the Weimar state were for a time under the influence of reformist, liberal elements, but the military, the judiciary, some elements of the bureaucracy, and above all the economy, were under the control of the authoritarian right. Furthermore the reformist, liberal elements had to labour under the considerable stigma of the Versailles Treaty. Economically this meant that the market for German goods was even further constricted, while ideologically an era of 'German decline' could be associated with the new democratic parliamentary system. The economic rationalisation set in train by the war-economy was exacerbated by the hyper-inflation which almost wiped out middle-class capital, leading to a new round of mergers and cartelisation and to the introduction of mass-marketing techniques.

It was in this climate that the principles of the pre-war völkisch movement once again flourished, as the attempt was made to 'hold back' the economic and political forces which threatened the traditional Mittelstand. Once more the petite bourgeoisie searched for a 'middle way' between modern finance capitalism and proletarian socialism, and called for a 'German dictatorship' which would guarantee the interests of the Mittelstand. But the first attempts to create a political movement which could articulate such demands were unsuccessful. The various organisations such as the Fatherland Party, the Stahlhelm, and indeed the pre-1923 NSDAP were to a considerable degree the tools of the old oligarchy and reliant upon a style of manipulative politics carried over from an earlier era. And yet in this early period Hitler and the NSDAP began to develop an organisational technique and an ideological style which was capable of creating an independent mass basis among the middle sectors of German society. This dilemma – a mass-based 'independent' Mittelstand movement, or a traditional conservative-led and financed party, was the tension at the heart of the National Socialist phenomenon, and understanding it is central to the problem of interpreting German fascism today. A detailed examination of the ideology of Nazism from 1919 until 1933 can throw new light upon the problem, providing that this goes hand in hand with a careful examination of the inter-relationship between ideology and practice during the same period. For, as we shall see, an understanding of the *appeal* of National Socialism must be tempered with the knowledge of how German fascism *exploited this appeal* to gain absolute power.

CHAPTER TWO

Nazi Propaganda, 1919-1933

This chapter looks in detail at the development of Nazi ideology during the Kampfzeit. It reproduces 54 documents – translations of Nazi posters, pamphlets and election leaflets – which illustrate the major themes and the style of Nazi propaganda during the struggle for power. Each document is dated, and where possible its place of origin is given.

Here we are dealing only with the ideology of National Socialism as reflected in the party's 'official' pronouncements and publications. In order to gain a fuller understanding of the evolution of Nazi ideology it is necessary to take into account the conflicts over the interpretation of National Socialism outlined in Chapter 3.

Translation of these documents has raised a number of problems, not least of which is the difficulty of rendering their original style into comprehensible English. If some appear turgid, or if the content seems open to conflicting interpretations (or no interpretation at all!) this is because the translation follows the style of the original. German also lends itself to a particular kind of word-association, which is often present in the originals, but is not translatable. Finally, the format of the originals is not reproduced. Where an italic typeface is used here, it indicates that the original used heavy capitals, often four or five times larger than the rest of the text.

The documents have been selected from the original 'Rehse Sammlung', which is now housed in various sections at the Bayerisches Hauptstaatsarchiv in Munich. Friedrich Rehse (1870-1952) was throughout his life a fanatical collector of memorabilia as well as a passionate supporter of authoritarian causes. He was introduced to Hitler in Munich shortly after the founding of the NSDAP, and at this meeting he apparently persuaded the future German Fuhrer to provide him with copies of all the posters and leaflets produced by the NSDAP, which Rehse promised to incorporate into a collection detailing the 'rebirth of Germany'. In 1929 the NSDAP incorporated Rehse's collection into its own archive, which in 1933 became the NSDAP Hauptarchiv. In 1945 the entire collection was seized by the American occupying forces in Munich, and shipped to America, where Rehse's collection was stored at the Library of Congress. Between 1964 and 1967 most of the collection was returned to the Federal Republic of Germany. The Rehse Collection totals many hundreds of examples, of which only a small sample is reproduced here.

Multiple examples of the same document in the Rehse Collection which are stamped with different dates and printed in a number of localities, indicate that many posters and leaflets were reproduced without major revision for a number of years. This is particularly true of election leaflets, which, especially after September 1930, were recycled for the numerous local and national election campaigns which took place over the following three years.

1
Political Awakening

Dear Colleagues,
It is a workmate who is speaking to you – one who still stands at the lathe.

What I have to say to you might seem rather strange and surprising; since it sounds very different from what you are accustomed.to hear ...

I am a socialist like yourselves. I want manual workers to gain equality with all other creative groups, as well as the annihilation of layabouts and drones and the confiscation of profits earned without work or effort.

I still hope for a true and just form of socialism, the salvation of the working masses and the freeing of creative mankind from the chains of exploitative capitalism.

But I have become convinced that we were not on the right path to reach this goal.

We haven't been told the whole truth! ...

Many of our leaders are indeed honest men, and want the best for the workers. But there are also a number who are in the service of a foreign power.

They have used the workers' movement as an instrument for certain special interests; they have used the workers' organisations as a bodyguard for *unproductive Stock Exchange and loan capitalism.*

As a result of my research, I am now convinced that:

> *There is a secret world-wide group who are always talking about freedom, humanity and tolerance, but whose single ambition is to harness the people to a new yoke.*

A number of workers' leaders belong to this group.

The leaders of this world-wide group are big capitalists.

They convinced the people that the aristocracy was an obstacle to freedom, and so we helped them to chase the princes out – but we will now discover how new tyrants – namely the money-princes – will take their place.

That's why the main banking houses financed the revolutionary movement.

Do you think that they did it out of love for the workers?

300 bankers, financiers and newspaper bosses, who are all inter-connected across the world, are the real dictators. They almost all belong to the 'chosen people'. They are all members of that secret world conspiracy which organises international politics – namely the international Freemasons' lodge ...

Their aim is the dictatorship of gold over work.

The revolution has not brought the worker freedom, nor will a second revolution be any more successful – if you don't turn upon the powerful moneyed interests, against the *finance-imperialists*, who until now have been the sole beneficiaries of the last war and the revolution.

These Bank and Stock Exchange dictators do nothing openly, for they have their agents in the workers' movement, and they pay them well. They turn people's resentment against them on to the small property owners, the factory owners and the farmers, who with all their money could hardly pay the interest owing to the big bankers.

The House of Rothschild alone owns more capital than the whole of German heavy industry together.

Why isn't the worker told that? ...

Working comrades! ... your hatred has until now been solely directed against factory and work-capitalism, whose exploitation I also ruthlessly fight against, but which is not nearly so dangerous as *invisible Stock Exchange* capital ...

The Jewish big capitalist always plays our friend and do-gooder: but he only does it to make us into his slaves.

We trusting workers are going to help him to set up the world dictatorship of Jewry. Because that is their aim, as is written in the bible:

> 'All the peoples will serve you – all the wealth of the world will belong to you – The kings will fall down at your feet, and the princesses will be your wet-nurses'

That is the aim of Jewish megalomania, for they regard themselves as a people born to lead, as the 'natual aristocracy of mankind'. So they want to make us all their slaves, since according to their Talmud-rabbis we are only a better sort of animal, fit merely to serve them. In the Talmud it says, 'a time is coming when each Jew will have 2800 slaves!'

Comrades, do you want to become Jewish slaves?

Help us so that the schemings of this power-crazy people, who have never worked, and who avoid all honest labour, finally come to nothing!

They are, in league with Jewified Christians, the worst kind of exploiters.

But their rule will only be broken when all honest men understand the situation, and join together to fight the real enemy of the people ...

An end to false pride! We workers always give it out that we have created all human culture with our bare hands. Is that right? ...

What about teachers, inventors, artists, researchers and technicians?

Are the middle classes (Mittelstand), the bourgeoisie and the farmers not productive? ... Don't they suffer under the dictatorship of big business, just like us? ... Wouldn't it make sense to offer them our hand and together turn on our common enemy? We workers alone can never hope to create a powerful enough body to crush world-capitalism. But if we stood together with the creative middle classes, then nothing could resist us. Then we could build a real majority in all countries against usurious (*Wucher*) capitalism.

It is the particular trick of the capitalist exploiters that they are able to play the workers and the bourgeoisie off one against the other, and thereby keep them powerless.

... Shake off your Jewish leaders, and those in the pay of Judas! Elect leaders from your own ranks and watch out that they don't become capitalists.

And one more thing. Don't expect anything from Bolshevism. It doesn't bring the worker freedom ...

In Russia the eight-hour day has already been abolished. There are no more workers' councils. All cower under the dictatorship of a hundred government commissars, who are nine-tenths Jewish.

Bolshevism is a Jewish swindle.

Anton Drexler, Toolmaker

2

All social classes tell us – your programme seems quite right to us, but one thing stops us from going along with you. We cannot understand why you are against the Jews. Aren't there some good Jews? Conversely aren't there some real *lumpen* elements among the non-Jews? Can't you see the Christian racketeers: the Christian usurers and the Christian exploiters? The Christian capitalist barons and the press?

Is it the Jew's fault that he is Jewish and not German?

We tell you plainly. We are against all forms of capital, whether Jewish or German, if it is not directed towards creative work, but instead is employed to gather interest and unearned income. And we fight against the Jew not as the one and only representative of this system, but as its instigator, and as the one who hinders its destruction.

We do not fight against the Jew as the one and only usurer, but because he is only one per cent of the population, yet makes up ninety per cent of all usurers.

We do not fight against the Jew as the only high-liver in our present crisis, but because he is one per cent of the population yet fills ninety per cent of the gourmet restaurants.

But above all we fight against the Jew as the one who always tries to avoid the blame, while leaving everyone else in the lurch.

...

We fight against the Jew as a foreign race – not because he is not German, but because he systematically lies in pretending to be German.

We fight against him, because as Mommsen has said, 'he is an enzyme which destroys races and nations'. And while he is destroying the state, and forcing its people to emigrate to foreign lands, then he comes in and settles down in their place.

We fight against his work as a racial tuberculosis in the body of a people (Volk), and we are convinced that peace will only come once this virus has been removed.

Therefore we appeal to you:

Come to our great public meeting, today, 13 August, in the Hofbräuhaus. Herr Adolf Hitler will speak on the theme: 'Why are we anti-Semites?'

3

German workers!

Two years have passed since you were promised that you would be freed from the claws of international capital.

The Revolution has reneged. You are poorer than before – but capitalism is stronger. Again they promise you help and explain that only the world revolution can help you. But once more you will be the loosers and capitalism the victor, unless you realise that:

The destruction of the national economy will not free you – it will merely deliver you into the hands of international capital.

No Revolution, no amount of blood or violence is going to help you! Only the struggle against the true origins of international capital – *the principle of unearned income, of interest*, can save you. If you do not understand that point, you can turn the whole earth into a heap of rubble, but international loan and Stock Exchange capital will still rule that heap of rubble!

Herr Gottfried Feder will speak on the theme: 'The breaking of interest-slavery!'

4

Who created the controlled economy? (war-economy)
but never stood in a queue!
Who financed the world war?
but was never in the trenches!
Who appoints the workers' leaders?
but shuns all manual work!
Who fights against church and religion?
but goes to the Synagogue every Saturday!
Who says we must tighten our belts?
but lives better than us!
Who preaches free love?
but only with Christian girls!
Who demands freedom of speech and the press?
but suppresses it at once when he is in power (see Russia)!
Who is against the death sentence for usurers and profiteers?
but shoots down thousands of striking workers!
   It is the Jew
      with the help of Jewish
         Stock Exchange capital!
      Are we now going to see the only non-Jewish
government in Germany overthrown, in order to make way for
         Bolshevism and those who have betrayed
           our Bavarian people?
            It's another Jewish swindle!
     Bring your representatives to account
         if they betray you.
    Out with the Bosses and power-seekers!!!

5

Berlin is being plundered! But it's not the Cohns who are being looted. Nor Wertheim or Tietz. Not Jewish shops. Not western shops.

And certainly not the Stock Exchange. No!

It's the small butchers, the small tobacconists and hatmakers, the bakers and the corner shop – they are being looted, and the farmers are being threatened!

But perhaps that is only justice. Aren't they responsible for the shortage of coal? Isn't the baker at fault if Germany is sold down the river? And when today the dollar is worth 295 Marks in New York, and tomorrow 254 and the day after 310 – isn't that a result of the evil deeds of our farmers?

And can't you see that while the common people are getting poorer by the minute, these small shopkeepers and these farmers trip off to the sea-side in their luxury cars, or travel to Switzerland in an express train, turning up on the Riviera, or wherever – never working, just living the high-life the whole time!

And you won't believe it, but they then have the affrontery to shift the blame on to others! Especially on to the innocent Stock Exchange and its harmless brokers – the speculators; the profiteers and asset-strippers! And you won't credit it, they even blame the Jews!

Racial Comrades (*Volksgenossen*), this is how it is. And there is little doubt that today only one city in the whole of Germany rejects this abject nonsense, because its people have learned to see the real enemy as a result of the untiring work and the explanations of National Socialism.

Not the shopkeeper. Not the baker. Not the farmer. Not the artisan. But

The Jew and his Stock Exchange!
that is the enemy!

Adolf Hitler will speak on the theme: 'The Jew as the world-enemy.'

6

...

For fifty years the Nationalist parties have fought for a free Germany. The result: Germany has reached rock-bottom.

For fifty years the Socialist parties have fought against international capital.

The result: Capitalism is stronger than ever; Germany is its colony; we are all its slaves.

Class prejudice and class consciousness have together driven Germany under.

Herr Adolf Hitler will speak on the theme: 'Class struggle – a Stock Exchange swindle!'

7

German comrades! German youth! Germans of all classes and occupations!

Today the terror of the Jewish Stock Exchange and its bloodhounds rages across Germany …

The völkisch resistance movement has taken up the struggle against the plundering of the German people by international finance capital. And now the Jew, unable to overcome this movement by non-violent means, has unleashed the parties of the Stock Exchange in an attempt to bludgeon it to death! Our meetings, festivals and outings have been set upon: the participants driven off by brute force! Blood flows! But the government ignores its duty to protect the lives of those who belong to a different political faction.

We've seen all this coming.

We never doubted for a moment that as soon as the völkisch movement became really dangerous to the international Stock Exchange race and its brood of exploiters, all manner of violence would be used against it.

As the only German movement we have taken the step of organising a Storm-troop. Its purpose and its task will be to protect the work of freeing our German people from Jewish terror.

8

When on 9 November 1918 the German people were driven into the German Revolution, it was explained to them that this was the beginning of the struggle to free our people from the gangs of world capitalism.

Today these same revolutionaries have to admit that the whole world is ruled by a gang of Jewish Stock Exchange bandits; and that it is no longer the people, but the world bankers who determine the world's fate.

And so the real purpose of the revolution has been fulfilled.

While the power of the international Stock Exchange dictators (thanks to the work of their Marxist and democratic bodyguards) grows from day to day, the last few survivors of millions of independent producers are being annihilated. The rooting out of our small producers and small businessmen is the conscious goal of our present-day so-called social policy.

Racial comrades, and all members of the middle classes condemned to annihilation – small businessmen, small producers, artisans and civil servants, workers of all occupations and status, come to a great public meeting ... Our party comrade Adolf Hitler will speak on the theme: 'The politics of the annihilation of the Mittelstand.'

9

Colleagues	Beware!	Comrades

THE ANTI-SEMITES WANT TO INCITE YOU
Workers, Bürger, Soldiers, Women!
SUPPORT US!
for:

Who are the big capitalists à la Rothschild, Bleichröder, Schwabach?	We Jews!
Who has a greater annual income than Krupp's fortune?	A Jew!
Who made the revolution, paid for it, and now wants the rewards?	We Jews!
Who led and paid the Spartacists and the Bolsheviks?	We Jews!
Who alone is 'international', yet is a united race among a divided and incited people?	We Jews!
Who offers you truly licentious art in the cinema,	

cabaret and theatre, and wants Christian morality to go to the Devil?	We Jews!
Who sees to it that you can buy on the black market all those goods which are supposed to be 'unavailable'?	We Jews!
Who destroys all bonds of honour, family, nation and society?	We Jews!
Who frees you from large families, just so that our own brood can develop nicely?	We Jews!
Who pushes taxes high, so that the banks need not go short?	We Jews!

Who frees you from ridiculous German honour, art and customs?
Who roots out both Protestantism and Catholicism?
Who protects instead his own Mosaic religion and secret Talmud teachings?

WE JEWS!

So join one of our Jewish controlled political parties.
We Jews are your Masters!
We will soon suppress the couple of Germans who want
to protect you:
the swastika-louts and the völkisch rabble-rousers.
We'll suppress them just like you.
We'll do it again with your help, dear workers!
Workers, you must be proud to be our slaves and our servants!
We'll pay for everything. You needn't do anything else,
We'll feed you for the rest of your life.

So workers, be our bodyguards! True until death! We have had to withdraw all our capital for your benefit, so that we are now quite poor.

Help us, dear worker! Cause a riot in every opponent's meeting! Rip any leaflet up, unread, that tries to open your eyes. You may not read it!

Make the Nazis despicable, by calling them Anti-Semitic rowdies, then the German bourgeoisie will fall into line.

A member of the Jewish race

10

Adolf Hitler will explain the following in a mass meeting, and demands *the destruction of the all-powerful international Jewish trusts through action.*

The armed struggle alone can make Germany free. It will be carried forward with a strength which comes from the broadest mass of her people. Without the German worker there can be no German Reich. The strength of the nation is to be found in the hands and minds, and in the will of the broad masses – not in political salons nor in parliamentary talking-shops.

It is always so; freedom does not come downwards from above, but is carried upwards from below.

How can the masses be won over to the German Volk? ...

To the right we must say, Away with your cowardice and your shopkeepers' spirit. Learn self-sacrifice for Volk and fatherland!

To the left we say, Stop the madness of self-destruction. Give up this ridiculous belief in other people!

In your own Volk lies your own strength!

Both must take account of the other ...

Manual workers and those who work with their minds belong together, and from both we must crystallise a new man – the man of the coming German Reich.

So I demand revenge, again and again. Revenge for every betrayal, for every atrocity and for every violation. A fanatically nationalist people is invincible!

To die or to triumph, that must be our only thought. Our only love, that of the fatherland. Our great holy belief – the Reich of the German nation.

11

GERMAN FARMERS!

What do Adolf Hitler and National Socialism want?! (Questions and answers for the German farming community)

1. The meaning of our name

Question: You call yourselves National Socialists. So are you socialists who want to abolish private property and take over our farms?

Answer: Mistake! You are thinking of the false Jewish socialism (Marxism) of the SPD and the Communists.

National Socialism accepts absolutely the principle of private property, providing that every owner relates his own private interests to the needs of the community (*Volksgemeinschaft*). For you, good farmer, this means that as long as you farm your land dutifully your entire property is sacrosant. If, however, you let your fields go to rack and ruin, then a better person will take over, because the common need comes before individual greed.

Question: Why do you call yourselves a workers' party? Are you a party like the Communists?

Answer: Not at all. We reject the Marxists' class struggle. A 'worker' in our opinion is the most honourable title for any German who earns his bread through honest work. It does not matter to us which class he belongs to, whether a worker with his hands or his brain. ...

2. Our struggle against the three parasites

Question: What in your opinion are the worst parasites in the rural economy?

Answer: ... The Tax-screw.

Usurious interest rates.

Speculation.

...

3. The settlement question

Question: How is it that German farmers today are so powerless? Their interests are almost always ignored. It was different before.

Answer: Fifty years ago the farming community represented two-thirds of the German people, but today hardly a quarter.

Question: How has that happened? The farming community has always produced the largest families.

Answer: Yes, but 25 million of our best sons from the land have left for the towns to help build up our powerful German industry. As a result a large proportion of them fell into the hands of Jewish leaders, and because of stupidity and ignorance, they now help these pests to carry out an anti-farmer policy.

Question: That is disgusting. So we are feeding our worst enemies with our own sons?

Answer: That is why something fundamental must be done so that at least a good proportion of our farmers' and land-workers' sons stay on the land. So we demand widespread resettlement, especially in eastern Germany, which in any case is threatened with being swamped by a mass of Polish itinerant workers. ...

6. Against the slanderers!

Question: they say that you are anti-Semitic hooligans, who want to blame everything bad in Germany on the Jews.

Answer: Lies! We fight against all shirkers, black-marketeers, and cowards, irrespective of whether they are German or Jewish. But we are convinced that the Jews are a dangerous, destructive bacillus in the body of the German people, who poison our economic security and our will towards freedom. That is why we are so fundamentally against the Jews. And if we give them our little finger, they'll take our whole hand ...

Question: They say that you want a dictatorship. That means that the people will not be free.

Answer: We want a dictatorship only as a transitional step – until the present filthy sump has been cleaned up. Then the people will be able to vote freely for their leader, as the German farmers once did. We want, as Hitler has said, a German democracy – free election of the leader, but strong powers for the elected Führer. ...

The people will gain their freedom not by wandering off to the right or the left, but by marching straight ahead with Hitler and Ludendorff.

Join the National Socialist German Workers' Party!

12

GERMAN WORKERS!

The November Revolution, the revolution of the Jews and the

Marxist party-rabble has delivered you into the hands of international loan capitalism. For years you have sweated so that the state can pay the interest on its loan capital. You are damned for all eternity to be wage-slaves, if you don't demand:

1. The nationalisation of the banks and the money economy.
2. The abolition of interest-exploiters and Stock Exchange speculators.
3. The abolition of mobile (share) capital.

Vote on 25 October for the National Socialist German Workers' (Hitler) Party, Völkisch and Revaluation Movement.·

13

GERMAN FARMERS!

In order that the state can deliver its burden of interest to international Jewish bank-capital, you have, for years, been robbed of the proceeds of your work in the form of taxes. No Landbund, no German Nationalist Party can save you from the total destitution of tax-Bolshevism! Your only hope is a true German peoples' community (*Volksgemeinschaft*) built upon the soil of National Socialism. Your only help can come from leaders like Adolf Hitler, who do not work for personal gain, but sacrifice themselves in the struggle for freedom of the German people.

Therefore, on October 25:

The Nationalist Socialist German Workers' (Hitler) Party, Völkisch and Revaluation Movement.

14

GERMAN COMRADES!

'Socialisation is on the March!' So the traitors of 1918 promised you.

Things have been socialised – but into the pockets of international crooks. Army provisions worth millions were stolen and put on the black market.

High finance, with the aid of the hyper-inflation, planned how it could make the Mittelstand into beggars. Taxes, and other forms of our national income were sold off, together with the railways.

But that wasn't enough! Now international big business wants to grab the aristocracy's property. Our people, bewitched and gormless, are supposed to lend their hand. The expropriation will bring in a few pennies for our people, who have been robbed of all that they have, while the Stock Exchange bandits make themselves comfortable in the castles of the royalty.

We call all thinking people to protest against this latest swindle of the international money-princes and their loyal Marxist party-bosses.

... Comrade Bruckner will speak on the theme: 'Expropriate the Princes – the Jew needs the money!'

15

IS THIS YOUR STRUGGLE AGAINST CAPITALISM, MARXIST?

The National Socialists have introduced into the Reichstag the following resolution, relating to a law for

THE EXPROPRIATION OF THE FORTUNES OF THE BANK AND STOCK EXCHANGE PRINCES AND OTHER PARASITES.

Article 1.

The total fortune of bank and Stock Exchange princes, the eastern Jews who since August 1914 have moved in, and other foreign elements, together with their families and family hangers-on, further the profits of war, revolution, inflation and deflation, will be expropriated without compensation for the well-being of the community.

The expropriated fortunes will belong to the states in which the owners live or are to be found.

Article 2.

The expropriated fortunes will be used to benefit:

(1) the unemployed
(b) war-invalids and war-widows
(c) old age pensioners
(d) the victims of inflation
(e) farm labourers, peasants, and subsistence farmers, who will settle the expropriated land.

By refusing this resolution the bourgeois parties, but above all the Marxist parties, have shown themselves clearly to be

CAPITALIST SLAVES

and that they don't give a damn about the plight of honest creative people.

Racial colleagues!

Our call goes out to you who earn your bread through honest work. If you don't want your children, and your children's children to be damned for all eternity as slaves of world capitalism, if you don't want to be made into the protectors of Stock Exchange bandits and other bloodsuckers by your treacherous leaders, if you are, on the contrary, filled with a fanatical will for freedom, then join the ranks of:

The National Socialist German Workers' Party

16

The Command of World Jewry!

World Revolution. A World Internationale. World Bolshevism. World Dictatorship. The death sentence against the white race in Europe.

Even today millions of ignorant people in Germany, England and France see Bolshevism as a force for social and economic justice. they have no idea that behind Bolshevism there lurks an international group of speculators, who misuse the good nature of the international Marxist parties and the trade unions for their own purposes. Through the racial alliance of these world conspirators, Bolshevism has been created as the final stage of a systematically organised racial struggle, whose aim is, through the

Slogan of Class Struggle

to annihilate all organic nationalist ideals, to rob every country of its nationalist leadership class; and then, after chaos has set in, to suppress the despairing and dispossessed creative classes by means of a fanatical terror – just as in Russia.

It is said that Germany is a democratic republic, that here there are

'Equal Rights for ALL'

That is not the real meaning of democracy, as we have once again had the opportunity to discover during the last seven years. We have seen that democracy is nothing but a hideous mask to disguise the pursuit of fiendish policies which have absolutely nothing in common, racially or spiritually, with the German people ...

No event in world politics can be understood without understanding this fundamental fact – control of world finance (which exploits all peoples) as well as control of all the Marxist parties (who are supposed to be locked in a life or death struggle with capitalism) lies in the hands of the Jewish race.

International democracy is the first stage in the destruction of the nations; Bolshevism the bloody means of breaking any resistance which cannot be broken through subversion alone. Democracy and Bolshevism are two means which serve the same end: Jewish money and Jewish world dictatorship. The revolution in Russia – imposed by the will of Jews throughout the world, financed from New York by Jacob Schiff and money from 'Germany', has created full-Bolshevism. First the deeply suffering masses were blinded by political agitation: they let loose a terrible blood bath among their own peoples. The Red Army then terrorised and plundered the nation – all without realising that it was a tool – used for the purpose of securing the dictatorship of the Jewish animal-leaders.

In western Europe it was different. Here the terrorist gangs of the

Third Internationale were not at the forefront. Rather it was the Versailles Treaty – imposed by the leaders of world Jewry and accepted by victorious and defeated nations alike – which allowed the Jewish bands violently to rob the creative people of their property.

This is the dictatorship of 'dry' Bolshevism. It was not the Communists in the working-class ghettoes who represented the Bolshevik danger. No! For us Bolshevism was the final aim of the world bankers – their political revolution didn't bring the working masses social justice, but instigated the dictatorship of the Jewish race over all other peoples. ...

What the world-Jew couldn't press out of Germany through the Treaty of Versailles and other innumerable swindles he later stole through the carefully planned inflation under the leadship of the Jew Parvus – whose friendships reached from Ebert to Barmat – with the aid of the leaders of the Social Democracy ... Thus our entire national wealth was surrendered, and the German economy 'socialised' in the Jewish manner – that is, thrown into chaos. So the wage earner was made into a multimillionaire, and shortly after, together with the Mittelstand, he was out on the streets begging for his living. The nationalist-thinking classes wanted to rebel, but even here the Jew had a trick up his sleeve which allowed him to hold on to his unlimited power.

It was Freemasonry, which infiltrated the nationalist organisations and destroyed them so successfully that they broke into hundreds of competing factions to be played off one against the other by the Jewish world swindlers.

... the struggle against the Jewish race is not itself sufficient, since non-Jewish organisations too form the backbone of its money-leadership. Thus we have 'dry' and 'bloody' Bolshevism. If we want to break the money-dictatorship – that is, the racial dictatorship of the Jews and the concentration of the riches of the world in the fingers of the Jews – then we must begin with a mass exit from the trade unions, the parties and the interest groups which the enemy controls.

If you honestly wish to see the rebirth of our nation, if you hold the fatherland in honour, then avoid all parties and organisations which, openly or secretly, are controlled by the Jewish world-octopus and join our ranks! Gather under our flag, the flag of Adolf Hitler with the election slogan, 'Germany Awake!'

17

International big business has won another victory!

As a result of the recently agreed International Steel-Trust, German steel production is to be reduced. This threatens mass lay-offs among German workers.

Unemployment continues to climb, while 75 per cent of our steelworkers must work in the factory for more than eight hours a day.

Workers – join in the public protest!

Party comrade Goebbels will speak on the theme: 'The revolution against the dictatorship of the money-bags!'

18

Proletarians! Away with the madness of the Internationale!

Are you going to fight for an Internationale of all nations when there won't be one?! When you should be looking after yourselves. ...

Bourgeoisie (*Bürger*)! Wake up from your sleep. Shake off your indifference!

Do you always want to prop up the reactionaries and capitalism?

On the eighth anniversary of the revolution come and join the new front which consists of all creative workers.

... Gregor Strasser will speak on the theme: 'Bourgeoisie or proletariat? Reaction or Internationale?'

19

THURINGIAN FARMERS!
CREATIVE PEOPLE FROM ALL OCCUPATIONS!
WORKERS OF HAND AND BRAIN!

On January 30 the people of Thuringia will vote for a new parliament (*Landtag*). The election is of the greatest importance politically! And not only for Thuringia's own affairs, for small businesses, or even for ambitious candidates, expectant Ministers and political big-wigs. No, in this struggle a part of the future of the entire German people is at stake. If the new parliament obtains a red majority then the

Stock Exchange Jews will triumph

all the way to the stronghold of their international financial empire –
Wall Street in New York! They they can rest assured that
the slave-state Germany
will once again place their bodyguards
the Marxists
around their golden throne.
Even the blind have seen, and the deaf have heard that wherever the
Marxists control the government, opportunities bloom for swindlers
and foreign-blooded races. Commerce and industry, artisan and
farmer, all middle-class economic existence, is socialised into the
pockets of international Jewish capital. Wherever the Marxists have
power, the Dawes army multiplies,
the million strong army of the unemployed!
That is the secret of the proletarian leaders – the thousands of
red-bosses *(Bonzen)* who live from agitation and hate. They need the
people to be in constant turmoil. Prosperity would make them
superfluous. So they refuse to support any plan which could rebuild
the economy or offer any real help to our starving out-of-work people.
The Marxist leaders
have always been good friends (and partly the corrupt aides) of
Jewish finance exploiters, e.g. the Barmat scandal. They have never
been true socialists or friends of the people.

As the deadly enemy of Marxism, we National Socialists are
therefore deadly enemies of all these political bosses ...

We National Socialists can honestly claim that we pursue a
consistent social policy – not one that is class-based, but one
designed for all our people. The stale old slogan of the Marxists, that
we are reactionaries, is a bare-faced lie and a slander. These people
are simply afraid of popular anger once they discover the truth. Our
attitude to the Jews
is unchanged: fight this pest, this parasite, until we have annihilated
its destructive influence upon culture and the economy. ...

Thuringian workers of hand and brain!
Think all this over and fight for this great cause!
Save our people from impoverishment!
Make Thuringia the heart of the coming National Socialist
state.

Vote List 5, National Socialist German Workers' Party.

20

Workers of hand and brain!
From the present eight-hour day that you work you keep little more than $2\frac{1}{2}$ hours worth – the rest must be given up as an offering to international high-finance.

Penniless savers and pensioners!
You thought that the inflation was a natural occurrence. In fact, according to an available protocol, it was agreed upon by a particular interest-group who did not want to have to demand direct socialisation ...
Instead they intended to expropriate everyone's money through hyper-inflation.

Small businessmen and shopkeepers!
Today you pay taxes and the like until your blood runs white – while huge concerns are making a fortune.

Are you still seeking salvation from one of the many parties or party-factions, who all dangle at the end of the strings of the international exploiters?
Gottfried Feder will speak on the theme: 'The state without taxation.'

21

Front-soldiers! Working men!
For four years you stood in trenches running with blood in the world war, as soldiers for a better Germany.

Now you know the truth – you were betrayed. Behind your back revolution was being plotted. And now we all stand on the edge of the grave.

You were promised 'freedom and honour'. But even a people in slavery have a right to one thing, and even that was taken away from you:

your honour.

And so the inevitable happened. You go to work, and the capitalists get the benefit.

Your property, your money, and your houses were stolen from you, and you were told that such things were just an inevitable first step.

You front soldiers, men who work with your hands and brains, believed all this, because you knew nothing of the crafty tricks of international capitalism ...
Dr Goebbels will speak on the theme: 'Jacob Goldsmith – the owner of the colony Germany.'

22

GERMAN FARMERS!
Farmers, it is a matter of your house and home!

We told you years ago but you didn't listen, just like the rest of the German People. The middle classes should have listened during the years of the insane inflation. Now they have been annihilated: their possessions and savings have been stolen – expropriated!

The German worker expected the revolution to bring honour and beauty into his life. Now he is (to the extent that he can find work) the starving wage-slave of the Bank-Jews.

AND NOW IT'S YOUR TURN, GERMAN FARMERS!
Factories, forests, railways, taxes and the state's finances have all been robbed by the Jew. Now he's stretching his greedy fingers towards the last German possession – the German countryside.

You farmer, will be chased from your plot of earth, which you have inherited from your forefathers since time immemorial.

Insatiable Jewish race-lust and fanaticism are the driving forces behind this devilish attempt to break Germany's backbone through the annihilation of the German farming community.

Wake up! Listen to something other than the daily twaddle printed in your local rags, which has hidden the truth from you for years.

Doesn't it open your eyes when you see the economy of the countryside being crippled by unnaturally high taxes, while you have no commensurate income to set off against this because of low prices for livestock and grain?

Don't you see the vile plan?! The same Jews who control the monopoly on sales of nitrogen, calcium and phosphorus, thereby dictating to you the high price of essential fertilisers, never give you a just price for your produce on the Stock Exchange.

Huge imports of frozen meat and foreign grain, at lowest prices, undercut you and push down your earnings.

The protective tariffs which the state has imposed are insufficient – not to say worthless. That same state is totally Jew-ridden in all its organs, and today can be called Germany in name only.

Nevertheless the prices of groceries are rising sharply in the towns day by day, driving your hungry German brothers to despair. Under the eyes of the so-called authorities the Jew is running a lucrative middle-man Stock Exchange.

And one thing more which is ruining you. You cannot obtain credit to tide you over these hard times. If you want money the usurious interest rates will wring your neck. Under the protection of the state it won't be long before the greater part of the land-owning farmers will be driven from their farms and homes by Jewish money-lenders.

The plight of the German farmer is desperate.

Think it all over in your last few hours, and remember – we have been telling you the same thing for years!

BUT IT'S NEVER TOO LATE!

A people that has the will to live and struggle will survive.

Don't stand on the sidelines. Join our struggle against the Jews and loan capital!

Help us build a new Germany that will be

NATIONALIST AND SOCIALIST

Nationalist because it is free and held in respect. Socialist because any German who works and creates will be guaranteed not just a slave's ration of bread, but an honourable life, decent earnings and the sanctity of his hard-earned property.

Farmers, it is a matter of the most holy possession of a people,
THE LAND AND THE FIELDS
WHICH GOD HAS GIVEN US.
Farmers, it is a matter of house and home,
Of life and death,
Of our people and our fatherland!
THEREFORE, FARMER – WAKE UP!
Join the ranks of our defence force.   Fight with us
in the NATIONAL SOCIALIST GERMAN WORKERS' PARTY.

23

Creative workers! Social Democrats! Communists!

Almost seventy years of struggle and sacrifice. And what are the results?

The bank-Jews stash away massive profits. The department store capitalists live the high-life without creating anything.

You slave and suffer! Why?

Because Marxism is madness. Your leaders are liars and traitors. We can show you the way to bread and freedom.

The miner and National Socialist, Comrade Kaufmann, will speak on the theme: 'The proletariat – the bodyguard of the bank-Jews.' (Members of the SPD and KPD who produce membership cards may come into the meeting free of charge.)

24

2000 OXEN
are led to slaughter every hour in American frozen-meat factories.

You too, good comrade, think that the Jews are mere cattle, because you believe the swindle of their press.

In the law-book of the Jews, the Talmud, it states:

'Only the Jews can be understood as human ... the Gentiles are not to be regarded as men but as animals.' (Sch A J D § 372) and so that he can deceive you, it also states:

'It is permitted to deceive a Gentile' (A Cho H § 227)

'Socialisation!' Marx-the-Jew and his prophets preached to the German workers for seventy years.

'Today the people have finally been set free' wrote Ebert, Scheidemann and Landesberg on 9 November 1918.

'A wonderful future' when you accept the Dawes Plan (David's Plan), said the Marxist Inflation Minister Hilferding.

'An incredible triumph of Social Democratic foreign policy' wrote the Jewish *Vorwärts* after it had been accepted.

The acceptance of the Dawes Report has put the creative German people into the chains of international high finance, i.e. of world Jewry.

A hellish laughter rings throughout Israel, the greatest swindle since the world began has been pulled off. An honest, hard-working people has been totally conned. Sacrifices have been offered up in the synagogues of New York.

But after the Dawes Plan had been accepted with the help of the Jewish wire-pullers of Marxism and democracy, they let the cat out of the bag.

'Can the German people fulfill the Dawes Plan?' The American banker and member of the General Council of the German (!) Reichsbank, Mac Garrah, made the following comment:

'If a people has the will and the endeavour to work ten to fourteen hours a day, as is demanded of it. If a woman is prepared to work with a horse or an ox to pull a load. And if a child is prepared to haul the plough while the father steers it, then something good must come from such industry and saving.'

Do you finally see that international high-finance and Marxism have the same aim; that Marxism is only a tool of the international Stock Exchange, and its personification, the World-Jew? ...

But the newspapers say otherwise. Yes, they lie, lie, lie ... and their leaders. They are also in the pay of the international leeches – whether consciously or not. And the real wire-puller, the Jew, controls them all!

...

Why is it increasingly difficult to make ends meet?

Because we must pay Dawes tribute!
Why is unemployment as never before?

Because it is the whip of the Stock Exchange leeches, so that you never think to strike for higher wages.

Why now, nine years after the Stock Exchange Revolution of 9 November 1918, is there still such a housing shortage?

Because housing finances are used for reparation payments.

Why is the tax office always after you, like the devil pursuing a sinning soul?

The tax office is simply the bailiff of the international Stock Exchange princes.

Why is nothing done for the pensioners?

You should be happy to have lost your savings as a result of the democratic-Marxist inflation swindle. Ask the international finance polyps, and their pimps the Marxist bosses, for your money back!

Why does the government not collect rates (housing taxes) directly from the tenant?

But how could the tenant be incited against the landlord then? No one would vote for the SPD if that happened. 'Voting cattle!' That's what you are! Who said that? A Jew!

And your voting-cattle drovers, the Marxist bosses who are in the pay of loan capitalism, and similarly the press-reptile Judas, will see to it (through lies, falsification and agitation) that your senses mist over and your head swims, so that like meek sheep you give your vote to the rapacious wolf.

But whoever has not lost his senses, whoever has not lost his solidarity with his people, whoever believes that the party and the bosses' economy should not hold sway,

Whoever believes that

the common need comes before individual greed, he will vote for the *Party of German Socialism*

the *National Socialist German Workers' Party.*

25

A Great Public Demonstration – Against the economic annihilation of the self-employed business community by the international department stores and consumer co-operatives.

– Against wage-cutting and exploitation: that means the 'buying-up' politics of the international Jewish department stores.

Gauleiter Fritz Saukel will speak on the theme: 'The crime-wave unleashed by the international department stores and consumer co-operatives.'

26

'Death to militarism!' they shouted ten years ago!

And so that it could die more easily Germany had to be the first to disarm. 'German disarmament is the precondition for world disarmament', the French said. Marxists, Democrats and Centrists carried out the order. The same Marxist traitors who were always telling us that the world was capitalist thereby delivered their own so-called socialist republic, defenceless, into the hands of world capitalism.

Stupidity or criminality?

And the consequences? The capitalist world has not disarmed. Germany, however, thanks to having been disarmed by the Marxists, is now ruled by the world. Our people are damned to be Dawes slaves. But who is surprised?

International Social Democracy and Jewish high-finance have always worked together and fought on the same side. The Frankfurt Stock Exchange newspaper and Marxist workers' papers have always supported the same politics. The whole of Marxism's struggle against capitalism has, until now, been directed solely at annihilating our national economy with the aim of delivering it into the hands of international high-finance. Even the German people's greatest nationalised industry – the German railways – was given away to a private syndicate by Marxists, Centrists and Democrats.

We have lost our weapons but won our chains. The rest of the world has re-armed as never before, and laughs at the stupid German idiots who have fallen victim to the Wilson swindle.

Those of you who want to drag still heavier chains around will vote for the parties of the Dawes-shame, but don't whinge about poverty, unemployment, the burden of taxation or deprivation.

Those, however, who want to smash the yoke of the international financiers will give their vote to

LIST 10   NSDAP.

27

'We will have absolutely nothing to do with the elections. Yet again we will be disappointed, whatever party we vote for. Enough of these election swindles!'

How often do you hear this – and not without reason. For the rule of the elected majority is the result of elections. And what is the majority? Majority is stupidity! Understanding (*Verstand*) is always the gift of the minority.

'Sooner or later the nation must go under where the majority wins and foolishness makes the decisions' (Schiller)

Government by the majority means the rule of irresponsibility ...

Instead of this parliamentary system, we National Socialists demand leadership by the best of our people. Nor do we care which social stratum (*Stand*) they belong to. ...

So we National Socialists will enter parliament, not simply to muddle along with all the others, nor to impose new taxes, nor to sit in armchairs at clubs and let the world wash over us until the next election.

No! We promise to fight to the last against this system – the rule of irresponsibility and stupidity. And we particularly promise that we will explain to our people, outside parliament, the nature of the treachery that has been practised upon them. The state makes it possible for us to carry out this task in our local parliaments because elected representatives get free travel passes.

If you don't vote, the old parties get the benefit – the ones who cling to this system – and you guarantee their dictatorship.   By voting anti-parliamentarians you make the most effective attack upon the Dawes-parties.

So vote for the NSDAP, the party that is against national betrayal, exploitation and parliamentary swindle.

28

In November 1918 we were told 'There will be no place for corruption in the republic.'

But the ten years since the revolution have in reality been ten years of corruption: ten years of robbery: ten years of deceit: ten years of swindle.

One scandal followed another. And the German republic has succeeded in doing what was never previously thought possible – a whole nation, millions of people, have been robbed of their savings without anyone having been identified as the culprit. And all the while small-time criminals have been put away behind bars!

What's more, those responsible for the greatest con-trick of all time now occupy the most exalted positions in our bureaucracy and in the government. While those who are fighting, at the risk of their lives, to put an end to today's corruption and to expose the betrayal of our fatherland, are locked up, thrown into prison and sentenced to death!

Our heroes in prison and the swindlers sitting on the throne! That is the statecraft of the new Germany.

If you want to put an end to this latest round of corruption, it's no good voting for those who live from it. If you want to see those responsible for the inflation and currency speculation really brought to justice, you cannot give your vote to those who are responsible for these crimes.

Anyone who wants to see integrity once again held in greater esteem than crooked self-aggrandisement; work greater than speculation; truth greater than deceit; but who still gives his vote again to the swindle-parties – he has no right to moan about the consequences.

Don't protest! Don't gripe! And don't blubber!

Fight for the NSDAP.   Vote List 10.

29

MIDDLE CLASSES AND SMALL TRADERS!

'Down with the Mittelstand! They must all shut up shop!' shouted the Marxist MP and co-operative leader Heinrich Peüss even in 1905.

And today all of us in the Mittelstand, traders and shopkeepers, are 'down', or else we are on the way down!

Or will anyone deny that year by year, month by month, things are getting worse? Or that we no longer know how we are going to pay for our small stocks of merchandise? Or that our profits hardly stretch far enough to feed ourselves and our families?

We slave from first thing in the morning till last thing at night –

We slave like nobody else – and yet we are going under.

Why is that?

Because we find it virtually impossible to compete against

co-operatives and department stores!

The way in which these co-operatives (usually founded by Social Democrats) have developed is shown in the following figures from their 'National Confederation':

	1903	*1927*
affiliated co-operatives	685	1,109
membership	575,449	2,918,369
turnover	167,456,549	1,276,573,556 RM
value of goods	18,773,198	122,761,342 RM

This does not include co-operatives in the Civil Service, buyers' co-operatives and the like.

The turnover even of those co-operatives confederated to the Social Democrats was

| 1924 | 548 million RM |
| 1927 | 982 million RM |

In three years an increase of 80 per cent!

The rapid increase in consumer co-operatives is not a consequence of them being more efficient than we are; nor do they have better goods. Rather they are supported and favoured by international finance capital, and the state accomodates them as far as possible through

tax reductions (concessions)

which can add up to 25 per cent. Yes, these concessions mean that

our own taxes

go to support these co-operatives! For instance, the following received:

1924	Beamtenwirtschaftsverein Berlin	90,000 RM
1924	Hannover Konsumverein	150,000 RM
1924	Grosseinkaufsgenossenschaft	750,000 RM
1927	Konsumverein Nordhausen	50,000 RM

So these organisations, built up with money from our own people, work partly against our economic interests. And because of importing from abroad our trade balance is made worse.

The Leipzig-Plagwitz co-operative sells only

Danish butter!

...

To the extent that the co-operatives have not yet ruined the shop-keeper, the

department stores

work in the same way.

Since the whole weight of Jewish high-finance is behind them, they can obviously look forward to the best possible concessions from the present-day authorities. Thus for instance, the Department Store Karstadt in Berlin received the sum of 150,000 RM in 'Extended tax-credits'! that is, they were practically written off! Already the news is getting into the newspapers that the East Galician Jew Hilferding (whom Germans have the pleasure of knowing as our Finance Minister) is preparing a tax amnesty for outstanding tax debts, which will benefit Karstadt and the like in the greatest measure.

Woe upon us Mittelstandlern and small traders if we are unable – even once – to fulfil our astronomical tax demands!

Thanks to the most obliging attitude of the tax authorities, operating costs for the department stores are lower – but not their prices!

This price difference can be seen in their massive profits. The total profits of the firm Karstadt in 1927 for instance totalled 75.36 million RM, the net profits 10.32 million RM, the dividend 6.12 million RM, while turnover in 1926 came to a total of 220 million. The other Jewish department stores such as Tietz, Wertheim, Jandorf, Emden, Schocken, Ury, Konisser, etc., do just as well!

These profits are in part used for expensive advertisements which are designed to kill off even further the competition from small shops. ...

Just like polyps the department stores keep sending out new suckers. So

Leonhard Tietz, Cologne, controls 37 other shops/stores

Karstadt-Althoff, Hamburg, controls 57 subsidiaries/branches

24 other shops/stores.

Behind the department stores ... stands Jewish
finance-capital

At the end of 1928 Tietz and Karstadt obtained new capital in order to introduce the single-price system thought up by the American Woolworth chain. (Who gives us credit when we need a couple of thousand marks?!)

Behind this financial manoeuvre lurks the Jewish Speyer-Elissen Bank. ...

... behind the French (!) department store Lafayette in Berlin is the Jewish bank Schlesinger Trier and Co. ...

To sum up, international Jewish finance-capital is pushing us under by means of the Marxist co-operatives and the large department stores. It throttles us by means of tax-laws which have been heavily influenced by its representatives. All the more so because the greatest share of this taxation flows back into the foreign banking houses of this same Jewish high-finance via 'reparations' and Dawes contributions.

So we ask ourselves, 'What can we do?'
Only one thing. As far as possible we must make sure that the only

party which has the courage to oppose international finance-capital gains in strength from day to day. This party is

the *National Socialist German Workers' Party*

... Point 16 of its Programme from 24 February 1920 reads:
... 'the creation and stabilisation of a healthy Mittelstand. Communalisation of the department stores; rent their premises to small traders at low cost; greatest possible support for all small firms through tendering local and national government contracts to small businesses ...'

We must work for the victory of this party by joining its ranks ... only its victory can bring us our salvation.

30

Stop!   Read!   Tell others!

Ultramontanism, Marxism and Liberalism – these are the three international powers which have brought Germany to its knees, and now keep it in slavery. They drain the nation of the strength to resist, and make us incapable of protecting ourselves from annihilation.

These three powers make up the Black, Red and Gold Internationale – A fact which is openly seen in the symbol of this state. The colour of the republic's flag is black, red and gold!
     But so that the broad mass of the people do not see through the deception practised by these international powers, these three enemies of our people hide behind dearly-held beliefs.

Ultramontanism pretends to protect religion. But in fact it has created a power-base in the Centre (Zentrum) Party which misuses religion to promote pro-capitalist politics.

Marxism pretends to help the working classes, but in fact it is merely the bodyguard of Stock Exchange capitalism.

Liberalism pretends to be in favour of democracy, but in fact it works behind our backs to establish the dictatorship of money.

All the parties serve one of these three international ideas.

The one and only party which recognises all three and attacks them head on is the NSDAP.

Our struggle against Marxism and Liberalism is recognised by all.

31

'The racial question is the key to world history' – so said the famous English Jew, Disraeli – later Prime Minister Lord Beaconsfield. Since that time many decades have passed and now the racial question – and with it the Jewish question – stands in the forefront of public concern.

Although maligned, derided, laughed at and slandered, the anti-Semitic movement continues upon its path.

Today it finds its most powerful expression in the NSDAP. Gradually, inside and outside the party, millions of Germans are discovering the meaning and the burning urgency of the Jewish problem in all walks of public life.

The Jew is guilty

So say many from instinct. Anti-Semitism is today a matter of feeling.

But it must become a matter of consciousness! We will show the way. We are not anti-Jewish out of spite or envy, but because of consciousness and knowledge.

Julius Streicher will speak on the theme: 'The Jew – the deadly enemy of the German people!'

32

FARMERS
You are going to be expropriated!
Taxes, usurious interest rates, debts to the banks, mortgages, all sorts of financial burdens, middle-man profit-taking and Stock Exchange dealings rob you of all that you have. You are forced to sell up. You must watch, with anger and bitterness in your heart, as you are tricked out of the rewards of years of hard work.

In the Town Hall and in parliament your complaints go unheard. That is understandable when you consider that the Social Democrats (who govern almost unopposed ...) said in Breslau years ago:

'We have no reason to support the farmer. Rather it is in the workers' interest if the peasants perish!'

German farmers!

You toil from morning till night, day in day out, week in week out, month by month; you toil and save, and yet it's more and more difficult to scrape a living, to pay the interest and to deliver your taxes.

Yet the price of everything you need for your farm goes up and up, and the prices you get for your produce cannot keep pace. So from day to day you need more cash.

Despite this you read in the newspapers that

Imports of agricultural produce

increase year by year, and that the total has now reached

4.2 billion gold marks

...

So ask your 'leaders', the men from the Landbund and the various Farmers' Leagues, why is this? And they will tell you all about customs duty and indexes, pacify you with promises and fine words, and console you with – 'You must be patient and trust in your representatives (*Standvertretung*); it will all be OK in the end.'

In the meantime despair is deepening, the burden of debt gets greater and greater, and the bailiffs and the Jews come more and more often to your door.

German farmers!

The real reason for your plight is the banking and Stock Exchange system. The cause of your poverty is the Dawes Agreement.

The aim of the Dawes Plan is to press

2,500,000,000 GOLD MARKS A YEAR

out of the German people for the next fifty years for the benefit of high-finance.

German farmers! The fulfilment of this plan means:

for you – expropriation,

for Germany – annihilation.

Bankruptcy proceedings and auctions have already reached record proportions. In one quarter alone from 1 October to 31 December 1928, court proceedings were started to liquidate

3071 farms with a total area of 43,652 hectares!

In the same period 432 farms with an acreage of

11,562 hectares were compulsorily auctioned off.

The rural economy is dying. Farmers, you have become the serfs of the

International bank and Stock Exchange princes!

Yes, you are slaves – no longer free farmers. Your property and your land is mortgaged. Every year, every month you go backwards. The total agricultural debt is now

13 billion gold Marks,

with a yearly interest of 950 million gold Marks,

and a yearly increase in the debt of

1 billion gold Marks.

And when you ask who committed this crime, who took up this murder-contract, the answer must unfortunately be: Your leaders! i.e., those who until now have been looked upon as 'leaders'. Because the following (apart from the Social Democrats and the Democratic Party, who self-evidently are in favour of this sort of thing) voted for the Dawes Plan:

the German Nationalists, and all these farmers' representatives and Landbund leaders:

George Bachmann, Franconia; Paul Bäcker, Berlin; Prince Otto von Bismarck, Friedrichsruh; Philip Christ, Hessen-Nassau; Friedrich Döbrich, Thuringia; Alwin Domsch, Saxony; ...

The German People's Party, led by the Landbund leader Hepp

The Bavarian People's Party, and all its MPs and farmers' representatives

The Farmers and Mittelstand League, with all its big-talking farmer-representatives

The Centre Party with all its farming representatives.

German farmers, this is at the root of your plight and poverty. Only we National Socialists who

Voted against the Dawes Plan

Fight against the banks and the Stock Exchange

Oppose the Jews

have the customary right to say to you:

'Our fight is your fight. You can only win if, together with us,
you oppose and overcome the causes of our crisis!'

We want to show you the real causes of the threatened collapse of the
German farming community, so

Get rid of the 'leaders' who have led you into poverty and despair!
If you and your sons want to be free farmers, then join our struggle
under the leadership of Adolf Hitler in the ranks of the

National Socialist German Workers' Party

33

The consequences of ten years of Marxist internal and foreign policy,
the consequences of red economic and tax policies, are as follows:

3 million unemployed on the streets.

The German rural economy in debt.

German farmers having to pawn their last possessions.

40,000 suicides in one year.

The livelihood of tens of thousands of workers disappeared.

The savings of the Mittelstand, the farmers and the workers
robbed by the inflation.

The Mittelstand annihilated.

Marxist co-operatives systematically destroying the artisans.

Department stores and consumer co-operatives robbing the small
businessman of his livelihood.

Industry bought out by foreign banks and Stock Markets.

Workers subject to foreign exploitation and tyranny.

Billions unwillingly paid in tribute, and German workers paying
for the armaments of the rest of the world.

Marxist teaching annihilating belief in the nation, destroying
Christian customs and morals, and opening the door to the
destruction of German art and culture.

That is the real face of Jewish-led Marxism. ...

German, wake up! Create a bulwark against the destructive
influence and the incompetence of the 300 Marxist party bosses in
Germany.

A new Bolshevik wave must be met by a Germany determined to fight! Police-captain Pflaumer of the Heidelberg police will speak on the theme: 'The destruction of society and the nation by Marxism'
NSDAP and NS Student League.

34

Mittelstand!   Businessmen!   Traders!   Artisans!
House-owners!

Article 164 of the Weimar Constitution states that
'The self-employed middle classes engaged in farming, business and trade must be protected, legally and administratively, against becoming overburdened and bled dry.'

Who's laughing? Certainly not the Mittelstand.
The Jew's laughing. The banks belong to the Jews.
The interest payments are eating you out of existence.
The department stores belong to the Jews. Tietz and Karstadt eat you out of existence.
You pay your taxes. The red consumer co-operatives pay no tax.
So the Weimar Republic tramples all over its own constitution.
Smash those responsible!

35

Evangelicals vote *Volksdienst*.
Catholics vote Centre.
Jews vote *Staatspartei*.
Workers vote Social Democracy.
Farmers vote *Landbund*.
Each his own interest-heap!
That's called unity!
Away with the swindle,
Create a German People's Community (*Volksgemeinschaft*)

36

SOCIALISM?

That is the terrifying word that sends shivers down the back of every peaceful citizen.

Socialism, that means to him, *expropriation and equality, Jacobinery* and the *guillotine*.

Socialism, that means to him *class-struggle*, because for sixty years the *Jew* has slyly put about this nonsense, both to the gullible worker and the ever-so-clever middle classes.

In reality *Socialism* means nothing other than *community: a people's community*.

Socialism can only originate from the principle of absolute justice: because without justice there is no community. But nothing is more unjust than equality, for man is in nature quite unequal. Man is not equal in fulfilling his duty. Therefore he cannot be equal in his rights.

But he should not be valued according to his money, rather according to his accomplishments for the community. Whoever accomplishes the greatest service for his people, he shall be the first among us. But whoever thinks only of his money, he is a pariah and an outcast.

THE COMMON NEED BEFORE INDIVIDUAL GREED
THAT IS SOCIALISM

Do you want to create a true and sound community within our German people, blooming with happiness and peace?

Then out with the swindle Marxism, and away with bourgeois selfishness!

Then join up with the party of the people's community.
German National Socialist Workers' Party

37

PERSECUTION OF CHRISTIANS
AND MURDER OF PRIESTS
IN THE RUSSIAN PARADISE!

Up to 1928, 28 bishops and 1200 priests were murdered. Between 1928 and 1929 another 30 bishops and 1348 priests disappeared. Nothing more has been heard from them. Additionally thousands of other clergymen have died a martyr's death and thousands of nuns have been raped and murdered. At present 37,000 priests and over 8000 monks are languishing in the dungeons of the Tscheka or in the hell of Siberia. This report and a list of other repulsive atrocities, carried out by Bolshevik animals, was made public by the St Elisabeth envoy in Nuremberg. The war is entirely directed against priests, nuns, the churches and schools. *Why this spiritual persecution?*

There are men who want to rule without God. Of them, Christ once said, 'The devil is their father. They are murderers from the outset. Hypocrites. Adders. These men are not like other men. In their secret texts they have set out how they will come to power, how they will come to rule the earth, how they will oppress the non-Jews. Their strategy is as follows:

The natural enemy of Israel is the Christian church. Therefore it is necessary to destroy it. Its own divisions make the task easier. Support freethinking, doubt, disbelief and conflict. *Therefore constant war in the press against Christian priests*; – promote suspicion, mock them. A major pillar of the church is the school. Gain influence over the Christian upbringing of youth. *Split the churches from the schools!* Under the slogan of progress and equal treatment for all religions, change Christian schools into confessionless (i.e. state) schools. Then Jewish teachers can work in all schools. Press for the abolition of all church and school property, its transfer to the state, therefore sooner or later into the hands of Israel.

BOLSHEVISM IS PERSECUTION OF CHRISTIANS BY THE JEWS!

Hundreds of thousands of examples could be given. So go to meetings of the National Socialists and hear the explanation. A leaflet is too small to set out all the various interconnections. Read anti-semitic newspapers and books, then check the facts by comparison with daily happenings! You can't change the Jew, any more than you can stop rust destroying iron. You can only keep it at bay. The Jew has to destroy. But you don't have to put up with his destruction.

First the monarchy must be abolished, then the military. After that the spiritual leaders and intelligentsia. Then the Jew is master and we the slaves – circus animals, beasts of burden for the Jews.

If you want that to happen, then stay with the present-day parties, who don't want to suppress this Jewish mania; then carry on reading those newspapers which remain silent about all this. But if you want things to change, fight with our leaders for a Germany under German leadership, join the

NATIONAL SOCIALIST GERMAN WORKERS' PARTY –
Vote for List 9.

38

Traders!
Small Producers! Artisans!

For a long time you have kept out of sight and let corruption, favouritism and the nepotism of others run all over you. You believed that obeying law and order was the first duty of the citizen.

But what has this led to? Ever more exploitation by those in power. The tax-screw being turned ever tighter. You are the helots of this system. Your only job is to work and pay taxes which go into the salaries and pensions of ministers.

What have your parties done for you? They promised the world but did nothing. They made coalitions, prattled away before the elections then disappeared into parliament until the next.

They didn't unite against the treacherous leaders of Marxism.

They horse-dealt over ministerial posts and never gave you a thought.

They have ruled with Social Democrats and forgotten the aim of that party – Death to the Middle Class!

Have you forgotten the inflation? How you were robbed of your savings and commercial capital?

Have you forgotten how taxes have slowly throttled your businesses?

Have you forgotten how the department stores and the co-operatives have ruined you?

... Middle classes, why is it so bad? Why are your shops empty? Why are you out of business?

Look at the banks and their massive profits! They are eating you out of existence!

Look at the co-operatives! They are free of taxation. You are slaving for them!

Look at the department stores which are springing up like mushrooms all around you, and who double their profits from year to year. They will be your graves!

The result of all this is *cold socialisation*. – Marxism is guilty of pawning the German economy to international high finance. Therefore citizens, you belong to the ranks of those who make no pact with Marxism, but fight it wherever it is to be found.

German National Socialist Workers' Party

39

To the Jewish People.

Through your statements, your pamphlets and your writings, you seek to make it clear to the good Fritz that anti-Semitism is a cultural slur contrived by anti-Semitic rowdies. That is a blatant lie! Anti-Semitism is as old as the Jewish race itself!

Some extracts from the golden words of a number of our greatest men will open your eyes, and you will see who is responsible for the real cultural slander – the Jews themselves!

[There follows a series of extracts from the writings of Bismarck, Kant, Sombart, Luther, etc. on the 'Jewish Question'.]

German people!
Are these men anti-Semitic rowdies?
Help us National Socialists in our defensive struggle against the Jews. They have attacked us, and not we the Jews!
The National Socialists are proud to be anti-Semitic, for we are at one with the spiritual and cultural greats of all time. If you want to free German customs, culture and the economy from the destructive Jewish spirit,
Vote National Socialist!

40

Maggoty meat!   Spoiled goods!
all offered with massive advertising by the department stores.
The buying public are being deceived.
Businesses ruined.   Artisans out of work.
Protest with us against the department store pest!

41

Is Germany on the brink of civil war?

The leader of the Reichsbanner, Hösing, has demanded that the Reichsbanner be ready to march on 22 February. Together with the hordes of Moscow it is going to launch a savage terror-attack upon the National Socialists' growing army of freedom.

Already the green grass covers the graves of hundreds of our best comrades – all gruesomely murdered because they allied themselves with Adolf Hitler, and thus the German nation.

In the dying hours of the present system our warning call must reach all creative racial comrades.

Stop the murderous beginnings of self-destruction!

Come over to us and build with us the true German *Volksgemeinschaft!*

42

Farmers!   *Workers!*   *Racial comrades!*

WARNING!

It is a fact that the Jew never puts up barns, but he earns more, far more through dealing in corn than you who have to slave to build a grain store.

It is a fact that the Jew never breeds cattle. He is never to be found working in the cow shed. But he dictates the price of cattle and food on the produce market.

It is a fact that the Jew is never seen among woodcutters, carpenters or furniture makers. So there are all the more in the timber trade.

It is a fact that no Jews are miners. But there are plenty who hold mining shares.

It is a well-known fact that the non-working Jew gets far more money than the productive farmer, the technician or the worker.

So it is true to say that the Jew is the exploiter of work. Therefore he is anti-national, because he steals from creative people and their work. That he is anti-social has already been proved.

It is a fact that these Jews, who as
court-Jews (Hof-juden)
whined, wheedled and fawned upon our leaders in the princes' courts, were at the same time working as revolutionaries, preparing the destruction of the aristocracy.

It is a fact that these same court-Jews today appear in the farmer's courtyard and discriminate against him while in the towns they incite the worker against the farmer.

It is a fact that the Jews, although giving themselves out to be Germans, evaded defending the nation in the war, and only rarely were to be seen at the front. And during our most difficult hours – during the war economy, during the inflation and now with the shame-treaties from Versailles to Young, they work in the most criminal manner against our people (Volk) and our fatherland.

It is a fact that the Jews worked closely with one another to carry out the revolution. In Bavaria for instance, Eisner, Toller, Mühsam, Kranauer and many others. In Prussia Aronson, Bernstein, Blumenfeld, Böhnheim ... As leaders of the banks and the press! Abraham (Vienna), Alexander, Bach ...

In Germany, in Austria and in Russia – everywhere the same picture – everywhere destruction, everywhere revolution, all brought about by the Jews.

It is a fact that all the parties in Germany, all the party leaders, and all the newspapers remain silent about this, and that alone the National Socialist German Workers' Party concerns itself with this vital question,
the racial question
Our newspapers have discovered the origins of our present-day plight, and therefore we
alone can show the way to salvation!
The Jew is the ruler of the Stock Exchange, the ruler of the nations, the leader of the world press, the reason for our decline, the reason for corruption and unemployment, the reason for the plight of the farmers and of the nation!

Without the removal (*Ausscheidung*) of the Jews
there can be no revival, no salvation!
Therefore away with the press which says nothing about the Jewish
Question. Away with the parties which know no Jewish Question.
Think for yourself and join the
National Socialist German Workers' Party.

43

NATIONAL SOCIALISM AND THE AGRICULTURAL ECONOMY
Party statement on the NSDAP's attitude
to the farmer and agriculture

Munich, 6 March 1930

I. The meaning of the agricultural community for the German
people

The German nation meets a substantial part of its food requirements
by importing foreign foodstuffs. Before the war we could pay for these
imports with the receipts from our industrial exports, our trade, and
from capital investments abroad. These possibilities have been
denied us by the outcome of the war.

Today we pay for our food imports mainly through foreign loans.
As a result the German people are being dragged ever deeper into
debt-slavery to the international financiers who give us credit. This
means – the longer it continues – the increasing expropriation of the
German people. By stopping these credits (and thereby our food
imports) or by hanging the bread basket higher, the German
proletarian in particular is forced to work for starvation wages, or else
he is shipped off to some foreign colony as a slave.

Only when the German people can feed itself from its own land can
we be set free from slavery.

Increasing the productivity of our home-based agriculture is
becoming a question of life and death for all the German people.

An economically sound rural economy is also of decisive
importance for the future prospects of industry, which in the future

will be increasingly oriented to the home market ...

We recognise not just the importance of maintaining a class of food producers for our people; we also see the peasant-farmer as the source of a healthy racial stock, the fountain of our people's youth and the backbone of our defensive strength.

The maintenance of a sound and strong ... farming class is a pillar of the National Socialist politik precisely because it is a matter of the well-being of the whole of our people, and of our future generations.

II.   Disregard of the farmer and the neglect of agriculture in the present-day German state

Because of the disregard for the biological and economic importance of the farming-class in the present-day German state, and in contradiction to the vital demand for higher agricultural production, the existence of an economically sound farming community is under the most serious threat.

An increase in agricultural production, although certainly possible, is prevented by the lack of necessary capital – a consequence of the farmer's increasing indebtedness, and the disincentive to increase production due to the fact that agriculture no longer provides any return.

The reason for the lack of profitability in agriculture can be found:
1. *In the present system of taxation*, which disproportionately affects the agricultural economy. This is a result of party-political considerations, and because Jewish world power, which in effect controls the democratic parliamentary system in Germany, wants to destroy German agriculture. Then our people, and in particular the working masses, will be totally at its mercy.
2. *In competition.* Our customs tariffs (which are unfavourable to home-based agriculture) do not stem imports from other countries where conditions are more favourable to agriculture.
3. *In unacceptably high profits* made by wholesale concerns which intervene between the producer and the consumer – these are mostly in the hands of the Jews.
4. *In usurious prices* which the farmer must pay for *fertilisers* and *electricity* to business combines which are mostly Jewish-owned.

The farmer can no longer pay high taxes from what he earns from agricultural work. So the farmer is forced to take loans for which he must pay usurious rates of interest. He is plunged ever deeper into interest-slavery, and finally loses house and home to the mainly Jewish providers of loan-capital.

The German farming-class is being uprooted.

III. In the coming German Reich for which we are fighting, the farmer's land will be his by right: ...

No substantial improvement in the plight of the rural producer or an upturn in the agricultural economy can be expected as long as the German Reich is ruled by international money-princes with the help of the democratic parliamentary system: for they aim at the annihilation of earth-rooted German strength.

Only in the *new and totally different German state* for which we are striving will the farmer (and the agricultural economy) be held in the respect to which he is entitled for he will be the cornerstone of a genuine German *Volksstaat*.

In this future Reich the German's right to his land and a German agricultural-politik will be guaranteed ...

V. Professional organisations cannot really help the farmer. Only the political German freedom movement of the NSDAP can do that.

The present plight of the farming community is a part of the plight of the whole German people.

It is a mistake to believe that any single group can separate itself from Germany's common destiny, and a crime to incite people in the countryside and the town against each other – they are, for better or for worse, bound together.

Temporary economic measures under the present ruling system can bring about no real improvement: the plight of the German people is rooted in its political slavery, and this can only be solved through political means.

The old political parties who have ruled until now and who have delivered our people into slavery cannot lead us on the path to freedom.

Professional organisations have an important part to play in our future state, and in this sense they can, even today, begin to prepare for this task. But they are not suitable to lead the struggle for political freedom (which alone can create the conditions for a new economy), because this struggle cannot be led from the standpoint of a single professional group, but only from the standpoint of the whole Volk.

The struggle for freedom against our oppressors and their taskmasters can only be led successfully by a freedom movement which takes into account the importance of the farming community and agriculture for the whole of the people and which unites all German-conscious people from all professions and classes.

This political freedom movement of the German people is the National Socialist German Workers' Party,

signed Adolf Hitler

44

German Landvolk, decide!

The old parties have reached absolute rock bottom! The farmers' own party, the Landvolk Party, has failed yet again at the crucial moment. Now there can only be one *final* decision

SWASTIKA OR SOVIET STAR

Do you want *your farm* to belong to all and sundry, even to useless layabouts? Do you want to lose control over your own harvest to the Jew in the Bolshevik party-office? Do you want to be chased from your old farm on the orders of the Jews, and be replaced by a foreigner, who has never been a farmer, who can do as he pleases in your property?

Do you want your Christian faith desecrated and spat upon by thieves and the scum of the earth and your church turned into a cinema as in Russia?

Do you want your beloved village priest to be murdered, with the result that at baptism, at marriage and in your last hours you have no spiritual comfort?

Do you want your family to be left defenceless, while Bolshevism satisfies its blood-lust throughout your homeland? And you, good farmer's wife, do you want your children to be snatched away from you at birth? Do you want to be fair game for every man; to lose your home; and to be herded together into barracks with tramps and vagabonds?

That's what the Communists want to do!

And yet the Soviet Five Year Plan is a total failure! In his last speech Stalin had to admit the total collapse of Communism. For fourteen years a billion-strong nation has been plunged into a sea of blood – only to collapse completely.

German Landvolk, your leader is Adolf Hitler

Only the Third Reich will make the farmers, and thus 'blood and soil' into the cornerstone of the nation. Only the Third Reich will fight to feed our people from our own land and refuse all imports of foreign food. Only the Third Reich fights for God and Family!

German Landvolk – it is the moment of decision!

Become National Socialists!

45

Shop-keepers!   *Businessmen!*   *Artisans!*

What are the aims of the Fighting League (Kampfgemeinschaft) against department stores and consumer co-operatives?

For twelve years we have waited for some improvement in our economic position. Burdened with cares and worries, we are now in the most desperate straits. Everywhere you go you hear that things cannot go on like this any longer. And you wonder, what can still go wrong? How are things going to get any better?

When we think back to the time of the inflation, when the exchange rate soared from hour to hour, when it was impossible for any businessman or salesman to cover his costs, then we can see just how serious the present situation is, for we are faced with the same problems with the present price-reduction swindle. At whose cost was the inflation? (Organised by that Saviour of Germany, Hilferding). And now who suffers most as a result of the present price-reductions and the economic collapse? The Mittelstand! The businessman!

And why? Because as usual, the various Mittelstand groups (in line with their rules) are politically neutral. So they lack any influence within the political parties.

The Mittelstand are attacked from left and right. From the left, through the co-operatives ... which in line with their Marxist dictum, means the annihilation of the commercial Mittelstand. From the right, through the establishment of monopolies and trusts, which cut the earnings of every businessman to the bone.

When will the Mittelstand finally see that politics affects the economy and that political neutrality means their extinction? Aren't taxes and laws made by the parties? And isn't it the various factions on the town council who give or refuse permission for the opening of new department stores?

Yes, Mittelstandler, there is only one course of action open to us – that is to be active politically and to take up the struggle against those who threaten our existence. There is only one party which proclaims upon its flag our highest duty – to fight and fight again against the oppressors of our people. That party is the National Socialist German Workers' Movement. In Hessen, this party has founded a Fighting League against department stores and consumer co-operatives ... This league represents not only the professional interests of the Mittelstand – it stands for a strengthening of all consumer interests as well.

First of all it is essential to create an organised group of consumers who will be duty bound to avoid all the department stores and consumer co-operatives. These consumers are only to be found in the NSDAP-movement. The Economic Parties and the Volks-Parties, although pretending to be friendly towards the Mittelstand, could never achieve this, because their voters (although artisans and members of the Mittelstand) give their custom to the department stores and the consumer co-operatives. ·

The second aim of this Fighting League is to bring the custom of National Socialists to Mittelstand business, and to give proper consideration to the political needs of this class. We declare open war upon the department stores and consumer co-operatives, and we will not be put off, even if counter-action is taken against us. We want to fight for our aims with all the means at our disposal.

So I ask you now, dear colleagues, what other Mittelstand organisation has been able to plan protest-actions against the department stores and consumer co-operatives? According to the

Marxist, comrade Engel, there has been no one for forty years ...

But our struggle goes further, for we know that only by destroying the present system can we clear the way to reach our final goal.

In the new Reich the Mittelstand will have a proper position in line with its vital economic role. Point 16 of the Party Programme shows you the right way ...

National Socialism not only represents the interests of professional groups. It also represents the interests of the customer, for we rely upon his trade. What use is a professional organisation without the support of the consumer? We must understand that the German people will only be restored to health once the interests of both are properly taken into account. The only party that can do this is the NSDAP.

Therefore, Mittelstand and business people, away with your reserve. Show that you are men. Create cells in your professional organisations. Only under the swastika will the economy, so badly crippled by the old parties, once again bloom and prosper. ... Join our ranks and fight with us. Then victory will be ours!

46

STALIN AS KING!

It is now the twelfth hour – the hour of decision about the future of the German fatherland.

We must choose between:

Swastika	or	Soviet Star!
Germany	or	Moscow!
Man	or	Machine!
Spirit	or	Materialism!
God	or	the Devil!
Blood	or	Gold!
Race	or	Half-caste!
Folk-Song	or	Jazz!
Family	or	Collective!

NATIONAL SOCIALISM OR BOLSHEVISM!

47

THE MITTELSTAND IS STARVING TO DEATH!

Nevertheless you still believe that you will be restored to good health by feeble resolutions and protests. Whoever wants to be master of his own destiny must take it into his own hands. You will never save yourselves with words, only with deeds.

THE GOVERNMENT PROMISED

when your so-called bourgeois parties (including the Economy Party) were attempting to explain away its acceptance of the Young Plan

Less taxation

900 million marks immediate tax relief

Lowering of real taxes, especially for the Mittelstand

Limitations on government expenditure

Waste-cutting in central and local government

To what extent has the government kept its promise?

Fourteen days after you in the Mittelstand, via your parties, signed the Young Plan, the same Minister explained that

TAX REDUCTIONS WOULD BE A MISTAKE.

The government is short of several million marks, which must be found from increases in taxation and new forms of tax ...

Mittelstand – put an end to it all!

Listen to the clear voice of statistics which report

1200 bankruptcies each month!

Those are not big capitalists going bust, but the small men, artisans, salesmen and business people.

700 court hearings every day in Berlin!

You can work out for yourself when it is going to be your turn.

About 20,000 suicides every year in Germany!

Those are not the mentally-ill – they are people with a high sense of self-respect, who can no longer stand the despair brought on by a life of misery and poverty ...

Instead of the tax reductions which the German people were promised, we have had instead
5,800 million in new taxes …
Do you still believe in promises?
Do you still believe in tax-reductions?
Mittelstand – think about it – this system is built upon cartels, trusts and syndicates, upon huge capitalist department stores, co-operatives, chain stores and single-price shops.

The turnover of the department stores is 2.5 billion marks a year!

The turnover of the co-operatives is 1.5 billion marks a year! That means: the annihilation of about 80,000 shopkeepers with a turnover of 50,000 marks each …

Hunger and misery for 100,000 workers.

What do you say? – 'It cannot go on like this any longer, it has got to change.'
Show that you have decided to change things by your own actions, and that you will no longer allow yourself to be fobbed off with promises.

SMASH THE DEPARTMENT STORE
SLAUGHTER-HOUSES!
DESTROY THE CO-OPERATIVE PARASITES!
ANNIHILATE THE MITTELSTAND'S GRAVEDIGGERS!

Thereby you destroy the system …
If you in the Mittelstand have had your fill of misery and bitterness, if you want to live again, then
Overthrow the Brüning system
by refusing to give your vote to its candidate, Hindenberg – the candidate of the enemy of the economy, the Social Democrats.
Your candidate is the Führer of the German Freedom Movement
The Supporter and Protector of the Mittelstand
ADOLF HITLER
To vote for him, Mittelstand, means once again to create work and bread, it means building a future for yourself and your children – and they will thank you eternally for it.
So no vote for Hindenberg, the candidate of the system-parties and the Red Terror …*All Vote ADOLF HITLER!*

48

German bank employees!!

Our people do not want rationalisation, nor training carried out by idiots with monster-sized machines, nor leadership from an American auditing machine ...

And if, for once, you feel secure in your job, who knows? In six months you could be out on the streets. In an economic system that understands only the profit motive anyone could fall victim to the profit-hunters from day to day.

An American machine; the idea that here a few marks can be saved; this is more important to such hyenas than the fate of a racial comrade.

49

Warning!   Warning!
'RELIGION IN DANGER!'

For twelve years, since 24 February 1920, the Programme of the NSDAP has remained unchanged.

For ten years, not one of the professional protectors of religion ever suggested that National Socialism was an enemy of the Catholic church. Only after the results of the September 1930 elections, and after the Centre Party and the Bavarian People's Party had decided upon an alliance with Marxism, did the struggle against the NSDAP begin.

'Religion in danger' – cry the 'Christian' politicians when their party stalls begin to empty.

'Religion in danger' – they cry, when they have no other weapon with which to attack their political enemies.

'National Socialism is heresy'

'National Socialism is a false belief' – say our opponents.

What is it really?

For the National Socialist politician it is a fundamental law never to become involved in church matters ...

Who really endangers religion?

Exactly those who complain that we National Socialists are anti-religious: the Centre Party and the Bavarian People's Party; as a result of their alliance with the Marxists who openly propagate atheism and call for a general rejection of the church.

Politicised priests; who under the protection of religious robes, and in 'Christian brotherhood' ... pursue their political adversaries with fanatical hatred – thereby genuinely seeing to it that God's houses are emptied.

Church authorities; who denied a good National Socialist *Gauleiter* a Christian burial, but who gave the mass-murderer Kürten the final rites of the church.

Who protects religion?

Adolf Hitler's Brown Army, whose struggle against church-destroying Bolshevism has already claimed 300 dead and thousands wounded. Adolf Hitler's Brown Army, in whose ranks most of the men march, who in 1919, under the leadership of General Ritter von Epp (now a National Socialist) destroyed Bolshevism in Munich.

National Socialism wants only to create a
sound, competent and upright people
and acts according to the law,
'Render unto the state what belongs to the state,
and to God what is God's.'
On 13 March bring down those who misuse religion for political purposes:

Vote ADOLF HITLER.

50

Vote Hindenberg – if you want everything to stay as it is.
Vote Hitler – if you want everything, absolutely everything, to change.

Artisans and business people!
You are standing on the edge of your grave!
You know your grave-diggers!
You know that
DEPARTMENT STORES, CONSUMER CO-OPERATIVES
AND SINGLE-PRICE SHOPS

are driving you to ruin.

So don't listen to the newspapers, which on the front-page recommend the re-election of the Field Marshal, while in the advertising section they gorge themselves upon juicy adverts for

DEPARTMENT STORES, CONSUMER CO-OPERATIVES AND SINGLE-PRICE SHOPS

Examine the Nazi newspapers:

You will never find adverts by your grave-diggers ...

The newspapers of the National Socialist movement refuse on principle advertisements from

DEPARTMENT STORES, CONSUMER CO-OPERATIVES AND SINGLE-PRICE SHOPS

Throw your prejudices overboard. Allow Hindenberg a peaceful end to his life. Do not allow those parties which have annihilated the Mittelstand to hide behind the honourable figure of the Field Marshal because they fear the day of reckoning.

Vote Hitler!

51

Adolf Hitler is going to be murdered!
Civil war in Germany!
The KPD murders women!

52

Already 40 pistols and 2500 rounds of ammunition have been found.
THE REICHSBANNER MEANS CIVIL WAR!

53

GERMAN WOMEN!   GERMAN MOTHERS!
GERMAN WOMEN!   GERMAN MOTHERS!
Our young people are being defiled:
Dr Zacharias, Dresden, reports as follows,

The present Prussian Welfare Minister, Hirtsiefer, has confirmed after questions were asked, that in a German grammar school for girls, 63 per cent of the girls had experienced sexual intercourse and 47 per cent had some form of sexual disease ...

The number of sexual offences and cases of incest pile up in the most gruesome manner! Since 1 January 1932, 92 convictions against sex offenders have been reported of which 12 were incest, 5 sexual murder, 40 offences against children and 35 offences against adults.

This is a result of many years during which our people, and in particular our youth, have been exposed to a flood of muck and filth, in words and print, in the theatre and the cinema. These are the results of the systematic Marxist destruction of the family. And all this despite the fact of having Hindenberg as our President, who watches over the constitution, which according to Article 122 is supposed to protect our youth against spiritual, bodily and moral harm.

Is there no possibility of salvation? Must our people, our youth, sink without hope of rescue into the muck and filth? No!!! The National Socialists must win the election so that they can put a halt to this Marxist handiwork, so that once again women are honoured and valued, and so that the theatre and the cinema contribute to the inner rebuilding of the nation.

German women and mothers, do you want your honour to sink still further? Do you want your daughters to be playthings and the objects of sexual lust?

IF NOT then vote for the National Socialists on 31 July.
Then vote for
Hitler Movement   National Socialist German Workers' Party

54

The NSDAP's Kampfbund of the Commerical Mittelstand.
Put an end now to the anti-Mittelstand post-war system.
While, on the one hand, all sorts of huge international concerns were

given care and protection by the state's tax incentives, on the other hand hundreds of thousands of hard-working German artisans and traders were reduced to begging because of an uncaring and pitiless tax-politik.

By putting into operation Point 16 of the National Socialist Programme:

> We demand the creation and preservation of a sound, viable German Mittelstand, conversely the removal of the huge concerns, department stores and single-price shops, etc.

the German artisans and small factories will once again blossom and flourish.

National Socialism will, on socio-political grounds, effectively *prevent moonlighting (Schwarzarbeit)* which does so much damage to the economy.

National Socialism will limit free competition, in order once again to promote the quality-work of the German artisan and to remove mass trash.

National Socialism will reduce the tax burden upon the Mittelstand, in order to make small enterprises viable once more, and to prevent the proletarianisation of the masses.

Only the National Socialists have demanded the creation of a corporate state from the day the party was created!

Therefore it is the only movement capable of realising the oldest wishes and desires of German artisanship and commerce.

The Kampfbund of the commercial Mittelstand has already gained the promise that a representative of the artisans and commerce will be appointed by the national government.

Those are deeds for the Mittelstand!

So on 5 March straight to the ballot boxes and give every vote to the

SAVIOUR OF THE GERMAN MITTELSTAND

ADOLF HITLER!

Original sources

These leaflets and posters are all to be found in the Bayerisches Hauptstaatsarchiv, Munich, Rehse Sammlung.

1. Leaflet, 1919/20. F1.
2. Poster no. 9659, Munich, August 1920.
3. Poster no. 9660, August 1920.
4. Leaflet, November 1921. F2.
5. Poster no. 9701, Munich, November 1921.
6. Poster no. 9714, Munich, March 1922.
7. Poster no. 9730. 1922.
8. Poster no. 9737. September 1922.
9. Leaflet, 1922. F3.
10. Poster no. 9770, June 1923.
11. Leaflet, 1924, probably produced for the Bavarian State Elections. F5.
12. Leaflet produced for Landtag (state) election, Baden, 25 October 1925. F6.
13. ibid.
14. Poster no. 9873, Göttingen, June 1926.
15. Leaflet, 1926, contents the responsibility of Gregor Strasser. F7.
16. Leaflet, 1926, issued by Central Propaganda Department, Munich. F7.
17. Poster no. 9884, Breslau, October 1926. F7.
18. Poster no. 9886, Hannover, November 1926. F7.
19. Leaflet produced for Thuringia Landtag Election, January 1927. F8.
20. Poster no. 9906, Brunswick, March 1927.
21. Poster no. 9909, Berlin, April 1927.
22. Leaflet 1927, contents the responsibility of Gregor Strasser, Munich. F8.
23. Poster no. 9919, Karlsruhe, May 1927.
24. Leaflet, 1927. F8.
25. Poster no. 9950, Brunswick, January 1928.
26. Poster no. 10013, produced for the Reichstag Election, 30 May 1928.

27. Poster no. 10014, produced for the Reichstag Election, 30 May 1928.
28. Poster no. 10022, produced for the Reichstag Election, 30 May 1928.
29. Leaflet 1928/9 (date not certain), Munich. F9.
30. Poster no. 10063, February 1929.
31. Poster no. 10092, June 1929.
32. Leaflet, probably 1929, Munich. F10.
33. Poster no. 10153, Heidelberg, February 1930.
34. Poster no. 10222, produced for the Reichstag Election, 14 September 1930.
35. Poster no. 10226, produced for the Reichstag Election, 14 September 1930.
36. Leaflet produced for the Reichstag Election, 14 September 1930. F11.
37. ibid.
38. ibid.
39. ibid.
40. Poster no. 10361, Hannover, January 1931.
41. Poster no. 10368, Gotha, January 1931.
42. Leaflet, Munich, 1931. F12.
43. Leaflet, Munich, 1931 (signed Adolf Hitler). F12. (But dated 6 March 1930.)
44. Leaflet, Darmstadt Hessen, July 1931. F12.
45. Leaflet, Darmstadt, October 1931. F12.
46. Leaflet, 1931. F12.
47. Leaflet, March 1932. F13. Produced for Presidential Election.
48. ibid.
49. ibid.
50. ibid.
51. Leaflet produced for Reichstag Election, 31 July 1932. F13.
52. ibid.
53. ibid.
54. Leaflet produced for Reichstag Election, 5 March 1933. F14.

PART II

The Struggle for National Socialism, 1919-1933

CHAPTER THREE

The Nazi Radicals

A study of the 'radicals' or the 'left-opposition' within the NSDAP would require a separate book in its own right.[1] My intention here is to examine the ideological characteristics of this tendency in order to balance the image presented by the party's 'official propaganda'.* The actual role played by the radicals in the evolution of National Socialism both during the Kampfzeit and under the Third Reich will become clear in future chapters.

The 'left-opposition' was most closely identified with the names of Otto and Gregor Strasser, although in fact the two brothers took up quite different positions in the conflict which developed in the NSDAP after 1925. None the less, the term the *Strasser-wing* can be used as shorthand to describe those elements, particularly within the SA and among rank-and-file party activists, who believed that Hitler and the NSDAP genuinely stood for national *socialism*.

However it must be emphasised from the outset that the 'socialism' of the Strasser-wing had nothing in common with the concepts of Marxism or even social democracy. Indeed the Nazi left was as implacable in its hatred of proletarian socialism as the most reactionary elements within the party. The 'socialism' of the Strasser group was a radical strain of the corporatist philosophy of the völkisch movement and was often known as 'völkisch socialism'. It represented par excellence the notion of a petit bourgeois 'middle-way' which claimed to bring together the 'healthy' qualities

---

[1] See R. Kühnl, *Die Nationalsozialistische Linke 1925-1930*, Meisenheim 1966.

* A complication is the fact that the KPD used black propaganda techniques to sow discord among disaffected SA units (see police report, Berlin, 25 April & 16 June 1931 (T175 357/2866883 & 2866928, MA2337).

of both bourgeoisie and proletariat. And although the roots of völkisch socialism can be traced to the pre-war völkisch Youth Movement, it was the experience of the world war which popularised many of its pseudo-egalitarian ideals.

Gregor Strasser traced his beliefs to his experiences at the front:

> In the war we became nationalists ... we became nationalists on the battlefield. When I saw all the nations of the earth rushing against the German trenches ... it became clear to me: if Germany is to survive, every German must know what it means to be a German and must defend the idea to the limits of self-sacrifice. Companies and batteries reduced from 250 men to 60 men did not have to be told about the 'community of need'; they knew it. If we do not stand together the blacks will be upon us ...
>
> And why did we become socialists? ... We learned all sorts of things at school. But nobody ever told us that half the German people were hostile to the nation because they had been denied the most basic needs of life by the other half. Not a word were we told about that tragic hour of the German people when the growing workers' movement was nothing but the cry of millions of fellow German countrymen for acceptance into the nation on equal terms. So these millions were left to the Jew Marx, who created Marxism out of the German workers' movement, who intended only to destroy the German nation with the strength of these millions and make it into a colony of world capital ... It was my experience that the best soldiers were frequently those who had least to defend ... We could not help coming home from the war with this resolve:
>
> Those who have fought together with us and who are hostile towards the nation because it has not bothered with them must be emancipated so that in future Germany will be strong and the master of her enemies.[2]

Thus Strasser's socialism was a means to an end. He identified the nation's weakness as being the result of class-ridden attitudes and of the conflicts which ensued. It was a desire to integrate the 'suffering masses' into the nation which inspired Gregor Strasser, rather than any wish to eliminate the causes of inequality by transforming society itself. This form of militaristic 'socialism' also found expression among the soldiers who served as mercenaries in the Free Corps after the war, and who, particularly in northern Germany, formed the first National Socialist cadres in the early 1920s.[3]

---

[2] Quoted by Albrecht Tyrell, *Führer befiehl ... Selbstzeugnisse aus der Kampfzeit der NSDAP*, Düsseldorf 1969, pp. 281-3.

[3] For Freecorps movement, see Robert Waite, *The Vanguard of Nazism*, Cambridge, Mass. 1952.

During the first phase of the NSDAP's development the radical wing was strengthened by the writings of petit bourgeois idealists like Gottfried Feder. Feder provided a pseudo-intellectual basis for völkisch demands by preaching against 'interest-slavery' and demanding a form of archaic capitalism purged of 'modernistic', 'rational' tendencies. Naturally the demands of the radicals did not find favour with the more openly reactionary elements who were also attracted to the NSDAP, but who merely sought a return to some form of pre-war authoritarianism. However, the increasing emphasis upon military preparations for the proposed 'March on Berlin' during 1923 effectively prevented political conflicts from taking substantial organisational form within the party.

After Hitler's release from prison in December 1924 the question of ideology assumed far greater importance. For Hitler was determined to rebuild the party so that it could attract a wider range of social support, even if at this stage he was still unsure about the viability of an 'electoral strategy'. The years of the party's reconstruction mark the high-tide of radical influence within the party, not only because the NSDAP pursued for a time the policy of winning over the working class, but because the structure of the NSDAP was not yet sufficiently tight to prevent local groups from promoting 'socialist' demands.

It was the Strassers' success in building a 'northern block', independent of Hitler and the Munich-based leadership, that led to the first major clash between the Nazi 'left' and 'right'. The northern Gauleiters under Gregor Strasser called an independent conference in November 1925 at which it was decided (among other issues) to side with the Communists and the Social Democrats in their proposal to expropriate the Hohenzollern estates without compensation. Furthermore, when the northern Gauleiters resolved to accept the Strasser Programme in place of the 1920 Twenty-Five Point Party Programme produced by Hitler, it was apparent that the National Socialist movement was in danger of breaking apart on the question of ideology.

Three months later Hitler counter-attacked at the Bamberg Conference, where he stage-managed the proceedings so successfully that he isolated the Strassers and won over Goebbels to his own position. In retrospect Hitler stemmed the radicals' tide, but initially at least he had neither the desire nor perhaps the organisational capacity to drive the Strassers out of the party. Certainly Gregor

Strasser was forced publicly to eat his words on the issue of expropriating the German aristocracy (see ch. 2, **15**) as the NSDAP campaigned against the plebiscite, and Goebbels was dispatched to Berlin to quieten the rebellious radicals. But Strasser remained a major power within the party, while in Berlin Goebbels merely outdid his rivals in radical anti-capitalist demagogy, although his act was always balanced by equally vitriolic attacks upon the Marxists and the Jews.

At its core the issue of the 'radicals' centred on control of the SA. Hitler needed the SA as the party's propaganda unit, as well as for its paramilitary strength and its ability to protect party meetings. But the SA cherished a radical independent ethos. Although its leadership was often drawn from military circles, including officers who were members of the old aristocracy, the SA's rank and file consisted of the more uprooted and dispossessed elements of German society, who were attracted by its cameraderie, its propensity for violence and its ethic of 'front-line socialism'. In the major cities, moreover, such rootless elements included many who drifted between the extremes of the political spectrum, voicing demands for 'revolution' and 'social justice' without regard for the finer points of political ideology.

Hitler certainly understood the importance of keeping these self-styled revolutionary elements within the National Socialist movement, and the evidence suggests that he only confronted them when their agitation threatened to spill over into controversy over political policy, thereby harming the party's wider organisational basis. However, as the NSDAP's emphasis changed during the late 1920s towards an open accommodation with the traditional right-wing voter and the nationalist establishment, confrontation became inevitable, especially as the onset of the economic recession sharpened the already stark political polarisation of German society.

The first public rift in the party occurred in mid-1930 when Otto Strasser's *Arbeitsblatt* (the official journal of the NSDAP in northern Germany) and the *Sächsischer Beobachter*, which he also controlled, openly proclaimed support for striking trade unionists in Saxony. Otto Strasser's outspoken support of working-class interests came at a particularly embarrassing time for Hitler, just after the arrest of the army officers Scheringer, Ludin and Wendt for spreading Nazi propaganda among Reichswehr soldiers, and as Hitler was desperately trying to plead the party's legality and (right-wing) respectability. Moreover Hitler had just begun to create contacts, through Kirdorf, with German industrialists.[4]

Hitler moved quickly to prevent Nazi party members from taking part in strike action, but he was unable to silence Otto Strasser's propaganda. Bringing matters to a head, Hitler travelled to Berlin in May and personally confronted the radical leader. To Strasser's accusation that he wanted to strangle the social revolution, Hitler angrily retorted: 'I am a socialist. ... I was once an ordinary working man. I would not allow my chauffeur to eat worse than (I eat) myself. What you understand by socialism is nothing but Marxism.'[5]

Otto Strasser's own views on the party which he had supported (and to which his brother Gregor still belonged) were made public in July when he left the NSDAP to found the United Revolutionary National Socialists (Black Front):

> We believe, and we have always believed, that National Socialism (as its name implies) should treat bourgeois capitalism and international Marxism as equal enemies. Its task must be the destruction of both. This follows from the fact that in Marxism the correct feeling for socialism is bound up with the false teachings of internationalism and liberal mechanism, whilst among the bourgeoisie the correct feeling for nationalism is bound up with false teachings about liberal rationalism and capitalism. Hence in this unblessed union, the authentic, characteristic strengths of both remain unfruitful for nation and history.
>
> We see no fundamental difference between our opposition to Marxism and the bourgeois spirit (*Bürgertum*), since in both the presence of liberalism makes them our enemy. We declare therefore that the increasingly one-sided slogan of the NSDAP leadership – 'Against Marxism' – is a half-truth, and we have begun to fear that behind this slogan lies a sympathy for the bourgeoisie and capitalist interests, which we refuse to have anything to do with.[6]

Interestingly, Otto Strasser's public break with the NSDAP did not provoke an immediate party crisis – this broke two months later, in September, when the Berlin SA mutinied and refused to protect

[4] See Chapter 4.
[5] See Otto Strasser, *Ministersessel oder Revolution* (pamphlet), 1930.
[6] *Aufruf* of the Strasser group, in *Der Nationale Sozialist*, 4 July 1930.

party meetings. Although the crisis was provoked by a dispute over finance between Berlin party leader Goebbels and SA Fuhrer Walter Stennes, there is no doubt that the crisis really concerned the issue of ideology and the party leadership's increasingly reactionary line. Lowly SA men did not take kindly to Hitler's courting of industrial interests, as an anonymous leaflet circulated in Leipzig makes clear:

> We tell you plainly, we cannot tolerate it any further. The Fuhrer is cooking his own soup. Can you still summon up the enthusiasm to fight for our cause – as we must do if we are to be victorious – when Adolf Hitler, swaying like a reed, is first influenced by one leader, and then another?
>
> It's a sad fact that things have got worse since Mücke left the party, and declared in an open letter: 'I set no hopes on the future of a party whose leader can carry no conviction among the leadership because ... he is under the influence and the obligation of the rich textile baron, Herr Mutschmann.'[7]

Hitler rushed to Berlin in an attempt to pacify the mutinous Stormtroopers. After listening to their complaints about the 'abuses' of party administrators, he appointed himself acting-chief of the SA and promised to correct the situation. In January 1931 Hitler appointed Ernst Röhm as the SA's new commander, hoping that Röhm's reputation as one of the 'old guard' would promote peaceful co-existence within the movement. But at the same time the SS was expanded from a personal bodyguard into a force that could act as a counter-weight to the SA.[8]

On 23 September 1930 the trial of the army officers Scheringer, Ludin and Wendt opened at the Supreme Court in Leipzig. Hitler was now the leader of the second largest party in the Reichstag, but he realised that unless he could assure the military establishment of his good faith and, equally important, counter the NSDAP's 'revolutionary image', he would face insurmountable obstacles to gaining power. Indeed the relationship between the Reichswehr and the SA was critical. If the army remained hostile to the National

---

[7] Copy of anonymous circular sent to Munich headquarters by Gauleiter of Hessen-Nessau-Süd, 10 September 1930. Cf. NSDAP Hauptarchiv MA 1226, Institut für Zeitgeschichte (IfZ).

[8] During the Berlin Crisis the SS had remained steadfastly loyal to Hitler and the Munich party leadership.

Socialist movement Hitler could never hope to achieve power through quasi-legal means; in which case the only alternative would be to lead the Stormtroops in open rebellion against the state. Yet the consequences of unleashing an SA revolt were incalculable; if it succeeded Hitler might become the prisoner of radical elements within the party; if it failed the movement could never hope to recover as it had after 1923.

In testimony before the Supreme Court, Hitler set out to reassure the Reichswehr generals that the SA were merely a propaganda troop, and that the National Socialists were not seeking to replace the army by a party-controlled militia. Moreover Hitler assured the judges that the party would henceforth not come into conflict with the law: 'Many party members have been expelled for such acts', said Hitler. 'Among them Otto Strasser who was planning revolution.'

It is against this background that Hitler issued an order on 20 February 1931 which forbade the SA to engage in street fighting with political opponents. For many rank-and-file members of the SA this was the last straw – final compromise with the hated 'system'. There were instances of wholesale defections to the Communists, while others set up a clandestine opposition within the SA in order to expose the 'treachery of the party bosses':

SA and Party Comrades!

Our fear that the building up of our bosses' SS bodyguard would be at the cost of the SA has been justified. The order, signed by the new C-in-C Röhm, to OSAF in January 1931 makes this quite clear. In Section II Part IV of this order it states that the new SS squads will be formed by the SA donating a leader and a corresponding number of men to the SS. The order further states that recruitment from the SS to the SA will cease. If however, in a particular *Gau*, the stipulated strength is not reached during a three month period, then the SS leadership can apply to the SA leadership for a further intake.

Do Hitler and Röhm really take us for such fools that we can't see which way the wind is blowing?! If so, they deceive only themselves. It is clear to anyone, even at first sight, just how divisive, unjust and deceptive this order is. They say, on the one hand, that recruitment from the SS to the SA should stop, while on the other they decree that the SA leadership and rank and file must obey the orders and demands of the SS. The order confirms only too clearly our belief that the SS is nothing but a bodyguard of the bosses.

According to parts 1/5 and 1/A of the order, the SS has been given the job of protecting the speaker, *the political administration and any leaders present as guests.* Moreover, they have to keep a watch on their cars. The SA have only to protect the meeting!! The nature of the SS, as a bosses' bodyguard, is seen even more clearly in the Rhineland, where SS units have been set up for the personal protection of the Fuhrer, the bosses and *their possessions.* (These bosses must have really earned a fortune if they need to have their possessions specially protected!) And as our Cologne party comrades can confirm, since the latter half of December, an 'SS Watch' has been created to accompany leaders of the party who are travelling in the Rhineland – the high-ranking ones, for the lower ranks there is nothing!

Party comrades! SA comrades! Surely we have the right to set off against the order to strengthen the SS the demand for the dissolution of the now completely superfluous SA! Is it not *unworthy of a revolutionary movement that their leaders* (bosses they should certainly not have) *should have organised a bodyguard at the cost of the movement? You have surely heard how the Communist leaders have servants and footmen!*

In the face of all this we must ask ourselves again whether or not our movement really is a revolutionary movement.

The time cannot be far away, when our parliamentary deputies, sliding down from their seats in the Reichstag, will crawl on their knees to the government benches, and leaning against Herr Brüning, will wring their hands and say ... 'Dear Reichschancellor, forgive us, for we knew not what we did. It was the fault of our stupid SA comrades! We will dissolve the SA at once! In future we will be quite legal and good!'

Party Comrades! SA Friends!

The relationship between the SA and the SS must lead to open conflict in the near future. If it comes to that, we SA men can look after ourselves. We will prevent any attempt to throw us out of the SA. Daily we are subject to the most unashamed attacks, especially from the SS and their arrogant leaders. And what do our own SA leaders do? They try to pour oil on troubled waters, instead of standing up to the SS and demanding its dissolution. But they will only achieve that if they are prepared to get their fingers burned!

The SA also faces an enormous leadership problem: a fact that was yet again demonstrated during our parade on 8 Feb. in Neustrelitz. The practice demonstrated their incompetence, even in the smallest things. While we were exposed to the cold, with chronic hunger pangs in our stomachs, our leaders were sitting around doing nothing in particular in the Mecklenberger Hof, or were nowhere to be found!

CAN WE ACCEPT SUCH LEADERSHIP?! NO! AND AGAIN NO!

Yet this leadership is supposed to be known for its so-called socialist opinions! It is a sad day for our party if it can tolerate such people when we're supposed to be a National Socialist party.

One man is quite unique in this aspect of denouncing socialist ideas. Furthermore he grossly insults the workers in our party, as our KÖNIGSBERG STUDENT PARTY COMRADES can tell you. And he still dares to be a party member and even an MP! He had better not be seen by us SA comrades who are proud to be workers, if he does not wish to end up as a mangled mess!

We are talking about party comrade, yes party comrade, Reichstag member Dr Usädel – a fine little fruit! This insolent patron spoke about us workers in his lecture on 'National Socialism and Knowledge' ... to the National Socialist Student League in Königsberg. He said:

'Nowadays all sense of responsibility is completely missing *because the worst elements are in control. Look at the proletarians for instance.* What is a proletarian? Proletarians are people who irresponsibly bring children into the world, then seek to achieve power by means of the democratic process. Such people must obviously make irresponsible leaders since they are quite irresponsible in small matters.'

Party comrades! Party friends! Has there ever been a more monstrous insult to the working class? Party comrade Dr Usädel, *this slut*, dares to define the procreation of children by the working class as 'a lack of responsibility in small matters'. His idea is that workers, instead of having children and bringing them up to face the prospect of starvation, should abort the child, just like SS leader Wregen (Rhineland) who was sentenced to prison for this very crime. We repeat, then – a fine little fruit!

This disgraceful statement fits entirely his further comments about socialism ... 'Socialism is the means by which we pass on inherited strength to future generations; our socialism must be understood as a question of race ... it is not the socialism of the workers!' That, word for word, is what Dr Usädel said to our Königsberg Students and Party Comrades! Doesn't he belong in a lunatic asylum? But watch carefully. This swine Usädel will never be put in an asylum, but he will remain, what is worse, a party comrade and a member of the Reichstag! Adolf Hitler has been told about this idiot's speech. Now watch, nothing will happen to him! Things are falling into place. Adolf Hitler has also ended up giving similar criminal explanations of national socialism.

We, however, must ask ourselves whether we can remain in such a party.

Heil! Several Party members and SA comrades![9]

At the end of March Walter Stennes was suspended for failing to obey Hitler's orders and the Berlin SA was dissolved. The

[9] Leaflet dated 25 February 1931. Cf. NSDAP Hauptarchiv, IfZ MA 1226 Reel 17, Folder 322.

disagreements between the SA and the Munich leadership over the question of co-operating with the 'establishment' now broke out into renewed conflict as the Berlin Stormtroopers attempted to seize the political initiative:

Berlin National Socialists!
Yesterday the NSDAP leadership in Munich announced
THE DISSOLUTION OF THE BERLIN SA
and dismissed SA leader Stennes, whom Hitler has constantly assured of his trust.

This news has provoked anger, bitterness and deep shock in the Berlin SA and in other SA groups throughout the Reich.

'Why has it happened?' Is it simply a clash of personalities – a 'leadership struggle'?

No! It is a question of the meaning of National Socialism. The entire SA is being attacked through the dismissal of Walter Stennes. Munich has forgotten that it was the self-sacrifice and solidarity of the SA that has built up the party to its present position. Today they are building the Brown House in Munich as a result of massive contributions to party funds, while the individual Stormtrooper hasn't even a few pennies to keep his tattered boots in good repair.

At a time of emergency decrees, when the blood-sacrifice of the SA, when the attack upon our movement and the terror have reached a high-point, the Munich party clique carries on
a civil war in the ranks of the party!

The SA has helped the party to gain thousands of seats in the Reichstag and local and parish councils.

Now the SA have done their duty – they can go. They are a heavy conscience, a reminder of the betrayal of the party programme and the struggle for the old ideals which National Socialism has always demanded, in contrast to the opportunist appeasement policies of Munich.

It is not a question of illegal putschism, as the Jewish press likes to present it, but quite simply a matter of
the betrayal of the SA by the party
in order to hold back National Socialism.

The SA leadership refuses to allow their unemployed comrades to be misused as cannon fodder for political self-seekers, or for the financing of the Brown House.

They are deeply responsible to every single SA man and to the entire German people, and conduct themselves according to the fundamental belief of National Socialism:
The Common Need before Individual Greed
and in line with the deepest law of comradeship
LOYALTY FOR LOYALTY!

Raise the flag!   Close Ranks!   The SA is on the March!
Stennes takes over command.[10]

But the rebellion failed. Branding Stennes as a police-informer, Hitler maintained his ban on the SA while Göring carried out a thorough purge. The SS was allowed to expand while the independence of the SA from the party apparatus was curtailed through cuts in the SA's budget and an order requiring that all appointments to its staff be vetted by a party leader. Once again Hitler managed to restore a semblance of order, but the rifts within the National Socialist movement ran deep. Opposition to the leadership's 'betrayal' of the 'old ideals', and criticism of its ever more reactionary political line continued, especially when Scheringer left the Nazi Party and went over to the Communists:

> Party Comrades, SA Comrades, National Socialists!
> Collapse!
> Betrayal by the party clique, headed by Hitler. How often have we denounced our bosses' betrayal of National Socialism, in the desperate hope of being able to turn around the rudder of our freedom movement? The die is cast.
> *Even our desperate hopes that our leaders' promises would be honoured have been dashed.*
> Hitler and his circle have made the party a cesspool of dried-up bourgeois bankrupts, while we, the committed party activists, must hold the reins for the ambitious traitors who now devote themselves completely to capitalism, so that they can fulfil their long cherished dream of becoming cabinet ministers at the age of forty.
> So we can starve? Like Hell!
> So we must ask ourselves once more if we can remain in the party under these circumstances. Is this not a betrayal of those voters who have put their hope in our courageous movement?
> *The bold soldiers of the Third Reich are sinking into the morass of our Fuhrer's double-dealings.*
> Do you remember how Hitler and the *Völkischer Beobachter* commended the Ulmer officers, Scheringer, Wendt and Ludin, saying that they were upright German men? At that time Scheringer and Wendt saw the Hitler party as the last hope of salvation. Well they soon changed their minds. Scheringer's resignation hit the party like a bomb, while in the meantime Wendt had also left the party and was speaking openly against Hitler. Hitler paled and almost collapsed when Scheringer threw the irrevocable party programme in his face with the

[10] IfZ MA 1226 Reel 17, Folder 325.

words 'You have obviously given up socialism within the last few months. You have spoken reverently of capitalism. In domestic politics and economic discussions you have represented the interests of big business, as opposed to the interests of the middle classes, the small farmers and the deeply suffering working class. You have nurtured inside the party a Byzantine ethic which stinks!'

In a miserable attempt to refute this proven betrayal of the National Socialist ideal, the *Völkischer Beobachter* wrote in Number 83 of 24 March 1931, that 'abolition of the capitalist system has for centuries been nothing more than a catchphrase'.

Can there be a more grotesque betrayal of socialism?

Hitler and his bosses must surely blush with shame. With this betrayal Hitler has declared himself conclusively in favour of the programme of the bourgeois parties who are already disintegrating, and has created an abysmal chasm between the party and millions of farmers and tradespeople and workers. In the last few weeks tens of thousands of disappointed and deceived party comrades and NSDAP voters have turned their backs on us. They have fled back to the camp of the indifferents or joined up with the ruling parties, who now have the reins of government even more firmly in their hands as a result of the emergency decrees which Hitler has so painstakingly obeyed.

'The old parties are winning the trust of our voters.'

Should we not be ashamed of ourselves?

'Hitler and his bosses declare themselves to be dictators of democracy.' Thus our great Adolf set out his aims. He has given our movement the kiss of death. The fanatical fighters for National Socialism, for our Third Reich, who fight as revolutionaries, will be labelled Bolsheviks, and will leave the movement. The SA has made the party great. Now it can disappear – vanish! Thus Goebbels' long cherished dream would be fulfilled. To him the SA has long been an embarrassment, and for this reason he does not want it to remain in its old form. So the betrayal moves from stage to stage.

Hitler tried to silence the real voice of NS militants by banning SA leaders from speaking. He particularly wanted to act against the Silesian Gausturmführer Kremser who is highly popular there. Only a few weeks ago he silenced Goebbels, because he knows that Goebbels is his most serious rival. With the row over the SA however, Hitler assured Goebbels of his steadfast trust and let everyone know that Goebbels was the Fuhrer's truest disciple. Will Hitler break his word – given 'forever' – in a few months? As he did to Stennes? Perhaps –

If Goebbels doesn't stab him in the back first!

If only Goebbels had managed to spread the rumour that Hitler himself had been behind the official ban on his public speaking. By doing this, foxy Goebbels was trying to discredit Hitler within the party. Goebbels had used such a tactic before. You Berlin NS members will recall the sly way in which Goebbels made a fool of Hitler shortly before the Reichstag elections in 1930, and showed himself to be the big shot. Hitler was completely exhausted after his speech in the Sportspalast, but he was still announced to speak in the Hasenheide. What did Goebbels do? He drove to the Hasenheide and declared to the capacity crowd that Hitler – the fighter! – was so exhausted by his speech in the Sportspalast that they had to put him straight into a bath and then into bed. Goebbels also adopted this double-dealing attitude towards Stennes. He promised him his fullest support shortly before the crunch. But then he suddenly went over to Hitler because Hitler had the money!

They're as bad as each other!

They will resurrect the nation as successfully as our chief of staff Röhm, who vanished somewhat unwillingly to Bolivia because he was one of two figures in a minor scandal which hardly fitted him for the SA.

Party Comrades! SA Comrades! NS! It is not a question of Röhm, nor Goebbels, nor even Hitler!

It is a question of the aims of our movement! Protect the old ideals!

Do not allow the betrayal of socialism by selfish politicians, for whom the party at this stage is only an end in itself.

The common need before individual greed!

It is a question of the freedom of our people! Not of treacherous bosses.

Several NS and SA Comrades.[11]

The 'opposition's' pamphlets are notable for a tone of incensed moral outrage and profound political naivety. But there can be no doubting their belief that National Socialism (or at least the 'old ideals') represented some kind of middle way between Communism and modern (big business) capitalism.

Yet the very criticisms levelled by the authors of these pamphlets are an indication of the 'opposition's' impotence. Unable to argue the case either for democratic accountability or for a genuine socialist transformation of society, they were forced to bemoan the (inevitable) consequences of the very policies that they sought – the leadership principle, political opportunism, etc. Indeed, in another pamphlet the authors maintain that Hitler's accomodation with capitalism was proof that the Jews had managed to infiltrate the National Socialist Party, and that the *Völkischer Beobachter* was being financed by the 'Jewish' Bayerische Hypotheken- und Wechsel Bank![12] – a charge reminiscent of Drexler's accusation during the 1921 leadership crisis that Hitler was in fact a Jewish agent.[13]

Thus the Nazi radicals were in a trap. Although proletarian

[11] Leaflet dated 8 April 1931, IfZ MA 1226 Reel 17.
[12] See *Freiheits Kampfer no. 2*, Hessen. Cf. IfZ MA 1226.
[13] See S. Taylor, *Germany 1918-1933*, London 1983, p.65.

elements initially attracted to the SA might leave the party for the KPD, the great majority of petit bourgeois militants still feared 'Communism' even more than they distrusted the double-dealing of the Nazi leadership. Moreover the very success of the NSDAP's image of 'radicalism' and its style of 'rejectionist' politics was largely responsible for the disintegration of the Mittelstand's traditional political representatives in the centre and moderate right-wing parties after 1930. In effect the Mittelstand radical had *no* political alternative to the NSDAP after the onset of the economic recession, for in 1928 the German Nationalist Party came under the control of the crassly reactionary Alfred Hugenberg and his political allies. In such circumstances most rank and file radicals must have preferred to carry on the fight for the 'old ideals' within the party rather than outside it. Besides, Gregor Strasser, Gottfried Feder and Otto Wagener still occupied leading positions within the party hierarchy, and there was every chance that an acceptable 'Mittelstand politik' would be implemented, even if the party programme was not implemented in full.

Hence, despite criticisms of the 'bosses' in the party leadership, the underlying ideological demands of the petite bourgeoisie for 'social peace' and 'political stability' (at the cost of the working class) tended to reinforce allegiance to National Socialism. The 'opposition' of course continued its attempts to 'expose' party corruption and the extravagance of Hitler and his clique, but in the absence of some form of organisational alternative, the radicals were little more than a running sore in the side of those who really controlled the NSDAP's destiny.

We had originally intended to suspend our criticism during the election period, but the situation within our party makes it necessary to issue a clear statement of our position before the election.

Have we not frequently warned you about Dr Goebbels, and marked him as an obstinate ambitious careerist? This has been shown clearly in recent events. Dr Goebbels is responsible for Hitler's candidature. Hitler hesitated for a long time, as he realised that he would be defeated, thereby damaging the party and above all detracting from the belief in its invincibility. Our Fuhrer has been publicly branded as a laughable marionette by Goebbels' tactics. Goebbels delivered a *fait accompli*, for without authorisation, he proclaimed at the end of February in the Sportspalast, 'Hitler will be Reichspresident!' Hitler could not turn back – he had to run into defeat. Foxy Goebbels planned this so that he could take a step nearer his goal of becoming leader of the party. If Hitler had won the first round of the election, for we cannot reckon with victory in the run-off, he would have become Reichspresident, and he would have had to hand over the leadership of the party to another representative. Goebbels saw himself as the man! But if Hitler is defeated he loses face as much in the party as in public.

Of course Hitler recognises Goebbels' perfidious tactics. However, he does not dare oppose them. Here again he is lacking in determination and strength of leadership. However Goebbels is not yet in sight of his goal, and we know how to ensure that he does not reach it!

With this we leave this dark point in the party's history. Who knows the resting place of this bragging insignificant Goebbels – so-called because of his Jewish appearance. There is, God knows, more important stuff than comrade Goebbels.

Have we, has our party for instance, any right to criticise extravagance, when our leaders do no better? Indeed with what right does Hitler on the one hand preach morality, while living in luxury himself? Is it not enough that he is a guest with a Berlin party member on his visits to Berlin, and makes do with his flat? Our party swarms with members who possess elegant flats in which our party leader could live. But he has got accustomed to princely comforts, and his stay in Berlin must be in the most luxurious hotel, the Kaiserhof. Is our leader already dreaming of a new coronation in the Third Reich? While tens of thousands of party comrades go hungry and cannot even find the rent for pitiful flats, he pays huge sums for hotel bills out of painfully saved-up membership contributions. In the Kaiserhof he lives in a whole suite of rooms, in which there is even a Roman marble bath. So Adolf Hitler spends 150 Marks a day solely for the rooms he occupies. To this sum must also be added the monstrously high price of breakfast, lunch and drinks which add up to hundreds, since our great leader will only eat with his retinue. Is this not simply provocative, in the light of our present needs?

And this man calls himself the leader of a workers' party, and is sufficiently without conscience to squander more on lodgings alone (from the painfully found pennies of party members) during a short visit to the capital of the Reich, than millions of unemployed German party comrades could spend on themselves and their families in six months. Should we fight for this?!

And now to the aims of these great bosses. In party meetings and rallies our leader has always declared that on gaining power he will tear up the shameful Versailles Treaty and the Young Plan and will withdraw Brüning's Emergency Decrees immediately. To the representatives of the foreign press, however, he has said the exact opposite. On the day before the first ballot for the presidential elections on 12 March, Hitler told the well-known American reporter Knickerbecker, Berlin correspondent of the *New York Evening Post*, the following:

'The moment that I take over the position of Reichspresident, orders will be issued for new elections in parliament. The notion that I will rule without Reichstag approval is absolutely false. I will certainly not rescind at once all the emergency decrees of the government, and even less will I immediately announce that the Versailles agreement will be ripped up. The Treaty of Versailles will be finished with, when, just like the earlier Dawes Plan, it is replaced by a new agreement at a new conference.'

With this Hitler has announced the bankruptcy of our party, for we are now doing the same as the former government parties have done – namely recognising the Versailles peace agreement and a programme of appeasement that until now we had fanatically resisted.

When the Reichschancellor, with the agreement of President Hindenburg, explained to the foreigners, 'We can no longer afford political payments', where was our party? Where was Hitler who could have taken up these words of the Reichschancellor and stirred the entire German people? ...

This single deed would have given our leader a further ten million votes in the Presidential election. Instead of this we said nothing, and the undoubtedly courageous words of the Chancellor went unheeded, for the voice of the inner impulse of a politically united German Volk was lacking.

We are now at the second ballot. Ashamed, we must 'do penance' for our leader's mistakes, for it must unfortunately be said, the Reichschancellor gave us every chance to exploit the issue. Is there any point in fighting the second ballot now that the Fuhrer's mistakes have handed our opponents the advantage? For us there can only be one slogan after missing our opportunity again.

Put an end to the divisions among the German people!

Gather under one flag and one leader who will rescue Germany in open battle!

The NSDAP opposition.[14]

Only during the final months of 1932 did the radicals' struggle within the National Socialist movement take on a meaningful organisational form. At stake was the fate of the so-called 'Immediate Economic Programme' much associated with Gregor Strasser, although in fact it had been largely drafted by Bernhard Köhler. The Programme was launched two months before the July

---

[14] Leaflet dated 4 April 1932, IfZ MA 1226 (the election referred to is the Presidential election which Hindenberg won on the second ballot).

Reichstag elections (in which the Nazis reached the peak of their popularity), and it was confirmed by the Munich leadership as being official party policy. At the heart of the programme was an attempt to create jobs and alleviate unemployment, but it was the method of achieving this aim which promoted the greatest interest.

According to Gregor Strasser the Programme's goal was the 'deproletarianisation of German workers' and the promotion of an 'active Mittelstand politik'. The decisive problem of the relationship between capital and labour was clearly spelled out (if in a somewhat unscientific manner) and a 'comprehensive regulation of profit-distribution' was promised 'as soon as the German economy, through the process of job-creation, is in a position once again to create profit'.[15] After the elections this Immediate Programme was further developed in co-operation with Gottfried Feder in his role as a leading member of the Economic Council of the Party Leadership. Feder's crackpot distinction between the 'sphere of circulation' and the 'sphere of production' did little to make the basis of the Programme any clearer, but by October 1932 Strasser was publicly expounding the theory of the National Socialist Economy to the electorate. Borrowing from his brother's pseudo-philosophical writings, Strasser spoke of the 'collapse of the Weltanschauung of the French Revolution' and the creation of a new Weltanschauung born of 'the experience of the war' which bound together nationalism and socialism. And although he repeated many of the stereotyped charges of Nazi anti-Semitism, Strasser went on to demand the creation of a 'state-economy' in which it was abundantly *unclear* whether the state would intervene in the free-market economy, or whether the free-market economy was the state! References to a 'planned corporate union of all strata and branches of production' and a 'state regulation of currency dealings with foreign countries, which is in no way the same as a nationalisation of exporters', did nothing to clarify this programmatic confusion. In fact the Immediate Programme was an attempt to ride a horse in two different directions by promising a populist Mittelstand politik with work-creation for the proletariat, without at the same time alienating the interests of big business.

The fate of the Immediate Programme was never *publicly*

[15] Cf. Ulrich Wörtz, *Programmatik und Führerprinzip*, PhD thesis, University Erlangen-Nuremberg. pp. 176ff.

determined, but as early as 12 September Hitler gave a secret guarantee to leading industrialists that it would never be implemented.[16] On 22 September the National Economic Council of the NSDAP, which included Feder, Köhler and Otto Wagener, as well as Theodor Adrian von Renteln, the leader of the Kampfbund (Fighting League) of the Commercial Mittelstand, was in practice deposed by an Economic Council of the Reich (Reichswirtschaftsrat) whose brief was to act as 'the highest National Socialist organ for the discussion of economic questions'. The old Economic Council was henceforth to work solely within the guidelines of the Reich's Council, and although Feder was appointed as the 'chairman' of this Council, it was a de facto relegation of Mittelstand political interests to the sphere of electoral and thus ideological expediency.

However, the radicals' struggle to implement the movement's 'old ideals' did not cease with the 'reorganisation' of the NSDAP's economic policy-making bodies, nor indeed with Gregor Strasser's resignation from the party in early December 1932. As we shall see, the accession of Hitler to the Chancellorship and the Nazi take-over of power let loose a renewed wave of radical demands from among the SA, and the threat of a second (anti-bourgeois) revolution was only finally put to rest in the Röhm Purge of June 1934.

But for all this the radicals' struggle against the 'betrayal' of National Socialism was a near hopeless contest against a shadowy or unseen enemy operating in a secretive twilight world. Otto Dietrich, who was to become the NSDAP's chief Press Officer, wrote in his memoirs that Hitler began to cultivate contacts with 'influential economic magnates' in the summer of 1931. 'In the following months he traversed Germany from end to end, holding private interviews with prominent persons ... either in Berlin or in the provinces, in the Hotel Kaiserhof or in some lonely forest glade. Privacy was absolutely imperative ... Success was the consequence.'[17] The substance of these 'discussions' will become clear in the next chapter.

---

[16] See p. 118 below.
[17] Otto Dietrich, *With Hitler on the Road to Power*, London 1934, pp. 12-13.

CHAPTER FOUR

National Socialism and Big Business

The early years

There are obvious problems in determining exactly who provided financial support for the NSDAP before 1923. During this early period the Nazi movement existed as an extreme right-wing grouping whose populist public image belied its real strategy of seizing power through armed counter-revolution. And although Bavaria was a safe haven for such groups, the central government in Berlin made consistent (if usually ineffective) attempts to expose the activities of such neo-fascist bands by bringing them to account through the courts. Thus the contributions which flowed into the NSDAP before 1923 were often given in secret, and certainly in the aftermath of the failed coup evidence of support for the National Socialists would have been destroyed by the party's benefactors.

It is very likely that the cost of provisioning and arming the Nazi SA was at least partly met by the Bavarian Reichswehr, especially after Hitler was appointed leader of the Bavarian Kampfbund early in 1923 (the Kampfbund was an alliance of right-wing Bavarian paramilitary units). Direct contributions to the party came through Hitler's personal contacts with Bavarian high-society, most notably from the wealthy Bechstein family. But financial support also came from industrial organisations. According to Haniel von Haimhausen (the Berlin government's agent in Bavaria), the Bavarian Confederation of Industry, and in particular one of its major figures, Dr Kuhlo, was responsible for 'providing the National Socialists and other organisations with money'.[1] A secret memo from the German

[1] Haimhausen to Reichschancellery, 18 March 1923, Bundesarchiv R43 1/2681. Haimhausen sent regular reports to the Reichschancellor on the activities of the far right.

Foreign Office suggested that Bavarian industrialists supported the Nazis because of Hitler's slogan 'Fight Stock-Exchange Capitalism, protect Industrial Capitalism. The one is termed Jewish, the other Aryan'.[2] More pragmatically Haimhausen notes that the industrialists wanted to 'reduce the power of the trade union movement', and so backed the Nazis because of their fanatical anti-Marxism.[3]

Funds also found their way into the NSDAP from abroad. On Hitler's birthday the *Völkischer Beobachter* (no. 74) claimed that in addition to a total of 11,000,000 marks from German sources, the Fuhrer also received 7431 krona from Czechoslovakia and a further 2,000,000 marks from other foreign countries. A secret service report confirms that considerable contributions came from abroad, and states that a Finnish woman had provided finance for the *Völkischer Beobachter* to be published as a daily rather than a weekly newspaper.[4] Much of this foreign money seems to have been sent from Latin America, for in April 1923 the German Foreign Minister Hamm requested his country's diplomats there to try to prevent money from Latin America reaching the NSDAP.[5]

Rebuilding the party

After Hitler's release from prison in December 1924 a number of his old benefactors once again provided the money to rebuild the party. Franz Hanfstaengel, the Munich publisher and art dealer, gave 30,000 Marks to finance the NSDAP's headquarters in Schellingstrasse, while Bechstein once again provided funds and attempted to persuade his fellow entrepreneurs to do the same. But during the next few years Hitler was not always received with total enthusiasm by leaders of industry. In order to understand why, it is necessary to examine briefly the political role of German industry in the mid 1920s.

Most industrialists either belonged to the ultra-nationalist DNVP or else formed the right wing of the German People's Party (DVP).

[2] Foreign Office to Chancellery, 13 January 1923, ibid.
[3] Haimhausen to Reichschancellery, ibid.
[4] Bericht der Reichszentrale für Heimatdienst an Staatssekretär Hamm, 20 February 1923, ibid.
[5] It is worth noting that Ernst Röhm disappeared to Bolivia after the trial of the Munich Putschists.

By 1926 the leading representatives of the western iron and steel industries, as well as sections of the mining industry, were openly demanding the institutionalisation of some form of authoritarian presidential government in place of parliamentary democracy – or as the leader of the League of Iron and Steel Industrialists stated: 'the government should rule with the help of Article 48 of the constitution' and the 'Reichstag should only be reconvened when the year has thirteen months'.[6] The most radical exponent of this demand for the reinstitution of a strong authoritarian state was Alfred Hugenberg, until 1928 the leader of the Mining Group of the Reichsverband der deutschen Industrie (Confederation of German Industry) and from 1928-1933 leader of the DNVP; he was supported by many leaders of small and medium-sized firms.

However, in opposition to Hugenberg and his circle, the leaders of the electro-chemical and machine-tool industries pleaded for an acceptance of the Weimar system, and called for co-operation with the bourgeois centre parties in parliament. During 1926, Hugenberg and the leading figures in Class's Pan-German League began their attempts to take over the DNVP and to direct the party along a totally 'rejectionist' path vis-à-vis democracy and the parliamentary system. In the process the old ideological characteristics of the Pan-Germans once again came to the fore: authoritarianism, ultra-nationalism and a latent anti-Semitism. This was the background to Hitler's first meeting with influential industrialists in Hamburg in February 1926.

It was largely through his contacts with the Bechsteins and the Bruckmanns that Hitler received his invitation to address the Hamburg National Club in person. Founded by the Hanseatic banker, Max von Schinckel, the Hamburg Club had already made public its demand for the founding of a 'nationally conscious' government, which would be 'anti-democratic, anti-socialist, conservative and authoritarian'. In his speech, Hitler concentrated upon his party's anti-Marxist and anti-socialist convictions, giving less emphasis to anti-Semitic agitation, and stressed his aim of building a mass party which could win support among the workers

---

[6] Statement by Reichert, 16 December 1925, in Dirk Stegmann, 'Zum Verhältnis von Grossindustrie und Nationalsozialismus, 1930-1933, *Archiv für Sozialgeschichte*, 13 (1973), p.408.

and the middle classes.[7] It was precisely this notion of winning a popular base for reactionary politics which most appealed to the audience, and for his speech Hitler received not only 'stormy applause', but also financial support for the party.[8]

During the summer of 1926 Hitler travelled through the Ruhr, and met leading industrialists Fritz Thyssen and Emil Kirdorf.[9] Twelve months later he spoke at a meeting of leaders of western heavy industry, where he again outlined his ideas. Kirdorf was so impressed with Hitler's speech that he requested him to outline his ideas in a leaflet which Kirdorf promised to circulate among 'leading personalities in industrial circles'. In this leaflet Hitler stressed that the NSDAP's 'socialism' was not the socialism of the working class parties but a form of 'social-politik' in which the worker would be integrated into society. Equally it was made clear that National Socialism would neither interfere in the economy nor alter property relationships.

Kirdorf joined the NSDAP in August 1927, donating 100,000 RM to the party at a time of desperate financial shortfall. But Kirdorf was not so much attempting to 'buy himself' into the Nazi movement as to create a bridge which would eventually allow the NSDAP to form some type of organisational alliance with Hugenberg's wing of the DNVP. Two months later, on 26 October, Kirdorf arranged a private meeting for Hitler with fourteen leading industrialists at his estate in Mülheim. According to Kirdorf's own appraisal, the industrialists were well pleased with Hitler's fanatical nationalism, but serious doubts were expressed about the NSDAP's attitudes to 'socialism' and 'anti-Semitism'.[10] Those present warned against taking on board any form of socialism, since it could ultimately lead to state capitalism, or even to nationalisation of the private sector. And although Kirdorf himself argued that the Nazis' exploitation of

[7] The speech took place shortly after the Bamberg Conference, and Hitler would have been keen to push home his appeal to the traditional right wing.

[8] According to a police report of the meeting, the exact amount was not known: see Police Report to Reichschancellery, 17 October 1928, Bundesarchiv R43 1/2252.

[9] Thyssen, born 1873; 1923 member of the Executive Committee of RdI and from 1926 Director of United Steelworks, the largest Steel concern in Germany.

Kirdorf, born 1847; leading member of Pan-German League; executive member of the Central Committee of German Industrialists.

[10] See Henry Turner, Jr, *Faschismus und Kapitalismus in Deutschland*, Göttingen 1972, p.70.

anti-Semitism only served a manipulatory function, which was acceptable from a tactical point of view, the majority complained that any attempt to couple anti-Semitism with anti-capitalism could backfire against Aryan entrepreneurs as well.

A year later Kirdorf left the NSDAP and returned to the fold of the German Nationalist Party, which was now under Hugenberg's leadership. The misgivings of the industrialists who had met at Mülheim seemed to have been justified, for in attempting to win over working-class support in the Ruhr, local NSDAP units were proclaiming socialist slogans and denigrating 'reactionary capitalists'. Yet Kirdorf's praise for Hitler was undiminished. Of his resignation he wrote: 'Despite my warm friendship with Adolf Hitler and the high esteem in which I hold him, I was forced to leave his party because his representatives in this region supported a political line which I cannot accept.'[11] And in 1929 he wrote to Hitler about the recent Nuremberg Party Rally, enthusing:

> Whoever was privileged to take part in this day must recognise the importance of your movement for the rebuilding of the German fatherland and wish it success, even if he has doubts about or indeed totally rejects certain points of your party programme.[12]

What fascinated Kirdorf and the western magnates was Hitler's capacity to move the masses. It was an aim which, as Dirk Stegmann notes, the right-wing parties and the Pan-German League had consistently failed to achieve. Yet for Kirdorf, as well as for Hugenberg and his allies, supporting the National Socialist movement 'could only be countenanced when it was certain that the "socialism" of the NSDAP contained no social-revolutionary dynamic'.[13] It is equally certain that Hitler himself recognised this obstacle to his political career.

A new respectability

Although the Reichstag elections of 1928 were hardly encouraging for the NSDAP, they did mark the consolidation of the party as the

---

[11] *Berliner Lokalanzeiger*, 23 August 1930.
[12] Letter printed in *Völkischer Beobachter*, 27 August 1929.
[13] Stegmann, op. cit., pp. 414-15.

strongest force on the ultra-right of German politics and ultimately led to the Nazis' participation in the campaign against the Young Plan. The alliance of the NSDAP with the new right-wing leadership of the DNVP (Hugenberg, Class and Kirdorf) marks the first stage of the so-called *Einrahmungspolitik* by which the DNVP hoped to bring the Nazi party into its own sphere of influence, with the ultimate intention of binding Hitler and his movement to the conservative establishment. By this manoeuvre Hugenberg hoped to widen his own power-base, and his massive press and cinema empire was used to build up the respectability of the National Socialist movement. The possibility that an *Einrahmungspolitik* could work in two directions does not seem to have troubled the elderly gentlemen in the DNVP.

However, if Hugenberg and his circle saw the way forward in terms of an extra-parliamentary, anti-republican alliance, the majority of western industrialists were following a different route. In order to prevent a disintegration of the bourgeois centre and right-wing parties under the impact of the deepening economic recession, industrialists such as Paul Reusch, Krupp (von Bohlen) and Ernst Poensgen advocated the consolidation of a liberal-conservative block in parliament to support a form of Presidential government which had been inaugurated by Hindenburg's appointment of Brüning to the Chancellorship in March 1930. Moreover this latter group were hostile to Hugenberg's leadership of the German Nationalists, believing that Hugenberg's rejectionist line would sabotage efforts to create a broad bourgeois alliance.

The National Socialist breakthrough at the polls in September 1930, however, threw the industrialists' calculations into chaos and provoked a confusion of responses within the ranks of big business. The director of Berlin AEG, Hermann Bücher, feared that the rise of the Nazis could only lead in the end to 'Communism', and he wrote to Reusch stating that any attempt to exert pressure upon the Nazi leadership would be in vain. (Bücher had failed to pressurise Goebbels to cut down on his anti-capitalist demagogy in Berlin.) Other business circles recognised the existence of two wings within the NSDAP. According to the Hanseatic League's experts, one wing, 'at present the major section of the leadership, concentrates upon nationalism and puts socialism second to that; other leadership elements, and the majority of the membership, are essentially romantic socialists ..."[14] Finally, the very success of the Nazis persuaded some industrialists that the only way to influence the situation was to become involved in the political struggle inside the NSDAP, and Tengelmann (Director of Essener Steinkohlen AG) and Thyssen both moved towards open support for Hitler.

In December 1931 Thyssen became a member of the NSDAP – his retort to the German Confederation of Industry's continued support for the Brüning government. In fact the mining industry (probably at Thyssen's instigation) had been providing finance for the NSDAP since the beginning of the year; but the manner of their support illustrates precisely the confusion that reigned among the leaders of heavy industry over the intentions of National Socialism. Thus the Bergbauliche Verein and the Zechenverband paid a monthly subscription of 10,000 RM not to the NSDAP's central offices, but to Gregor Strasser and Paul Schutz![15] This apparently illogical support for the 'radicals' within the party is not what it seems for, according to the economist August Heinrichsbauer, the magnates of the Ruhr saw Goebbels and Göring as the more 'dangerous' elements within the NSDAP, and believed that Strasser, for all his socialist rhetoric, was more 'reasonable' than other Nazi leaders (as did General Schleicher later). Equally, such financial support was a useful insurance policy in the event of Strasser's wing winning the struggle for control of the National Socialist movement's political direction.

Yet at the same time the mining industry was also giving money to

---

[14] Definition of 'National Socialism' in *ABC of Economics for Commerce and Industry*, Berlin 1931, p.138. Even more illuminating is Paul Bang's letter to von Lüttichau, 8 April 1930:

> The political relationship is quite variable according to locality ... It is necessary to differentiate between the National Socialists, i.e. the Munich leadership, and the agitation of local organisations ... it will be a matter of whether Hitler has the party in hand, or not ... Scheibe has told me (in confidence) that leading National Socialists are increasingly taking advice from us on economic matters ... A movement, at whose head Prince August Wilhelm of Prussia marches, cannot be dismissed as unreliable from a nationalist point of view. Equally, a movement in which a greater part of our academic youth has gathered, in which Kirdorf is extremely influential, and ... in which a great number of sons of our leading industrialists (for instance Vögler's) are active, cannot be shrugged off as pure Marxist ... And in order to show you how far this has gone already, I enclose some documents (which I ask you to return) which demonstrate that even big landowners stand behind the movement today (AdV Nr 232 Bl 90-93).

[15] Cf. August Heinrichsbauer, *Schwerindustrie und Politik*, Essen-Kettwig 1948, p.40.

Walter Funk (1000 RM per month, according to Heinrichsbauer[16]), one of Hitler's closest personal advisors on economic matters. This money was to counter the influence of Dr Otto Wagener, the leader of the NSDAP's Economic Council.[17] Funk was the editor of the Berlin Stock Exchange Newsletter, and a trusted emissary of the interests of heavy industry, who provided a secret 'information service on economic matters' to the Nazi leadership. Wagener, on the other hand, was a supporter of corporatist economic proposals which were regarded as 'insane' by the Ruhr industrialists.[18]

The nature of the relationship that was gradually evolving between the Ruhr coal and steel barons and the NSDAP is well illustrated by the case of Hans Reupke, a member of the RdI's Central Committee *and* of the NSDAP. In 1931 Reupke produced two brochures entitled 'National Socialism and the Economy' which aimed to reassure industrialists that the Nazi movement's 'socialism' had become 'aristocratic socialism' which 'accepted the hierarchical and the aristocratic principle in government and the economy'. Hitler praised Reupke's work highly, and it clearly influenced many industrialists, including Albert Vögler.[19] But when, at Hitler's insistence, the *Völkischer Beobachter* also expressed its satisfaction at Reupke's ideas, there were loud protests from a number of SA leaders, who roundly denounced this latest 'betrayal' of the National Socialist ideal.

The Harzburg Front

The Harzburg Front was supposed to embody a new unity of purpose among the leaders of heavy industry, the landed aristocracy, the military and the right-wing parties (including the NSDAP), in their opposition to the republican system. But the coalition evaporated almost overnight. Hitler's snub of his partners-to-be may have been a fit of pique, but it was surely well calculated, for he had seen at first

[16] ibid. p.42.

[17] For the significance of this, see Chapter 3.

[18] For instance, Blank to Reusch 10 June 1931, in Stegmann, op. cit., p. 419. And in a 'Syndikus' meeting on 9 September 1932, Paul Bang quoted Funk as having said 'Don't get excited ... that is all a swindle for the exterior ... everything that Feder comes up with is madness (*Unsinn*) (AdV Bd 165 Bl 20).

[19] Vögler, born 1877; 1926–1935, General Director of United Steelworks.

hand the disarray which reigned within the conservative ranks. Alfred Hugenberg undoubtedly saw himself as the future Chancellor of a great nationalist coalition, but although the group around Reusch, which included Vögler, Krupp and Poensgen, were prepared to support the Harzburg Front to depose Brüning from the Chancellorship, they were still implacably hostile to Hugenberg. If they could remove Hugenberg from the leadership of the DNVP, they believed that it would then be possible to form a centre-right block against both the SPD (the trade unions) and the Nazis.[20]

Hitler's unconditional demand for leadership of the conservative coalition set up a wail of anguish amongst the nationalists, who regarded his 'arrogance' (*Sturheit*) as unacceptable. 'Who', asked Otto Furst zu Salm-Horstmar, 'can make Hitler see sense?'[21] But Hitler needed to take account of his political power base among the petite bourgeoisie, for whom a coalition with the nationalists under the control of the arch-reactionary Hugenberg would have been unthinkable. Besides, the electoral tide of the NSDAP was still running high, and Hitler believed that he could bide his time, secure in the knowledge that the conservatives could offer no real alternative to the populist Nazi movement and its Fuhrer.

With the exception of a minority who joined the Nazi party, the prevailing mood among German industrialists vis-a-vis National Socialism at the end of 1931 was one of 'wait and see'. Only a tiny sector of big business, representing the chemical, electrical and machine-tool industry, still placed any reliance upon a 'moderate' course, based upon support for Brüning and his cabinet. Yet the procrastination of the industrialists was not due to moral scruples – a result of misgivings about the ethical standards of Hitler and his party. Rather big business was still afraid of the influence of the 'socialists' in the NSDAP, fearing that after the Nazis had crushed the power of the Marxists and the trade unions in their 'first revolution', there might be a 'second revolution', and that powerful industrialists would then be the victims. For 'the party seemed to be speaking with two voices, and it was a matter of conjecture which

[20] See letter from Reusch to Supervisory Council of Krupps, 27 April 1932 (Historisches Archiv der Gutehoffnungshütte, Oberhausen, (HA/GHH) No. 400101290/39), ending 'it is high time that the bourgeoisie woke up instead of surrendering to National Socialism!'

[21] Salm-Horstmar to Class, 26 October 1931, Stegmann, op. cit., p. 423.

side would win through'.[22]

In an attempt to allay these suspicions, Hitler undertook to speak personally to the Dusseldorf Industry Club in January 1932. Out of this meeting the NSDAP received a contribution of 100,000 RM for the April election campaign for the Prussian *Landtag*.[23] But Hitler did not achieve the immediate breakthrough that he was seeking. Success came two months later in the form of a letter from Dr Hjalmar Schacht, President of the Reichsbank.

12 April 1932

Dear Herr Hitler,

... Although I have not yet been able to persuade the extremely powerful gentlemen in the west to side openly with you, I can nevertheless report that you command a great deal of support. But there are two issues which come up time and time again. The first is the worry that you are going against the government ... the second is the lack of clarity over Nationl Socialism's economic programme. Concerning the latter point I have been successful to the extent that a number of persons have declared their willingness to finance, with me, an office (*Stelle*) which will study the economic and political concepts of National Socialism, to see if there is a possibility of bringing them into prosperous union with the demands of the privately owned economy. The single-minded struggle against the word socialism, as pursued by Herr Hugenberg, is obviously too simple. I am quite certain that as a result of working together we could reach accord between the fundamentals of National Socialism and the possibilities of a privately owned economy, because the contradiction is not between socialism and capitalism, but between individualism and collectivism ...[24]

The organisational links

Schacht's proposal to set up such an 'office' was willingly agreed to by Hitler, and he appointed Wilhelm Keppler and Leopold Plaichinger to represent the NSDAP.[25] In fact two NSDAP business circles were

[22] Stegmann, op. cit., p.424.

[23] The contribution came from the mining industry and iron and steel industries, see Heinrichsbauer, op. cit., p.44.

[24] Reproduced as document VII in Stegmann, op. cit., pp. 449-50.

[25] During May, Hitler in fact gave Keppler (the proprietor of a Bavarian photo-chemical firm) the brief of creating a 'circle' of businessmen who could advise him personally on economic matters, irrespective of the theories emanating from the NSDAP's Economic Committees in the Brown House. In this circle were Keppler and

1. An SA column on the march through a village in Saxony in 1929. (Weimar Archive)

2. Propaganda meeting in Glauchau, Saxony, June 1930. (Weimar Archive)

3. 'The March into the Third Reich,' as portrayed by Nazi propaganda in 1931. (Weimar Archive)

Wo ist der Jude?

Auf der Börse, wo Millionen ergaunert,

Oder in der Fabrik, wo Pfennige verdient werden?

4. A cartoon from *Der Stürmer* asks, 'Where is the Jew? In the Stock Exchange where swindles make millions? Or in the factory where pennies are earned?' (Weimar Archive)

5. The octopus of the 'Jewish' department store strangles the small German trader. Propaganda leaflet, 1931. (BayHStA)

6. Hitler consecrates a new party standard at Reichsparty day in Nuremberg by holding it against the

7. The Celebration of 9 November in Munich, 1935. The 'old fighters' (including Hitler, Goering, Streicher, Hess and Himmler) march towards the Feldherrnhalle past the pylons inscribed with the names of the NSDAP's 'martyrs'. (BayHStA)

8. The newly built Thingplatz at Borna (near Leipzig) during the first performance of Curt Heynicke's

eventually formed. The group known as the Keppler Kreis (Keppler Circle) met for the first time in Berlin on 20 June 1932, when Hitler informed the assembled businessmen that he was a politician, not an economist, and promised to give the industrialists a free hand in formulating an economic policy to overcome the recession. At the same time he repeated his guarantee that he would crush the trade union movement, and announced that he would dissolve the political parties once he had assumed power.[26] Nobody at the meeting expressed dissent at these policies.

According to Helfferich, the Keppler Kreis eventually included the following: Max Luyken and Gottfried Graf Bismarck-Reinfeld (representing agriculture); August Rosterg (potash industry); Albert Vögler and Ewald Hecker (iron and steel); Hjalmar Schacht, Friedrich Reinhart and Kurt von Schroeder (banking); Emil Helfferich and Franz Heinrich Witthoeft (Hamburg financiers) and Keppler and Plaichinger for the NSDAP. Schacht's 'office', which also started work in June, was far more representative of western heavy industry (Reusch, Thyssen, Springorum, Vögler and Krupp).[27]

The attempts of these industrialists and aristocrats to reach some form of accord with Hitler was not solely motivated by the desire to strengthen the Hitlerite wing of the party against the 'radicals', and thereby prevent the Nazis from pursuing an economic programme that might be hostile to a private-sector economy. Equally worrying for big business was the possibility of some form of alliance between the Strasserite wing of the NSDAP, the trade union movement and small and medium-sized capital, which would dissolve the huge industrial trusts and create a state-regulated economy to guarantee the demands of the commercial Mittelstand. Strasser's 'Immediate Programme' was announced in May, and the spectacular gains of the Nazis in the July Reichstag elections must have alerted industrialists to the danger that such corporate policies posed to their monopoly position in the economy. The elections also highlighted the

Kranefuss for the NSDAP, Helfferich (Hamburg businessman), Rosterg (potash industrialist) and the banker von Schroeder. See Emil Helfferich, *Ein Leben*, vol. 4, Jever 1964, p.12.

[26] See G. Schulz in Bracher, Sauer & Schulz, *Die Nationalsozialistische Machtergreifung*, Köln 1962, p.395.

[27] Helfferich, op. cit., pp. 15ff.

threat that the NSDAP might find sufficient coalition partners to be able to rule without the need for a presidential cabinet – in that case the influence of the conservatives could be shut out completely.

But although the success of the NSDAP at the July elections made it the strongest political faction in the Reichstag, Hitler was unable to exploit the situation to make a strategic breakthrough. In an interview with Hindenburg on 13 August, the old president once again flatly refused to make real concessions to the NSDAP, and Hitler realised that he would have to influence those who could influence the President if he was to become Chancellor. Furthermore, although the conservative establishment might be looking to build bridges with the NSDAP, they were no longer in such a hurry. The replacement of Brüning by von Papen and his 'cabinet of barons' in May meant that the nationalists now had 'their own man' in office, and the continuity of right-wing authoritarian government seemed assured for at least the immediate future.

So politically the situation was deadlocked. Big business was prepared to flirt with Hitler because his party could offer a mass basis for a savage attack upon democracy and the left. But under existing circumstances they were not prepared to abandon their new bride, von Papen, given the fact that they were unsure about what Hitler could offer. As Hindenburg told Salm-Horstmar, 'Hitler can talk to great effect, but he cannot deliver what he is promising ... when they come to power the Nazis will nationalise the great estates'.[28] The conservatives may have trusted Hitler, but they did not trust the NSDAP. As ever they feared that the Fuhrer might not be able to control the radicals in his own party.

In order to break the political stalemate, Hitler intervened decisively in support of big business and agriculture. On 12 September Schacht was able to write to Reusch that Hitler had told him that 'the Immediate Programme will be pulped. It will no longer be circulated'.[29] Shortly afterwards the NSDAP's Economic Council was 'reorganised'[30] to weaken Feder's influence and to tilt

[28] Letter from Salm-Horstmar to Heinrich Class, 23 October 1932, DZA, AdV no. 45.

[29] HA/GHH no. 4001012290/33a.

[30] See above, Chapter 3.

the balance towards Funk and the Keppler Kreis.

Hitler's obvious desire to reach an accommodation with big business now proffered a further dilemma for the industrialists. Failure to back the reactionaries in the NSDAP politically and financially in practice supported the radicals. Already the SA was four times stronger than the regular army (400,000 men compared to 100,000), and the demands of the Stormtroopers for power were becoming increasingly difficult to hold back. Indeed it seemed that only Hitler was capable of restraining them. Moreover the difficulty of keeping von Papen in power in the teeth of popular opposition was becoming apparent. The conservatives' dilemma was forcibly stated by von Papen himself at the Berlin Herrenclub: 'a conservative course can only be followed by an authoritarian government, but it is absolutely essential to anchor this politik in the psychology of the people.[31] The mass following of the NSDAP offered the solution, but thereby posed the problem: How could this mass following be kept in check?

The danger that the Strasserite wing of the NSDAP might conclude an alliance with liberal political elements was spelled out clearly in the weeks before the November Reichstag elections, when Strasser began behind-the-scenes negotiations with the Centre Party and the leadership of the German trade unions. This was anathema to many industrialists, and alienated the support of Reusch, Springorum, Poensgen and Krupp. They put their trust (and their trusts' money) fully behind von Papen, as did the electrical and chemical industries whose policy of supporting the moderate centre was now in complete disarray.

On the face of it the November election results seemed to confirm von Papen's hunch that the Nazi tide was on the ebb. The NSDAP's share of the vote fell by nearly two million to 33.1 per cent (from 37.3 per cent in July), while the nationalist parties gained fifteen seats. But the conservatives' elation was tinged with alarm, for the KPD now commanded 100 seats and had polled nearly six million votes.

The rise of the Communists and the apparent demise of the Nazis created a shift of opinion within conservative circles, who suddenly saw 'the grotesque face of communism beating at the door'.[32] The

---

[31] Stegmann, op. cit., p. 433. Blank to Reusch, 6 October 1932.
[32] Bruno Linder to Staatssekretär Otto Meissner, 25 November 1932. See E. Czichon, *Wer verhalf Hitler zur Macht?*, Köln 1972, p.73.

issue of bringing the Nazis into the conservative court took on a new urgency, and in view of Hitler's uncompromising demands, this meant giving him the post of Chancellor. Indeed just a week after the elections Wilhelm Keppler wrote to von Schroeder that von Papen himself was in favour of a government under Hitler, and that von Papen should intercede for such a solution since this would have the most telling effect upon the 'old man' (Hindenburg). Keppler added however that one 'great difficulty' remained – namely the 'economic guidelines'.[33] In order to overcome this barrier it was decided to send a letter to Hindenburg in favour of Hitler's appointment, signed by the widest cross-section of industrial, financial and agrarian leaders.

This letter to Hindenburg, dated 19 November 1932, demanded that 'the greatest possible popular strength should be lined up behind the cabinet' and pointed out that the rebuilding of the German economy would demand great sacrifice. 'Such sacrifice will only be made willingly if the largest element of this national movement takes a leading part in the government.'[34] The roll of signatories was impressive; not only were leading names from heavy industry, banking, finance, retailing and export industries included, but also powerful agrarian landowners such as Graf von Kalckreuth (President of the Reichslandbund), Graf von Keyserlingk and von Rohr-Manze, whose opinions could be expected to carry particular weight with Hindenburg. Another industrialist, Friedrich Flick, who did not sign, nevertheless provided 50,000 RM for the NSDAP in the same month.[35]

Hindenburg, however, could not be persuaded to accept Hitler as Chancellor, and upon dismissing von Papen he nominated General Schleicher to the post. Only a very small section of German industry had any sympathy for Schleicher's attempt to tread a path that was 'neither capitalist nor socialist'. Even the chemical industry and the Hanseatic Bund, who had once sought to build a middle-ground bourgeois block, were hostile to Schleicher, whose intention was clearly to disengage the Strasser-wing from the Nazi party and create a popular coalition with dissident Social Democrats, members of the

[33] Keppler to von Schroeder, 13 November 1932, reproduced by R. Kühnl, *Der deutsche Faschismus*, document no. 89.
[34] See document no. PS 3901 in Proceedings of Nuremberg Trials, vol. 33.
[35] Stegmann, op. cit., p.435.

Centre Party, the leadership of the German Trade Union movement and the Stahlhelm.

Schleicher's appointment, and the fear that this would ultimately lead to some form of state-controlled capitalism, finally created the conditions for a closing of the ranks in industrial and business circles. Ironically the very weakness of the Nazis during the final months of 1932 strengthened Hitler's demand for the Chancellorship of a nationalist coalition. The NSDAP was virtually bankrupt; at the end of the first week in December, Gregor Strasser made his final break with the other Nazi leaders; and the set-back in the November elections had dented the myth of the movement's 'invincibility'. At a stroke the NSDAP seemed to have been purged of its most powerful 'radical' influence, and it was now in desperate need of finance (and hence allies) to shore up its whole top-heavy structure. Certainly the dismissal of Strasser from a position of great influence within the party was seen as the crucial move in the bargaining process by powerful sections of German industry. Suddenly substantial funds began to flow into the coffers of the NSDAP, lifting the threat of bankruptcy and allowing Hitler to concentrate a massive propaganda barrage on the electors of the tiny constituency of Lippe in the New Year.[36]

The final negotiations between Hitler and the conservatives took place during early January when von Papen was also brought into the talks. On 4 January a crucial meeting took place at the house of the banker Kurt von Schroeder in Cologne. According to von Schroeder's testimony at Nuremberg, Hitler outlined his intentions quite clearly: there was to be a fundamental change in the style of government, most obviously the 'removal of all Social Democrats, Communists and Jews from leading positions in Germany and the re-establishment of order in public life'. And Schroeder went on to elaborate upon the reasons why industry supported Hitler and the Nazis:

Before taking this step (arranging the meeting in Cologne) I discussed the matter with a number of business leaders ... The general aspirations of these men ... were to see a strong Fuhrer coming to power, who would build a government which would remain in power for a long time. After the NSDAP had experienced its first set-back on 6 November 1932, thus falling from its high-point, the support of

[36] See Schulz, in Bracher, Sauer & Schulz, op. cit., pp. 405ff.

German business became especially urgent. Fear of Bolshevism was the common concern of the business community, and they hoped that the National Socialists – once in power – would create a permanent political and economic base in Germany.[37]

Three days later, on 7 January, von Papen met Reusch, Springorum, Vögler and Krupp for further discussions.[38] It is barely conceivable that von Papen failed to repeat Hitler's conditions or report upon the Fuhrer's intentions once in power.

It was not the German industrialists who finally broke Hindenburg's resolve to refuse Hitler the Chancellorship, but the president's friends in the Reichslandbund (notably those in the Keppler Kreis), together with von Papen and a section of the Reichswehr. However, the pressure exerted by the industrialists was crucial, for even at the last moment, on the day before Hitler's appointment, Hindenburg enquired whether Hitler still had the trust of broad conservative circles in banking, industry, commerce and agriculture.[39]

The conservatives and German industry saw the appointment of Hitler to the Chancellorship as the crowning achievement of their long-term strategy of 'hemming-in' the NSDAP (*Einrahmungspolitik*). At first glance the new nationalist coalition was merely the old 'cabinet of barons' with a populist image – Hitler, it seemed, was constrained by colleagues who were the flesh and blood of the old establishment: von Papen, Hugenberg, von Neurath, von Krosigk etc. Few industrialists saw the danger of new elections in which the NSDAP could control vital sectors of the bureaucracy, while the terror unleashed against the left by the SA and the SS appeared to be proof merely of Hitler's promise to 'clean up the state'. Indeed the Nazis' willingness to crush 'Communism' in Germany by means of brutal terror, seemed finally to consolidate the unity of all sections of big business in backing the National Socialist movement. Nowhere is this trust better expressed than in the meeting that Hitler and Göring held with the most influential men in German industry on 20 February 1933.

---

[37] Reproduced as document no. 96 in Kühnl, *Der deutsche Faschismus*.

[38] Turner, op. cit., p. 150.

[39] See Helfferich, op. cit., p. 21, although he mistakenly believed that Hindenberg first saw the November letter in January 1933.

Among the 27 business leaders who gathered to meet the new Chancellor were Krupp, Springorum, Tengelmann, von Schnitzler (IG Farben), Stinnes, Opel, von Winterfeld (Siemens and Halske) and von Loewenstein. In his speech Hitler clearly stated that the coming (March) election would be the last for the forseeable future, regardless of the outcome. Life was a constant struggle; only the NSDAP could save the country from the Communist danger, and only a militarily strong people could overcome their enemies. Moreover, only a nation that was militarily strong could expect to create a successful and expanding economy.[40]

At the end of Hitler's speech Krupp rose spontaneously to thank the Fuhrer on behalf of those present. Göring then stressed the problem of financing the coming election, but left the task of deciding the amount that industry should contribute to Schacht. Schacht proposed that industry should raise three million RM for the election expenses of the government parties, three-quarters of which would go to the NSDAP and the rest to the other coalition parties. The sum would be gathered in equal amounts from three sectors: the western coal and steel industries, the chemical and potash industries, and the machine and electro-technical industries.[41]

The day after the meeting Springorum wrote personally to Reusch (Director of Gutehoffnungshütte) with the bill for his company's contribution:

> under the agreed formula Gutehoffnungshütte is to pay   34,271 RM
> already paid   19,930 RM
> outstanding   14,341 RM
> ...may I ask you to transfer this sum to the agreed account ...
> With my best wishes to your very honourable wife, Frau Gamahlin ...[42]

In the event the 34,271 RM which Reusch and Gutehoffnungshütte 'invested' in the Nazis' election fund was a small price to pay for the economic and political benefits which the NSDAP were able to deliver after March 1933. In 1936, three years after the meeting with Hitler, Gutehoffnungshütte was able to report pre-tax profits of 123

---

[40] For details, see Nuremberg document D203.
[41] HA/GHH no. 4001012024/11. See document XVIII in Stegmann, op. cit.
[42] HA/GHH no. 400106/105. See document XIX in Stegmann, op. cit.

million RM which rose to 148 million in 1938. Other contributors to the fund could claim even more spectacular results. The net profits of the Krupp Concerns rose from 6.65 million RM in 1933/34 to 17.22 million in 1936/37, while Siemens and Halske saw an increase from 185 million in 1933/34 to over 474 million RM in 1936/37.[43]

---

[43] Figures from Kühnl, *Der deutsche Faschismus*, p. 264.

CHAPTER FIVE

National Socialism and German Society

The first stage, 1919-1924

As we have seen, the early Nazi party was an unlikely symbiosis of aristocratic authoritarianism and petit bourgeois radicalism. Age was a factor which even cut across class boundaries in determining this ideological allegiance.[1] Thus the party drew extensive support from ex-soldiers, but although many of the older membership could be regarded as political reactionaries, the younger elements, irrespective of social background, more often identified with the radical wing of the party. The young radicals combined a fanatical hatred of Bolshevism with a deep resentment of decadent, class-conscious bourgeois society.

Rabid anti-Marxism often co-existed with a profound belief in national *socialism*, which painted a romantic image of the workers as the only force capable of achieving a rebirth of the German nation. A number of Nazi militants had actually been involved in the revolutionary struggle waged in central Germany during 1919. Otto Strasser, for instance, fought with the Red Army against the Kapp Putsch. His disillusionment with the SPD and the Communists brought him into contact with National Socialism.

On the other hand the percentage of Nazis from a working-class background was consistently low. Only about 10 per cent of the early members of the NSDAP could be described as proletarian, compared

---

[1] The average age of NSDAP members between 1919 and 1921 was 33, while the median age was 18-26. Cf. D. Douglas, 'The parent cell, some computer notes on the composition of the first Nazi groups in Munich, 1919-1921', *Central European History* vol. 10, no.1, 1977, pp. 55-72.

to 23 per cent of the party membership who came from the commercial Mittelstand.[2] For small traders and producers, the appeal of National Socialism was bound up far more urgently with the promise to restore some form of archaic capitalism which would rid them of their most powerful competitors. Their demands were expressed in a populist anti-capitalism, which bemoaned the power of big business to monopolise the market and denounced anonymous finance capital as an agency of 'Jewish domination.' The first attempts to integrate the demands of the working class and the Mittelstand – the creative strata who would compose the corporate state – were championed by Anton Drexler (**1**)[3] and Gottfried Feder (**3**).

Clearly anti-capitalist and 'socialist' ideals (however circumscribed) were anathema to the NSDAP's powerful backers in industry and the Reichswehr. Yet, as the Pan-German League had discovered, creating a mass basis for authoritarian politics was impossible unless the movement could 'go out on to the streets' and 'find the ways and means of getting to the masses'.[4] In turn, this meant adopting some form of pseudo-socialism, for according to Anton von Rieppel (Director of M.A.N. in Nuremberg), 'the people will only listen to socialist leaders. Appeals from professors, aristocrats, industrialists and army officers simply evaporate into thin air; or, what is worse, they can do the greatest damage if it is suspected that the influence of the Pan-Germans, conservatives or reactionary forces is at work.'[5] It must be presumed therefore that the NSDAP's patrons were realistic enough to accept that the party's radicalism was the necessary price of success, although they would have demanded some form of guarantee that the NSDAP would remain within the orbit of the authoritarian right, despite its apparent 'socialism'.[6] By the time he had established his position as the First

---

[2] ibid.

[3] Numbers in bold type in this and following chapters refer to the numbered documents in Chapter 2.

[4] DZA, AdV no. 121, Sitzung des Geschäftsführenden Ausschusses, 19/20 October 1918, Bl 45.

[5] DZA, Nachlass Gebsattel, Bd 5, Bl 238.

[6] Max Maurenbrecher's editorial in the *Deutschen Zeitung* (the newspaper of the Pan-German League) on the day after Hitler's abortive coup noted the importance of the NSDAP's ideology: 'It was quite right that this worker-socialism should look different from, and take on different forms vis-à-vis the nationalism of the old ruling classes.'

Chairman (dictator) of the NSDAP in July 1921, Adolf Hitler was the industrialists' guarantor: a fact which is clearly documented in the correspondence of Heinrich Class.

In January 1921 Heinrich Class wrote to Otto Gertung (von Rieppel's fellow director at M.A.N.) pleading with him to provide the National Socialist movement 'which under Drexler and Hitler's leadership has had great success in Munich and southern Bavaria'[7] with the finance to launch the newly acquired *Völkischer Beobachter* as a daily newspaper. Gertung's reply to his friend Class, written a month later, was distinctly evasive; for although Gertung stated that 'M.A.N. was not against supporting the party', he added that the necessary money would have to be properly approved and that the matter would have to be put before M.A.N.'s board at its next meeting.[8]

On 1 March 1921 Class wrote to his personal emissary in Munich, Dr Paul Tafel, asking him to inform 'Herrn Drexler and Hittler [sic]' in confidence, that it would be some time before the matter in Nuremberg 'comes to maturity'.[9] In fact Hitler was able to find the money for the *Völkischer Beobachter* elsewhere, but the reasons for Gertung's procrastination can be gleaned from a letter which Class wrote to Paul Tafel on 8 June 1921:

> I have been told that according to reports from reliable sources in Munich ... the movement around Hittler [sic] and Drexler is taking the same direction as all previous so-called national socialists' attempts; they are unable to make significant inroads into the working class. The membership indeed is confined to petit bourgeois circles, and in Munich it is certainly possible that white-collar workers and above all students will become thoroughly confused and infected with socialist ideas. It is said that this danger has already shown itself in Munich, and as a result (they) want to have nothing to do with supporting the movement.
>
> My objection, that at present the main task is to mobilise the broad masses against the Jews and to make a breach in the socialist parties, is countered with the advice that the damage caused by such an infection of the student-body is, in the long term, a greater risk than the short-term fulfilment of both other aims.
>
> I would therefore be most grateful if you could inform me whether

[7] Letter from Class to Dr Gertung, 29 January 1921. AdV no. 258, Bl 238.
[8] Letter from Dr Gertung to Class, 27 February 1921. AdV no. 258, Bl 239.
[9] Letter from Class to Dr Tafel, 1 March 1921. AdV no. 258, Bl 240.

things really are going the way that has been reported. I will, although I am reluctant, write again to Gertung in Nuremberg, and I ask you to try to get Baron von Pechmann to give something – if you yourself have no connection with Pechmann, then try to rope Lehmann in, as he and Pechmann are great cronies.[10]

Unfortunately no copy of Tafel's reply has survived, but a letter to Class from a Fritz Schwartz, with the letterhead of J.F. Lehmann's publishing house, dated 30 July 1921, provided the information that Class was seeking. The letter is in fact a report of the Extraordinary Membership Conference of the NSDAP held on the previous day, at which Hitler's appointment as First Chairman of the party was unanimously approved. Having enthused over the role which Hitler played at the conference, Schwartz continued:

> I have given you this short report simply to let you know that there is not a word of truth in the various rumours which are circulating about the National Socialist party. The two leaders [Hitler and Drexler] are as one, and the membership are solidly behind them.

Lehmann himself added the handwritten comment: 'I have spoken with Dr Tafel today. He arranged for a shorthand copy of the speeches to be made. Delighted at the outcome. JFL.'[11]

During these early years Hitler was walking a tightrope between the industrialists and the party membership. The skill of this balancing act becomes apparent if we look at the style of his speeches. Compare for instance Drexler:

> Working comrades! ... your hatred has until now been solely directed towards factory and work-capitalism, *whose exploitation I also ruthlessly fight against*, but which is not nearly so dangerous as invisible Stock Exchange capital ... (**1**)

and Hitler:

> We are against all forms of capitalism *if it is not directed towards creative work*, but instead is employed to gather interest and unearned income ... (**2**)

[10] AdV no. 258, Bl 243.
[11] Fritz Schwartz to Class, 30 July 1921. AdV no. 232 Bl 1 & 1a.

Drexler hopelessly confused his audience and their interests; workers who fight against 'factory capitalism' must by definition be close to proletarian socialism: they would have little or no idea of what Drexler meant by 'Stock Exchange capital', which is a concept designed to appeal to the consciousness of the petite bourgeoisie. And if Drexler fought against factory capitalism, then he was in danger of alienating the small businessman whom the NSDAP was also trying to attract, not to mention big business, which was paying the party's bills! Hitler makes no such mistake. He is against 'all forms of capitalism' but then only if it is not directed towards 'creative work'. The qualification is cunningly vague, but plainly the 'hard-working capitalist' whether large scale or small (provided he is not Jewish) is socially acceptable. Yet at the same time Hitler still manages to appeal to a sense of injustice felt by proletarian and small businessman alike – the notion that wealth can be created by 'some capitalists' (whether Jewish or German) without work or effort. Having first raised the resentment of his audience against such 'drones' Hitler then suggests that it is the Jew, who is one per cent of the population but makes up ninety per cent of the usurers, gourmets, etc.

Of course Hitler's exploitation of anti-Semitism was in no way original. In this he was merely drawing upon the cultural tradition of völkisch thought, not to mention Class's attempts to manipulate the 'Jewish question' to prevent social revolution (see p. 17). But Hitler's ability to present the common theme of anti-Semitism as the means of linking together radicalism and traditional authoritarianism within the National Socialist movement was crucial not only to the party's ideological appeal, but also to his strategy of seizing and holding dictatorial power within the party. Thus at the 1921 Extraordinary Party Congress (having gained near unanimous support for his appointment as First Chairman), he refused point-blank to be drawn into an ideological debate over the relative merits of nationalism and socialism. He turned instead to 'the central importance of the Jewish question', arguing that the party's struggle was a 'racial struggle' not a 'class struggle'; destructive Jewish capitalism and false Jewish socialism were the forces responsible for the demise of the nation and the plight of its 'creative classes'.

A memorandum signed by Hitler in January 1922 notes that other völkisch groups 'are not able to draw together the practical conclusions from correct theoretical ideas', [12] while in *Mein Kampf* (1924) he writes that 'by making the völkisch revolution into the anti-Jewish revolution ... the ideology is crystallised and made attractive to the masses'.[13]

The decision to move towards armed action by the NSDAP's paramilitary units is presaged by Hitler's speech in June 1923, in which he demands 'the destruction of the all-powerful international Jewish trusts through action' (**10**). It is noteworthy that Hitler's diatribe is peppered with the sort of traditional nationalist rhetoric that he otherwise avoided. And he finishes upon a tacitly militaristic note: 'to die or to triumph, that must be our only thought.'

As it turned out Hitler neither died nor triumphed, but found himself the centre of attraction at a circus-like trial for high-treason – a trial which gave him the opportunity to launch the myth that he alone was capable of leading the struggle against the 'Jewish republic'.

The twelve months that Hitler spent imprisoned in Landsberg Castle were clearly dedicated to reappraising the position of the National Socialist movement in post-war Germany.

The NSDAP had successfully projected an image of youth, dynamism and radicalism, and as a result the party had become a major force within the German völkisch movement even before the Munich Trial. Yet this initial political success had been compromised by the Nazi movement's reliance upon the armed forces to lead a rebellion against the republic. Moreover, as the inflationary crisis of 1923 receded, and the Weimar political system began to stabilise, the chances of success for a military coup declined accordingly. None the less, Hitler's decision to move over to an attack upon the republican system through the ballot box came only slowly, despite the electoral success of the Völkischer Block (an alliance of Nazis and other völkisch parties) in 1924.[14]

The ideology of the National Socialist movement during the first

---

[12] Werner Jochmann, *Nationalsozialismus und Revolution. Dokumente*, Frankfurt 1963, pp. 88-9.

[13] Adolf Hitler, *Mein Kampf*, p.279.

[14] The Völkischer Block received half a million votes, and became the third largest party in the Bavarian parliament.

stage of its development was dominated by an unresolved conflict between means and ends. The NSDAP's organisational strength had been built upon a radical ideological appeal which had found support among some sections of the Bavarian Mittelstand. Yet this radical image was at odds with an organisational reliance upon traditional authoritarian forces to create the conditions necessary (through military rebellion) for the party to become a major force in national politics. Moreover, the NSDAP's ideological 'concepts' needed to be more carefully expressed in its propaganda. The pre-putsch ideology of the party lacked sophistication: too many different voices were talking, and they were talking with different tongues. This wide spectrum of ideas needed somehow to be centralised and co-ordinated, although without restricting the party's appeal. To this end the image of the leadership needed to be altered, for if the party was to seek support from a wide range of socio-economic groups, conflicting ideological and organisational demands would have to be regulated by a supreme arbitrator. So the appeal to sectional interests had to be allied to the seductive promise of a state freed from disruptive political struggle *between* conflicting interests. As such Adolf Hitler could not continue to beat the drum for the German Nationalists – he had to become the leader of a German nationalist revival.[15]

The second stage, 1925-1929

The relative influence enjoyed by the radicals during the years immediately after the reconstruction of the party is amply illustrated by the tone and the nature of the NSDAP's propaganda during this stage. Although the demands of the Mittelstand were not ignored, there is a heavy emphasis upon slogans designed to appeal directly to the working class. Posters headlined 'Socialisation is on the March' (**14**) or 'Proletarians! Away with the madness of the Internationale' (**18**) can only be interpreted as attempts to win over proletarian socialists to the message of National Socialism. The Nazis even offered Social Democrats and Communists the opportunity (upon production of their membership cards) to hear their leadership and

[15] For an appraisal of Hitler's self-image in the early years of the NSDAP's development, see A. Tyrell, *Vom Trommler zum Führer*, Munich 1975.

political principles vilified free of charge! (23) – there was usually a small entry-fee to political meetings.

The type of propaganda directed at the working class was basic in the extreme – identify the failures of socialist policies as being the result of infiltration by the Jews, and make the 'connection' between 'Jewish Marxism' and 'Jewish capitalism'. This approach is amply illustrated by the NSDAP's response to the dilemma afforded by the Bill to Expropriate (without compensation) the German Princes. The Strasser-dominated northern Gauleiters had initially opted to support the campaign, but Hitler's counter-attack at Bamberg ensured that the party was in no way associated with an attack upon the sanctity of private property.[16] The propaganda department in Munich produced a wholly predictable response to the measure – 'Expropriate the Princes – the Jews needs the money' (14). Hardly more subtle was Gregor Strasser's attempt to save face and salvage his 'radical' credentials by diverting attention from the real issue of expropriating the estates of the German aristocracy to the question of expropriating 'the fortune of the Bank and Stock Exchange princes' (15).

We have suggested that the influence enjoyed by the radicals during this second stage of the Kampfzeit was at least in part a result of Hitler's still weak organisational control of the party after his release from prison. Indeed the jumble of frequently contradictory working-class and Mittelstand-directed propaganda, so evident in the NSDAP's output during these years, indicates an inability on Hitler's part to impose his authority upon the radical strongholds rather than any substantial organisational strength on the part of the Strasserite-wing.

Only as the failure of any sort of 'radical-urban' strategy became apparent in the poor voting figures obtained by the NSDAP in major industrial centres, and conversely, the party found unexpected support in rural areas, did the balance of propaganda swing decisively towards a 'Mittelstand-politik'. At the same time, Hitler's consolidation of his absolute authority within the movement was the precondition for strengthening the ideological appeal of National Socialism, for it harnessed the radical image of the party to its organisational drive. In other words, Hitler's dictatorial power made it possible for him to control many of the negative political

[16] See p. 91 above.

consequences of radicalism, without at the same time destroying or weakening a vital organisational pillar of the party's propaganda effort – namely the SA. This, however, was a process of control which could only be perfected gradually, and which the very strength of the party after 1930 consistently threatened to disrupt, as mass unemployment and economic recession strengthened both the appeal of radicalism and the power of the SA.

The farming community

The Nazis achieved their first real breakthrough among the farming communities of northern Germany towards the end of the 1920s. In order to understand why the NSDAP was so successful in its appeal to the farmers we must look first of all at the patterns of political loyalty in the countryside.

Patterns of political loyalty

Election statistics clearly indicate that the size of agricultural unit was the most important factor in determining political allegiance among the farming community.[17] Thus in Schleswig-Holstein in 1919, areas with a predominance of small and medium-scale farms (from 2 to 20 hectares) voted *en masse* for the liberal parties in the elections for the first National Assembly. Areas where larger farms were the norm (20 to 100 hectares) demonstrated a similar pattern of voting, although the identification with the 'new' liberal parties was definitely less pronounced. Conversely, where large-scale agricultural estates were predominant, voting figures show a clear rejection of liberalism in favour of class-based political allegiance; here the landlord maintained his traditional support for the conservatives (DNVP) while the farm-worker gave his vote to one of the working-class parties (SPD or USPD).

Just as the swing to the liberal parties in 1919 was most pronounced among small farmers, so the sudden swing from liberalism to National Socialism was decisive in areas of small and medium-sized farms by 1930; in the areas of larger farms this swing

[17] For the following, see R. Heberle, *Landbevölkerung und Nationalsozialismus*, Stuttgart 1963, p.116.

was not so obvious until 1932, and even then it was far less pronounced. On the estates traditional patterns of political loyalty remained fairly stable, with the Communists replacing the USPD as the most radical of the working-class alternatives.

According to Rudolf Heberle, a more exact breakdown of the statistics for Schleswig-Holstein suggests a farm of more than 50 hectares was the 'critical threshhold' for socialist parties, while the most favourable size for the National Socialists was one of between 2 and 50 hectares. By early 1932 the NSDAP had achieved an almost total penetration of rural communities characterised by farms of 2 to 20 hectares, with voting figures showing anything from 70-100 per cent support for the NSDAP in a number of localities. Indeed the most fundamental characteristic of support for Nazism in rural areas was that it increased in *inverse proportion* to the size the community: in other words, the smaller the community the greater the support for the NSDAP. Heberle suggests that the factor of 'social control' in the small village or hamlet, allied to the greater homogeneity of interest in such settlements, almost certainly accounts for this relationship.

The agricultural debt

In general the North German farming community had overcome the worst problems of the war-economy and the dislocation which followed by the mid 1920s, although nationally it was not until 1928 that the average levels of pre-war production were reached. After the stabilisation of the mark in 1924, credit once again became available to the agricultural sector, and particularly in Northern Germany this was taken up to capitalise and intensify small units which provided produce for the livestock and vegetable market.

The availability of credit corresponded with an upswing in industrial production and an increase in the gross domestic product, so that during the mid-1920s the demand for agricultural produce grew apace as small farms were intensivised. Indeed even without re-capitalisation, most farmers found it necessary to take credit if only to replace working capital which had been decimated during the hyperinflation. Allied to this was a promotion campaign by the state authorities and various farming groups to modernise and capitalise in order to increase national agricultural production.

For the farmers of Schleswig-Holstein, working with loan capital was nothing new, for they had been accustomed even before the war to take loans in order to increase their productive capacity. But the sudden availability of loan capital in the late twenties, coming as it did after a period of credit starvation, set off a trend towards intensivisation.

By 1928 Schleswig-Holstein farmers had taken up 7.2 per cent of the four 'America Loans'; yet Schleswig-Holstein accounted for only 4 per cent of the land area of Germany. The total debt of the German farming community was 9.88 billion marks, but the debts of Schleswig-Holstein farmers were 25 to 30 per cent higher than the average. And although total indebtedness was in fact lower than before the war (a fact probably accounted for by the inflation), the cost of servicing a post-war debt was considerably higher. Thus, for instance, the total cost to a creditor of the First America Loan was about 14 per cent p.a. (*Jahresbericht der Generallandschaftsdirektion*).[18]

In effect the agricultural creditor was taking a far higher risk in his business by the mid-1920s, for the return on capital had to be quite significant to allow for a profit after interest payments had been taken into account. A failure in the harvest, an outbreak of disease or a fall in market prices became potentially catastrophic. But in the optimistic mood of the mid-twenties, the first period of sustained growth since the beginning of the century, few considered the effects of such a failure.

Another factor of great psychological significance in encouraging the taking up of new loans was the experience of the hyper-inflation, for although it had decimated many of the rural credit agencies, it had done so to the benefit of those already holding loans. Hence the belief gained ground that inflation was a built-in factor which serviced agricultural debt, so that any farmer taking out a long-term loan could count upon the effects of even a low inflation rate to *reduce* the real cost of that debt. Again few considered the possibility of chronic deflation which would in effect *increase* the cost of a loan.

Finally the general availability for the first time of modern technology and consumer goods persuaded many farmers to use readily available agricultural loans for purposes that were less than agricultural. Telephones, automobiles and modern machinery might

[18] ibid., p.122.

well lighten the burden of work around the farm, but their purchase was often related to the effects of modern advertising techniques rather than cold-blooded business sense.

The Landvolk

A major agricultural crisis gathered momentum in late 1927, as a sharp reduction in market prices coincided with a poor harvest and the outbreak of foot-and-mouth disease in Northern Germany. The first major stirrings of discontent followed in the summer and autumn of 1928 and coalesced in the Landvolk movement.

The Landvolk drew its greatest support from small farmers in the areas most affected by the crisis, and the movement soon became infected by a wild radicalism which rejected any form of dialogue with 'the authorities'. The Landvolk demanded direct action against evictions and the 'extortionate' demands of the taxation authorities. Action also extended to boycotts of farmers and farming agencies who did not support the Landvolk's aims and methods.

The heavy-handed reaction of the local authorities, with the mass conviction of farmers for failing to pay taxes and the use of heavily armed police to enforce evictions, merely intensified animosity and the 'rejectionist' attitudes of the farmers.[19]

The Landvolk stubbornly refused to form any organisation to represent their demands, fearing a watering-down of the ethic of 'natural solidarity' and direct action. But in 1929 'Emergency Committees' (*Nothilfe-Ausschüsse*) were formed in many regions under the leadership of Landbund members, Stahlhelm leaders or Nazis, depending upon the political character of the particular region. In the more radical communities these committees proclaimed a total boycott of all state institutions in the name of 'the revolutionary will' of the people. At about the same time a terrorist group within the Landvolk movement began a series of bomb attacks on tax offices, and incidents of violent confrontation rose accordingly.

Unnerved by this development, many farmers drew back from the Landvolk, and by late 1929 the movement was in decline: discredited by the violence of a minority and a lack of tangible

---

[19] For a detailed examination of the Landvolk movement, see G. Stoltenberg, *Die politische Stimmungen im Schleswig-Holsteinischen Landvolk 1918-1933*, Düsseldorf 1962.

success. The failure of direct action unco-ordinated with any form of effective political mobilisation, and the ineffectiveness of the old conservative farming organisations to represent the small farmers' interests, left a political vacuum in the farming community which the general economic recession accentuated after 1929. The NSDAP moved in to fill this vacuum, and the success of its propaganda among the rural community was spectacularly demonstrated in the Reichstag elections of September 1930.

National Socialism and the farming community

In the May 1924 elections in Schleswig-Holstein the NSDAP gained just over 7 per cent of the vote. The notable feature of this result was that the Nazis received greater support in the towns than in the countryside (7.8 per cent as against 6.4 per cent). Elections in December 1924 showed an overall fall in support for the Nazis to less than 3 per cent, but support was still stronger in the towns than in the countryside. This is particularly interesting given that the Nazis' success after 1928 was consistently *greater* in the countryside than in the towns (in 1930, 35.1 per cent compared with 23.2 per cent; and in July 1932 63.8 per cent compared with 44.8 per cent).[20]

This variation can probably be accounted for by the change in ideological direction within the NSDAP that we have already noted, from the ill-defined radicalism of the early years to the specific Mittelstand-oriented ideology of the late 1920s.

Of vital importance to the farming community was the NSDAP's far from clear attitude to the question of land ownership and the demand for socialisation which Article 17 of the Party Programme raised. The defensive attitude of the National Socialists towards this issue is demonstrated in Chapter 2 (**11**); this pamphlet goes to great pains to disclaim any suggestion that the NSDAP would take over the farmers' land.

So Hitler's 'reinterpretation' of Article 17's demand that land be expropriated without compensation was an essential first step in consolidating the Nazis' campaign in rural areas. The local elections held in 1928 show that the party was beginning to draw greater support from the countryside, but in general support for the Nazis still

[20] Heberle, op. cit., p.38.

lagged behind the results of the May 1924 elections. Thus it was between 1928 and 1930 that the NSDAP made its major breakthrough among the rural population, and Heberle's study confirms that Nazi agitation in Schleswig-Holstein began with the first signs of the agricultural crisis.

The most identifiable characteristic of National Socialism's propaganda offensive in the farming community after 1928 was its tone of impending doom and disaster:

> You, farmer, will be chased from your plot of earth ... The plight of the German farmer is desperate ... Think it all over in your last few hours ... it is a matter of house and home, of life and death ... (**22**).

> In the meantime despair is deepening, the burden of debt gets greater and greater, and the Jews come more and more often to your door ... you are slaves, no longer free farmers (**32**).

Deliberate falsification of the facts certainly helped to promote this vision of imminent disaster (for instance, the total agricultural debt was claimed to be 13 billion marks in 1928, when in fact it was less than 10 billion), but in general the Nazis did not need to invent the farmers' plight; they needed only to 'interpret' it.

The National Socialists' apocalyptic tone was calculated and deliberate, for the NSDAP was in an especially favourable position vis-a-vis the 'traditional' farming parties which the Landvolk movement had identified as being responsible for the farmers' plight. In particular, the tendency of the government parties (the SPD, Centre and liberal parties before 1930, and the conservatives during the presidential cabinets) to underrate both the depth and the effects of the crisis, played into the hands of the NSDAP as the crisis in agriculture deepened and merged into the world slump.

In the autumn of 1931 a second wave of spontaneous farmers' protest swept Schleswig-Holstein. As the movement threatened to get out of hand, the Nazis moved to organise Common Destiny Committees (*Schicksalsgemeinschaften*) in villages throughout the region. On 10 October, at over 1000 meetings, these Common Destiny Committees were called into being. Their task was to press for a moratorium on farming debts and to prevent any further foreclosures and evictions. The mood of the farmers can be judged from a revealing statement by the Süderdithmarschen Farmers' League:

> Never before has the position of the agricultural community on the west coast been so serious. Previously it was the incompetent and careless who went out of business, as they still do today. But in even greater numbers, those competent and hard-working farmers, whose life-styles are beyond reproach, are going bankrupt. Their only mistake was to believe that we ... could go forwards ... by intensivisation, rationalisation, increasing production and bettering quality.[21]

We have already noted the comment of the sociologist Theodor Geiger, who, writing in the early 1930s, suggested that the German peasant farmer was 'less concerned with creating more or better than with keeping his own individual possessions and property'. This sense of 'earth-rootedness' obviously accounts for the strength of protest which accompanied the first major wave of foreclosures and evictions in the agricultural community after 1927.

Between 1924 and 1931 almost one million hectares of mortgaged land was compulsorily sold by the courts to pay off farming debts. And given the fact that three-quarters of all German farmers worked an area of less than five hectares, the threat of foreclosure touched every agricultural community in Germany. By eulogising this notion of 'earth rootedness', Nazi propaganda was able to exploit the threat of eviction in a highly emotive and effective manner:

> Farmers! It is a matter of the most holy possession of a people, the land and the fields which God has given us (**22**).

The Nazis' success in exploiting the specific emotions and consciousness of the small farmer did not happen by chance, for the NSDAP perfected a propaganda technique which was minutely tuned to the needs of the farming community. Darré in particular developed a network of 'agricultural advisors' (*Fachberäter*), whose task was less to advise the farmer than to supply the leadership in Munich with detailed information on the mood of the rural population. They were to be 'the eyes and ears of the leadership ... to discover what particular needs and cares weigh upon the population of the community'.[22]

[21] ibid., pp. 165-6.
[22] Stoltenberg, op. cit. p.97.

The exploitation of religious imagery also proved highly effective in the small farming community where adherence to religious tradition was stronger than in the towns or cities. The suggestion that 'God-given' land was being taken away, and that the 'sanctity' of the farmers' property was being desecrated, was designed to create a feeling that the strictest taboos of rural society were being violated. This fear was further exploited by pamphlets which represented National Socialism as the only defence against the destruction of religion and spiritual values by 'Bolshevism'.

The tax problem was presented in a similar manner, in that heavy taxation was seen as part of the same 'Bolshevik' threat, although in this case it was claimed to be part of the plot to install 'dry Bolshevism' (**16**). Thus the question, 'Why is the tax office always after you ...' is answered with the suggestion that, 'the tax office is simply the bailiff of the international Stock Exchange Princes'. (**24**). Tax demands were therefore only one more symptom of the plot against the farmer by the forces of international finance, who were also responsible for usurious interest rates, and hence the Dawes and the Young Plan.

The parties and the 'system'

The German Nationalists (DNVP), as the traditional representatives of the farming community, were the most obvious obstacle to the NSDAP's penetration of the rural community. But Hugenberg's accession to the leadership of the party in 1928 merely heightened the disillusionment of the small farmer with the Nationalists, who were increasingly seen as the party of big business and 'reaction'. Even when landed interests within the DNVP were able to influence government policies in favour of agriculture, this was not necessarily to the good of the small farmer. Thus when Schiele, the Nationalist Minister for Agriculture, succeeded in supporting cereal growers with subsidies (a result of pressure from Junker landlords) this was of no benefit to the farmer in Schleswig-Holstein who demanded lower prices for animal feed. The collapse of support for the DNVP in Schleswig-Holstein was as spectacular as the Nazis' rise: in 1924 the DNVP took 43.4 per cent of the vote in agricultural communities, by 1930 this had dropped to 7.9 per cent. The Landbund also lost ground over the same period, although their reverses were not as severe as those of the Nationalists. The Landbund's influence lay less in its electoral power than in the influence wielded by its leaders upon Hindenberg and the presidential cabinets.

The Landvolk Party was a quite different proposition. Not only did it draw its support from the small farmer (like the NSDAP), it also raised its national vote from half a million in 1928 to over 1,100,000 in 1930 – thereby posing a direct threat to the Nazis during their first period of growth. Because of this, all attempts by the Landvolk Party leaders to ally themselves, either nationally or locally, to the NSDAP, were vigorously resisted.

As we have seen, the nature of the NSDAP's ideology, with its total attack upon the 'system', gave it a cumulative advantage over the other farming parties as the crisis deepend. The NSDAP's strategy was twofold. First, it set out to create an absolute dichotomy between National Socialism and the 'corrupt and degenerate Weimar system' in which all the other political parties and their leaders were in some way implicated:

> And when you ask who committed this crime, who took up this murder contract, so the answer must unfortunately be: your leaders … the Social Democratic Party and the Democratic Party … the German Nationalists and the Landbund leaders … the German People's Party … the Bavarian People's Party … the Farmers and Mittelstand League … the Centre Party … Get rid of the 'leaders' who have led you into poverty and despair! (**32**).

Secondly, National Socialism's image as a spiritual crusade rather than a political party allowed the NSDAP to project itself as a movement expressing the 'natural' social solidarity of the Volk. Therefore Nazi propaganda suggested that by supporting a farmer's pressure group (the Landbund or Landvolk Party, for instance) the farmer was exacerbating social and class conflict – which in turn furthered national disintegration and promoted the interests of the 'Marxist' and 'Jewish' parties who were conspiring against the Germanic peasant-community. In place of socio-economic conflict, the NSDAP offered a utopian Reich in which social solidarity would guarantee the farmers' well-being:

> Farmers Vote Landbund – each his own interest-heap.
> That's called unity.
> Away with the swindle,
> Create a German People's Community (**35**).

This ideological mirage of social cohesion (bolstered by the visual imagery of the SA) was probably the vital factor in the remarkable success of the NSDAP among the rural population. Heberle alludes to this when he refers to the effects of communal crisis upon the traditional 'king in his castle' (*Königtum auf dem Hofe*) mentality of the Schleswig-Holstein peasantry:

> At the end of 1931 it was the problem of debt which was clearly in the foreground of consciousness. Of interest psychologically, and essential for an understanding of political developments, was the denial of the traditional individualistic ideology of the farmer as the 'king in his castle', and the bitter disappointment over the failure of modern capitalistic farming methods, which immediately after the war, at a time of real hunger, were encouraged by the administration and the various farmers' organisations themselves.[23]

Thus the collapse of the agricultural system, and in turn the dislocation of traditional patterns of 'community' among the rural population, was reflected in the collapse of the traditional individualistic consciousness of the peasant-farmer. Nazi propaganda constantly played upon this denial of traditional values in order to heighten the farmer's sense of outrage at the loss of his 'sacrosant' property and his personal sense of 'worth'. But most important of all, National Socialism offered an alternative to dislocation. The Third Reich would guarantee the restitution of *individual* rights, but within a society which guaranteed social harmony and communal honour. And this particular image of utopia found favour among the small farmers precisely because they were discovering (in the Landvolk movement and in mass demonstrations against evictions) a new sense of social solidarity through communal action against the 'external' threat – the threat from the money-lenders, the courts, the bailiffs, the tax-office – everything that represented 'the system'. Furthermore, Nazi ideology compensated for the loss of the individual's *personal* integrity by elevating the peasantry as a whole to the status of an elite within the Volk-community:

> We recognise not just the importance of maintaining a class of food producers for our people; we also see the peasant farmer as the source of a healthy racial stock, the fountain of the people's youth and the backbone of our defence strength (**43**).

[23] Heberle, op. cit., p.166.

So the Nazi movement *expressed and exploited* the spirit of the farming community, both in crisis and in its response to crisis. Ideologically speaking, it gave vent to real feelings of bewilderment, bitterness and betrayal, and offered hope of a utopian Reich in which the farmer would once again regain prosperity, honour and freedom. But in offering this 'positive myth' of community and freedom, National Socialism also created a 'negative myth'. Moreover, this negative myth, which purported to explain the origins of the crisis which afflicted the rural Mittelstand, was in effect an *integral part* of the positive myth, for it determined the manner in which the utopia of the Volk-community could be reached.

The commercial Mittelstand and the artisans

It was not until the NSDAP had made its first major breakthrough and consolidated its support among the farming community that its campaign among the commercial Mittelstand gathered momentum. Obviously major elements of this commercial Mittelstand-politik are to be found in earlier years: indeed before the Munich coup Hitler was preaching on 'the politics of the annihilation of the Mittelstand' (**8**), while in 1928 Fritz Saukel was complaining of a 'crime wave unleashed by the international department stores' (**25**). However, it was only as the economic recession deepened in the final months of 1929, and as political polarisation became more pronounced under the Brüning government, that the commercial Mittelstand and the artisans became increasingly susceptible to Nazi propaganda.

As in the farming community the NSDAP did not have to invent the grievances of the traders and small manufacturers. Declining turnover, low profitability, high taxation, the fear of bankruptcy and the spectre of Communism were all factors which predisposed the petite bourgeoisie towards some form of conservative radicalism. But, as in the case of the farming community, Nazi propaganda deliberately fanned these grievances into a syndrome of fear and impending doom in order to reinforce the image of National Socialism as the only alternative to 'the system'. There were also certain specific cultural reasons for the success of the NSDAP's propaganda campaign, so we must look briefly at the background to the crisis of the commercial Mittelstand at the beginning of the 1930s.

In its campaign to win over the commercial Mittelstand the NSDAP concentrated its attack upon exposing the 'ruinous' effects of two particular competitors – the department stores and the consumer co-operatives. Both were branded as the 'enemies' of the small independent trader. The success of the NSDAP's propaganda in lumping together these two quite different organisations requires explanation, for although the department stores could rightly be presented as the embodiment of 'big business practices' and 'modern' capitalism, the consumer co-operatives could hardly be tarred with the same brush.

Before the war there had been strong animosity between the small shopkeepers and the first department stores, which led the imperial authorities to impose limits upon the growth of department stores through taxation policies and the curtailment of advertising.[24] After the war, in the wake of the revolutionary events of November 1918, Karl Kautsky's Socialisation Committee was given the task of recommending action to nationalise the marketing system. In response, the department stores and the small traders made common cause to protect their interests, and formed the Association of, German Traders in March 1919.

The consumer co-operatives, on the other hand, which were formed almost exclusively out of working-class initiatives (many co-operatives were associated in some way with the SPD) were seen by the small trader as the natural allies of a socialised marketing system. Thus even in the aftermath of the revolutionary events, the consumer co-operatives were seen as either ambivalent to private enterprise and the small trader or, worse still, as the Trojan horse of a Marxist state. And although the tactical alliance of the department stores and the small traders fell apart as soon as it became obvious that the SPD had neither the will nor the capability to introduce any measure of socialisation in Germany, the fear of the 'worker co-operatives' remained.

The hyper-inflation also left a severe impression upon the psyche of the commercial Mittelstand. However, with the stabilisation of the mark in 1924, a period of relative prosperity set in, which saw turnover in the retail trade rise from 25.8 billion marks in 1924 to

---

[24] The first department stores were Tietz (1879), Karstadt (1881) and Althoff (1885).

33.8 billion in 1927.[25] More importantly, the number of small traders continued to rise in absolute terms from 695,800 in 1907 to 847,900 in 1925 – a rise of 21 per cent, which was all the more remarkable given the drastic drop in gross domestic product during these years. In effect, the statistics suggest that the existence of a great many of these new small traders was highly marginal, and many would have been pedlars and hawkers rather than shop-keepers.

None the less the gradual rise in prosperity between 1924 and 1929 helped to absorb these petty traders into the economy despite the expansion of large stores and chain shops with modern marketing techniques. So until 1929 the increase in turnover of the small traders more or less matched that of the department stores.[26]

	Turnover of small shops	*Turnover of department stores*
1925	100	100
1926	104	103
1927	115	114
1928	123	128

But after 1928 the disparity in growth already evident in the previous year began to widen.

The effects of the world recession upon the small traders were therefore disproportionately severe. While large concerns were able to maintain or even increase their percentage turnover, the small trader could claim only a declining share of a rapidly contracting market, as total retail sales fell from 36.6 billion marks in 1929 to just 22.7 billion in 1932.[27] The inevitable consequence was that many thousands of small traders, and the small manufacturers who traditionally supplied them, went out of business. If anything, the recession hit the artisans even harder than the commercial Mittelstand:[28]

[25] Heinrich Uhlig, *Die Warenhäuser im Dritten Reich*, Köln 1956, p.27.

[26] ibid., p.24.

[27] ibid., p.41.

[28] C. Krohn & D. Stegmann, 'Kleingewerbe und Nationalsozialismus in einer agrarisch-Mittelständischen Region', *Archiv für Sozialgeschichte* no.17, 1977, p.50. These figures do disguise major variations between different trades.

Artisan production (Handwerk)

	total turnover	profitability
1928	100	100
1929	98	91
1930	86	68
1931	65	58
1932	50	35

National Socialism and the commercial Mittelstand

The heterogeneity of the commercial Mittelstand and the small producers makes it far more difficult to appraise the ideological appeal of National Socialism to them than to the rural Mittelstand. Certainly there are broad similarities of propaganda-style and content, but there are also interesting differences.

First of all, the NSDAP was not able to exploit an existing movement of radical social discontent among the urban middle classes and the artisans as it had been able to exploit the Landvolk movement among the farmers. Thus it is noticable that Nazi propaganda devoted considerable effort to breaking down the reserve of the commercial middle class to any form of political action:

> When will the Mittelstand finally see that politics affects the economy and that political neutrality means their extinction? (**45**).

The Kampfgemeinschaft (later Kampfbund) for the Commercial Mittelstand was therefore a particularly important instrument in generating support among the small traders for the NSDAP, since it effectively initiated 'direct action' against the department stores and set in train the process of political militancy which was vital to the success of National Socialism. In turn the evidence of direct action could be pointed to as proof that the NSDAP was the only *effective* opposition to the forces which threatened to 'annihilate the Mittelstand':

> We declare open war upon the department stores and the consumer co-operatives, and we will not be put off, even if counter action is taken against us ... What other Mittelstand organisation has been able to plan protest actions ...? (**45**).

Of course the NSDAP maintained its attack upon the Weimar 'system', constantly hammering home the point that a real improvement in the lot of the commercial Mittelstand and the small producer could only come about once a thorough (National Socialist) transformation of society had been achieved:

> We know that only by destroying the present system can we clear the way to reach our final goal ... Only under the swastika will the economy, so badly crippled by the old parties, once again bloom and prosper (**45**).

And, equally, the Mittelstand's traditional political parties and their professional interest groups are denounced for having failed the crisis-ridden businessman:

> What have your parties done for you? They promised the world but ... did not unite against the treacherous leaders of Marxism (**38**).

However, the highly specific propaganda onslaught against the department stores and the consumer co-operatives is an indication of another difference in the way in which the Nazis approached the task of winning over the urban middle classes. In the farming community the crisis itself appeared to be the work of relatively anonymous market forces. The small farmer could not see a competitor who was driving him out of business; he was merely faced with an apparently universal collapse of the agricultural economy. In the towns and cities, however, the 'little man' could identify his antagonist – another retailer or manufacturer who appeared to be gaining business at his expense. All in all, then, it seems that the propaganda directed at the urban petite bourgeoisie was far more direct in its appeal to sectional self-interest. For instance there is no equivalent of the ideological elitism which we find in the attempt to eulogise the peasant as the 'backbone of the nation' and the fountain of youth. Instead the commercial Mittelstand are promised salvation from their many cares through the institution of the corporate state:

> In the new Reich the Mittelstand will have a proper position in line with its vital economic role (**43**).

Even more apparent is the relative degree of 'politicisation' of Nazi propaganda where the commercial Mittelstand are concerned. Thus the issue of anti-capitalism raises its head time and time again:

> You pay taxes and the like until your blood runs white, while huge concerns are making a fortune (**20**).

> Look at the banks and their massive profits. They are eating you out of existence! (**38**).

And most notable of all is that even in the March 1933 election leaflets, we find an example of this anti-capitalism which actually falsifies the NSDAP's own party programme to provide evidence that the Nazis will tackle the issue of big business by 'abolishing large concerns' (**54**). In fact Point 16 of the Party Programme makes no such mention of 'large concerns' (see **29**), referring only to the 'communalisation of the department stores'.

Ideology and Weltanschauung

So far we have concentrated upon what could be termed the positive appeal of National Socialism: its promise to break the existing 'system' and create a utopian Third Reich in which the nation would be rejuvenated and the Mittelstand would find economic prosperity. But we have suggested that in offering this 'positive myth' the National Socialist movement necessarily created a 'negative myth' – an aspect of its ideology or Weltanschauung which did not evolve in isolation, but which was intimately bound up with the Nazis' explanation of the crisis, and indeed with its intended solution.

This negative myth was of course centred upon anti-Semitism and the stereotype of the Jew and 'Jewishness', and we can see exactly how positive and negative myth relate to each other within the Nazi Weltanschauung by examining its structure. Before doing so however, we must look briefly at what we mean by a Nazi Weltanschauung.

Hitler consistently characterised the ideology of National Socialism as a Weltanschauung – literally 'a way of looking at the world'. At best this is a somewhat fanciful description of what was in effect a hotch-potch of ideas and obsessions which varied according to various factions and individuals within the party. That having been said, there is a sense in which National Socialism did create a

Weltanschauung precisely to enclose these multifarious beliefs within an all-encompassing cosmological myth which attempted to explain not only the crisis of post-war German society, but indeed the whole of history, as a consequence of racial struggle. So in analysing this Weltanschauung we must bear in mind two particular points. First, we are identifying an ideological *structure* only for the purposes of analysis: to illustrate a number of tendencies specific to Nazi ideology. We are not attempting to give this Weltanschauung the status of a philosophy. Secondly, although Nazi ideology cannot be reduced to its ideological 'function', it must be understood that it was a specific function of this Nazi Weltanschauung to obscure and mystify the real contradictions between its various elements.[29] In other words Nazi ideology attempted to cement a political alliance of social factions and classes whose objective historical interests contradicted one another.

This Nazi Weltanschauung can best be represented diagramatically, for its structure relies not upon logical progressions but upon a series of 'associational links' which were enforced by propaganda and psychological manipulation. This structure rests upon a 'racial' axis – the dichotomy (separation into two conflicting and *mutually exclusive* elements) between:

German   and   Jew

or more exactly between:

German Racial Community   and   Jewishness
(*Volksgemeinschaft*)   (*Judentum*)

All social, economic, political and cultural criteria are in turn related to, or enclosed within, these two elements.

---

[29] Thus although ideology cannot be reduced to the 'function' it serves in the social structure, since this ignores the dialectic between ideas and material conditions, in the case of National Socialism we are clearly dealing with an 'ideology' which, at least in part, was organised to perform a manipulatory function. The real problem of interpretation exists in detailing the degree to which manipulation and dialectic interact in the case of Nazi ideology, and this is clearly the major issue in any interpretation of Nazi anti-Semitism.

German Racial Community	Jewishness
Capitalism	
All creative social elements	all anti-social parasitic elements
'creative' or 'productive' capitalism	'exploitative' capitalism
small Mittelstand capital	finance or loan capital
small shop/artisan	department store/trust
creation of goods, food or raw materials	profiteering from 'middle man activity – Stock Exchange, merchant, etc.
Socialism	
German socialism	'Jewish' socialism, i.e. Marxism/Bolshevism
social justice	corruption
racial solidarity	disintegration
economic prosperity	economic collapse
Further social, political and cultural aspects	
nationalist	internationalist
traditional	modernistic
authoritarian state	liberal-democratic or Bolshevik state
military strength	pacifism

Economic criteria

The dynamic of this Weltanschauung is the economic sphere. The distinction between 'creative' and 'exploitative' capital generally expresses the consciousness of an archaic, economically inefficient petite bourgeoisie under threat (at a time of chronic market contraction) from modern, capitalist enterprises. This threat is expressed at the point of production (or exchange) in the problems of *credit and competition*.

Thus the German Mittelstand concretely identified the threat to its existence as:

1. Lack of credit – a particular effect of the hyper-inflation and the sudden withdrawal of foreign loans in the late 1920s.

2. Overbearing competition from conglomerate companies with:
    (a) Highly capitalised (and hence more 'efficient') methods of production – and the power to create cartels or monopolise major branches of industry.
    (b) Highly rationalised methods of marketing.

In turn these two threats found everyday expression in the denunciation of:

1. Finance capital, the Stock Exchange, the banks, or more immediately 'usurious interest rates' and 'profiteering'.
2. Resentment against (a) trusts and syndicates (b) department stores and chain shops.

So the negative economic aspects of the Nazi Weltanschauung relate to objective criteria and to a specific consciousness which developed out of crisis conditions.

The sleight of hand, or the trick of propaganda, came in identifying these negative aspects exclusively with the Jews and 'Jewishness', and it was the *specific task* of Nazi propaganda to fasten this 'racial' link. Again we can identify two types of approach. First, there was a generalised denigration of the Jew and his effect upon the workings of the economy. For instance:

> It is a fact that the Jew never puts up barns, but he earns more, far more through dealing in corn ... the non-working Jew gets far more money than the productive farmer ... so it is true to say that the Jew is the exploiter of work ... he steals from creative people and their work ... (**42**).

Secondly, there was the identification of the Jews (and 'Jewishness') as the power behind the various economic threats to the Mittelstand's existence:

> Don't you see the vile plan, the same Jews who control the monopoly on sales of nitrogen, calcium, etc. ... never give you a just price for your produce on the Stock Exchange ... it won't be long before the greater part of the land-owning farmers are driven from their farms and land by Jewish money lenders (**22**).

> Behind the department stores ... stands Jewish Finance Capital (**29**).

> The Jew is the ruler of the Stock Exchange ... the reason for corruption and unemployment ... (**42**).

Political criteria

Just as the negative aspects of economic existence for the Mittelstand are associated with 'exploitative' or 'parasitic' capital, and hence the Jew, so the various objects of the Mittelstand's political animosity are linked to 'Jewishness'. Most of all their hatred was directed towards the forces of socialism: in the vocabulary of National Socialism – 'Marxism' or 'Bolshevism'.

> In Germany, in Austria, in Russia – everywhere the same picture – everywhere destruction, everywhere revolution, all brought about by the Jews (**42**).
>
> ... control of all the Marxist parties lies in the hands of the Jews (**16**).

And finally we learn that the 'Jewish' socialist parties (KPD and SPD) are in league with the forces of 'Jewish' capitalism in the conspiracy against the 'German' Volk:

> Do you finally see that international high-finance and Marxism have the same aim; that Marxism is only a tool of the International Stock Exchange, and its personification – the World-Jew (**24**).

Indeed all the non-Nazi parties, especially the bourgeois parties for whom the Mittelstand traditionally voted, are wittingly or unwittingly involved in this same racial conspiracy:

> Your parties ... didn't unite against the treacherous leaders of Marxism ... they have ruled with the Social Democrats and forgotten the aim of that party – Death to the Mittelstand! (**38**).

Eschatology

Because the various elements of the Nazi Weltanschauung are linked together by a process of psychological 'association', the ability of the NSDAP to gain support was heavily reliant upon the degree to which party propaganda could enforce and reinforce these images in the minds of its potential supporters. Political ritual (mass rallies, etc.) was certainly one method of maximising this type of psychological manipulation, and we shall discuss this in Part III. But during the Kampfzeit, and especially after the onset of the recession, another aspect, which might be termed the *eschatological* factor, was clearly important.

We have noted time and time again how the Nazis' bid for electoral support concentrated upon exposing and attacking the evils of the Weimar 'system' and offering the image of a National Socialist millennium as the *only* alternative to 'chaos' and 'Bolshevism'.

> Vote Hitler, if you want everything, absolutely everything to change! (**50**).

And we have argued that the negative and positive aspects of the Nazi Weltanschauung were implicitly bound up with one another to the extent that the promise of the Nazi utopia was presented as the historical antithesis of the Jews' 'destruction and chaos'. So it follows that in order to maximise the appeal of the Thousand-Year Reich, and to generate the 'enthusiasm' and the commitment upon which Nazism flourished, it was essential to promote an atmosphere of deep foreboding and fear among the NSDAP's social base. If the Mittelstand could not be enticed into the Third Reich, then they would have to be panicked into it.

It was the onset of the agricultural crisis in 1927 and the world slump after 1929, together with the political polarisation of German society, which created the essential preconditions for the success of Nazism's eschatological propaganda. Again, this eschatology exploited both the economic and the political insecurity of the Mittelstand, while its tone of apocalyptic hysteria intensified year by year after 1929:

Economic:

> Today all of us in the Mittelstand are 'down' or else we are on the way down (**29**, 1928/1929).

> Middle classes, why is it so bad? Why are your shops empty? Why are you out of business? (**38**, 1930).

> The Mittelstand are starving to death! ... 700 court proceedings every day in Berlin – you can work out for yourselves when it is going to be your turn (**47**, 1932).

> Artisans and business people! You are standing on the edge of your graves! (**50**, 1932).

Political:

> Farmers, you are going to be expropriated! (**32**, 1929).

> Now there can only be one *final* decision, Swastika or Soviet Star! ... do you want to be chased from your old farm ... your village priest to be murdered ... your family to be left defenceless while Bolshevism satisfies its blood-lust? (**44**, 1931).

> It is now the twelfth hour ... we must choose between God or the devil, race or half-caste ... family or collective, National Socialism or Bolshevism! (**46**, 1931).

> Adolf Hitler is going to be murdered! Civil war in Germany! The KPD murders women! (**51**, 1932).

Of course the apocalyptic imagery of the written word was heavily reinforced by the visual imagery of the movement – the massed ranks of the brown-shirted SA preparing to do battle with the 'system-parties', or party-day at Nuremberg where Hitler stood aloof from the masses below him – called by God to save the nation from Bolshevism. And here we come to the heart of the eschatological appeal of National Socialism, for it was not necessary for the potential 'convert' to the Nazi cause to accept rationally or even consciously every facet of Nazi ideology in order to identify the NSDAP as the only hope of rescue from the threat of 'imminent' ruin and Bolshevism. This fact was clearly recognised by a perceptive employer as early as 1930:

> The mental rejection of certain parts of the party programme ... weighs less heavily than the notion that only the National Socialists are strong enough to pull the cart out of the mud.[30]

Therefore the 'appeal' of the Nazi Weltanschauung has to be understood in this light, for although the NSDAP clearly detailed its 'racial' explanation of the crisis of German society (and indeed offered a racial solution) it also gathered support on the basis of its eschatological style. But those who did put their shoulder to the wheel, in the belief that the first priority was 'to get the cart out of the mud', were to learn a bitter lesson. For in their enthusiasm to push with the Nazis, it seems that few questioned just what was inside the cart that they were struggling to free.

---

[30] Cf. *Nordwestdeutsche Handwerks Zeitung*, September 1930. Even more important, see Kirdorf's statement on the NSDAP and the party programme, p. 111 above.

PART III

Power and Ritual – the Forging of the Nazi State

CHAPTER SIX

The Betrayal of the Mittelstand

In this chapter we shall look at the policies of the NSDAP after 30 January 1933, examining to what extent the party's ideological pronouncements during the Kampfzeit were put into effect under the Third Reich.

Obviously a thorough analysis of the social policies introduced by the Nazi state is beyond the scope of this work; indeed analysis of the socio-economic history of the Third Reich is still in its infancy.[1] Therefore we shall concentrate upon examining the fate of National Socialism's Mittelstand-politik – that aspect of Nazi ideology which we have identified as the most important source of electoral and organisational support for the NSDAP during the Kampfzeit.

The power struggle within the administration

Even before Hitler's accession to the Chancellorship, National Socialism's much-trumpeted Mittelstand-politik had come under attack from big business. In December 1932 Hitler ordered the newly created Kampfbund of the Commercial Mittelstand (the old Kampfgemeinschaft against Department Stores and Consumer Co-operatives) led by von Renteln, to be merged into Section IVa of the NSDAP's Economic and Political Department, thereby cutting back its independence and its ability to pressurise for purely Mittelstand objectives. Kampfbund leaders were forced to concede that National Socialism 'could only pursue the interests of a single economic group (*Berufsstand*) ... when this was not detrimental to the

---

[1] For a bibliography of works on the social policy of the Third Reich, see H.A. Winkler, 'Der Entbehrliche Stand: zur Mittelstand Politik im Dritten Reich', *Archiv für Sozialgeschichte* no. 17, 1977.

whole of society'.[2] Similarly, the Programme for Economic Regeneration published by the NSDAP in the autumn of 1932, largely under Funk's influence, named the 'stimulation of industrial production' and 'protection of agriculture' as top priorities for a new National Socialist government; while the Immediate Programme published in July 1932 had contained a catalogue of specifically Mittelstand demands.

In the euphoric aftermath of the take-over of power, however, it seemed for a time as if traditional Mittelstand elements within the National Socialist movement would be able to assert considerable influence upon the direction of socio-economic policy. Certainly, as Winkler suggests, 'boycott demonstrations and acts of terror against department stores and Jewish businesses were the expression of the feeling of victory on the part of National Socialist small traders and artisans'.[3]

After the March elections, local and national Mittelstand pressure-groups prevailed upon Hitler to appoint a minister to represent the interests of the petite bourgeoisie. In April, Weinbeck was given a post as Junior Minister for the Middle Classes in Hugenberg's Ministry of Economics, and Wagener was appointed as Commissioner for the non-Agricultural Sector of the Economy. In turn Wagener appointed von Renteln to head the newly-created Reichsstände of German Handicrafts and Trade, which was in effect a Nazified (*gleichgeschaltet*) central organisation designed to regulate traders and artisans. This organisation was seen as a necessary first step in the creation of occupational groups (or councils) which would eventually form the structure of a corporate economy.

In the boardrooms of commerce and industry, however, attempts at Nazification were vigorously resisted.[4] Using Göring's influence, and the offices of the Ministry of Economics (under Hugenberg), industrialists and senior civil servants largely succeeded in blocking or forestalling the attempts of local SA units and party militants to gain influence within large commercial organisations. Schacht in

---

[2] Flugblatt des Kampfbundes des Gewerblichen Mittelstandes, in Bundes Archiv, Sammlung Schumacher 242 a.

[3] Winkler, op. cit. p.3.

[4] Although the Confederation of German Industry (RdI) was eventually Nazified, this was done voluntarily at Krupp's suggestion, and under Krupp's leadership. In fact the RdI simply changed its name to the Reichsstand der deutschen Industrie, without undergoing any change in personnel, function or ideology.

particular saw to it that the party's Kampfzeit slogan – 'Against international finance capital' – found no expression in policy. As early as 27 April Wagener was forced to issue a statement forbidding SA units from 'arbitrarily installing commissioners of any sort' in the industrial sector of the economy.[5] And when at the beginning of May Hitler was informed that a Nazi party member, with the help of the SA, had tried to force himself onto the board of the Dresdner Bank, Hitler ordered the offender to be dismissed from the party and put on trial.

Also symptomatic of the pressure which big business brought to bear upon the Nazi leadership was Hitler's decree of 31 May 1933 to the Reichs-Governor and the Minister-President of Prussia. The decree sought to stop the wave of denunciations of corrupt businessmen and business practices which were being voiced by the NSDAP's rank and file, especially by small traders and radical members of the SA. Ignoring the party's fifteen-year struggle against 'the bosses' economy' and 'financial swindle', Hitler ordered all investigations against corruption to cease, suggesting that behind such allegations lay nothing but 'a desire for revenge and the pursuit of self-interest'. Indeed the Fuhrer effectively apologised for the past misdemeanours of businessmen, suggesting that their failings were 'less a result of pure greed' than a side-effect of 'their very struggle for existence'.[6]

In the second half of May Wagener announced the dissolution of all Fighting Leagues (Kampfbünde) with the exception of the Mittelstand Kampfbund – but the latter was forced drastically to review its role. Thus the Kampfbund's Munich leadership warned against 'any sort of meddling in economic affairs, above all, attempts to Nazify employers' associations'.[7] And in July Röhm publicly announced that the SA 'must not meddle in the running of the economy', and that it was expressly forbidden to work with any Kampfbund for such purposes.[8]

At the end of June Hugenberg was replaced as Minister of Economics by Kurt Schmitt, previously managing director of

[5] Martin Broszat, *Der Staat Hitlers*, Munich 1969, p.219.
[6] ibid., p.220.
[7] Statement of Kampfbund Leitung, Gau München-Oberbayern. See Winkler, op.cit., p.5.
[8] ibid.

Germany's largest insurance company, the Allianz. In return for allowing Walter Darré a free hand in agricultural affairs, Schmitt gained important trade-offs from the Nazi leaders with respect to the industrial sector. In July Schmitt issued a joint party and ministerial decree to the effect that all National Socialists who had gained positions of influence on the boards of companies or in the management of business concerns, purely as a result of their party connections, were to be dismissed. Simultaneously Otto Wagener was ousted from his position on the NSDAP's Economic-Political Council and replaced by Wilhelm Keppler. Equally notable was Schmitt's success at this early stage in gaining the power to determine the wage-rates set by the Ministry of Labour.

As Minister of Economics Schmitt was instrumental in shaping the course of co-operation between the state and private industry. On 15 July a new Cartel Law was proclaimed 'for the purpose of market regulation', which gave the state bureaucracy the power to determine pricing policies and the structure of the newly introduced (compulsory) industrial cartels.[9] Such a law worked decisively in favour of existing monopoly groups in heavy industry, and gave a firm indication of the increasing harmony of interest between the political demands of the Nazi state and the economic interests of big business. Schmitt further secured the creation of an 'economic advisory council' to help determine the Nazi state's future strategy, whose eighteen members were to be drawn almost exclusively from the leaders of heavy industry and banking.[10] It was Schmitt too who announced that the government's intention to create work must take priority over attempts to lay the foundations of a corporate economic structure. In this he was supported by Hitler's private Secretary, Hess, who informed the party that all public discussion of corporate plans and similar measures was banned.[11]

The National Socialist Revolution formally came to an end in July

[9] Kartellgesetze, *Reichsgesetzblatt* I, pp. 487/8.

[10] A similar fate befell the committee appointed to investigate the banking system in April 1933. Schacht was appointed as chairman, and the panel of experts was drawn almost exclusively from bankers and academic economists. The committee did not report until the end of 1934 (after the Röhm purges) and its recommendations were against Feder's demands to nationalise the German banking system. See A. Schweitzer, *Big Business in the Third Reich*, Bloomington 1964, pp. 128ff.

[11] Winkler, op. cit., p.5.

1933. On 6 July Hitler announced to the Reichs-Governors that 'the full spate of revolution must be guided into the secure bed of evolution ... the main thing now is the daily bread of five million people'.[12] A month later the Mittelstand Kampfbund was dissolved and its members taken *en masse* into the 'National Socialist Handicraft, Trade and Commerce Organisation' – NS Hago.

The first issue of the NS Hago's newsletter (*Führerbriefe*) made it abundantly clear what the leadership expected from the membership, who were now part of Robert Ley's German Workers' Front (DAF). According to the leading article, the Mittelstand had taken precious little account of the sufferings of the German workers for a hundred years, but as soon as the middle classes too began to suffer, they adopted 'a policy of self-interest that was laughably egoistical'. Therefore, the article concluded, the task of NS Hago was not to promote the interests of small businessmen, but to educate the Mittelstand to National Socialist attitudes![13]

The assimilation of the Mittelstand Kampfbund into NS Hago was plainly designed to blunt the campaign waged by the commercial petite bourgeoisie for the introduction of a corporate economic structure. Even so, organisational manoeuvres could not completely suppress such demands. In March 1934 the NS Hago leadership of Mainfranken had to 'remind' its local branches of the order by the Fuhrer's Secretariat (Hess) that the texts of posters and placards displayed in demonstrations must first be approved by 'the relevant political organisations'. Posters with slogans such as 'Whoever buys from a Jew is a traitor' would not be permitted. Furthermore 'demonstrations should not lead to boycott-actions against department stores, single-price shops or Jewish establishments. Boycotts such as this ... must first be approved by the Ministers of Economics, Propaganda and Education, as well as by the President of the Reichsbank!'[14]

But the decisive defeat of a National Socialist Mittelstand-politik had occurred before March 1934, and certainly before the physical liquidation of the radicals in the SA which Hitler ordered three months later. Indeed the political struggle waged within the

---

[12] H.A. Jacobsen & W. Jochmann, *Ausgewählte Dokumente zur Geschichte des Nationalsozialismus*, Bielefeld 1963.

[13] Führerbriefe der NS-Hago, 1 September 1933. Sammlung Schumacher 242a.

[14] Sammlung Schumacher 242a.

administration between May and August 1933 was decisive in defeating the attempts of the NSDAP's grass-root supporters to institutionalise the Mittelstand policies for which the Nazi party had campaigned with such vigour during the Kampfzeit. We can demonstrate this by looking at the fate of the department stores, the co-operatives and agriculture under the Third Reich – remembering how these issues had been presented by Nazi propaganda before the take-over of power!

The department stores

During the second week in March 1933, the Mittelstand Kampfbund, with the enthusiastic support of SA units, organised the first widespread boycott of department stores, consumer co-operatives, chain stores and Jewish businesses. These boycotts were intensified in April with the sanction of the party – the Nazi leadership's response to foreign press reports of Nazi brutality and the suppression of democracy and human rights. The strength of support mobilised by the boycott actions (voluntarily and through coercion) led many party members to believe that the NSDAP had both the ability and the will to 'grasp the snake of finance capital' and to close down the department stores.

In mid-April the *Völkischer Beobachter* reported that Fritz Reinhardt, Secretary of State at the Ministry of Economics, would shortly announce a number of laws which would promote the interests of the Mittelstand in the economy.[15] However, when the 'Law for the Protection of the Small Trader' was published on 12 May, its sole administrative power contained provision for a short-term ban on the opening of new department and chain stores, and a clause giving local authorities the right to limit the development of commercial enterprises where there was 'a lack of demand' or where competition was deemed to be 'fraudulent or unfair'.[16]

Despite, or more likely because of, public disappointment at the limited nature of these powers, boycott actions continued during May, with Nazi militants pointing to Point 16 of the party's 'unalterable' Twenty-Five Point Party Programme to support their

---

[15] *Völkischer Beobachter*, 15 April 1933.

[16] The ban on new stores was extended at the end of the six-month term and eventually enshrined in a new law in 1935.

actions (see **29**). At the same time small traders and businesses, emboldened by the new political atmosphere which seemed to favour middle-class militancy, used the opportunity to increase their hard-pressed profit margins by raising retail prices. The result was a sudden surge of price-rises which created an outcry among the mass of unemployed and the low-paid. The National Socialist Factory Organisation (NSBO), fearful lest a sudden spiral of price-inflation should alienate working-class opinion at a crucial stage in efforts to Nazify Factory Councils (and prevent moves towards a General Strike) was particularly loud in its condemnation of 'middle-class profiteering'. And, ironically, the NSBO's protests were echoed by many of the SA units actually responsible for the boycott actions.

The party leadership could not afford to ignore this popular reaction. In Bavaria the state cabinet met on 16 May and decided to proceed 'with the most severe police measures if necessary' against 'anti-social price-rises'.[17] During the next few days some 200 shop-keepers were rounded up in Munich alone, their businesses closed down, and a sign erected which read 'Business shut down by police on account of profiteering – the owner in custody in Dachau'.[18]

However, the boycott actions initiated in March and April had a severe effect upon the turnover and hence the profitability of the department stores. Further legislation was promised by the NSDAP for the early summer to increase drastically the taxation on large stores. But pressure was building up against these discriminatory measures from two powerful sources. First, the NSBO, fearful of the political effects of making thousands of department store staff redundant, began to voice misgivings about forcing the department stores into liquidation. Secondly, the banks, finance houses and trusts who had considerable funds invested in the new retail stores warned that the threat of insolvency in one part of the economy would damage business confidence in other sectors, and leading businessmen began to exert their influence upon ministers and party officials to curtail further punitive action.

By early June the promised legislation had still failed to materialise; and then, at the end of the month, the Hermann Tietz Konzern announced that it was teetering on the edge of bankruptcy.

[17] *Völkischer Beobachter*, 20 May 1933, Supplement.
[18] Heinrich Uhlig, op. cit., p.106.

The new regime was faced with a stark choice – sanction a financial rescue, or let the concern collapse and with it the livelihood of 14,000 employees.

The Hermann Tietz corporation was Jewish-owned, and its Hertie department stores had been one of the NSDAP's prime targets in its campaign against 'Jewish finance capital' (see, for instance, **29**). So at first Hitler refused Schmitt's pleas to save the ailing company through a state-financed rescue. But within a matter of days Hitler was forced to back down as the financial and political implications of the situation were made crystal-clear to him by his economic advisers.

The plan to rescue Hertie was leaked in early July, provoking the sort of uproar among the Nazi rank and file that Hitler had obviously feared. Dr Hilland, the deputy leader of the Mittelstand Kampfbund, unaware that Hitler himself had sanctioned the deal, angrily demanded in the National Socialist press that 'ruthless action' should be taken against the 'irresponsible' interests behind the rescue.[19] On 7 July Hitler's Secretary, Rudolf Hess, was forced to make a public statement in which he announced the party's new attitude to the department stores:

> At a time when it is the first priority of the National Socialist government to help as many as possible of our unemployed comrades to find work and bread, the National Socialist movement should not stand in the way by denying work to the hundreds and thousands of workers and staff employed in the department stores and businesses dependent upon them. NSDAP organisations are therefore forbidden to take action against department stores and similar businesses until further notice.[20]

On 15 July the long-awaited 'Law for the Regulation of the Taxation of Department and Chain Stores' was finally published. The intention to increase taxation drastically had been abandoned: instead the relevant local authorities were empowered, at most, to double existing taxation rates. In Prussia, where Göring and his Finance Minister Popitz held sway, even these limited powers were ignored.[21]

[19] ibid., p.116.
[20] *Völkischer Beobachter*, 10 July 1933.
[21] Uhlig, op. cit., p.100.

Nor did the appointment of Gottfried Feder to the post of Under-Secretary (Staatssekretär) to Schmitt at the beginning of July produce any change in government policy towards the department stores.[22] Indeed one of Feder's first tasks as Under Secretary was to inform the Bavarian State Chancellery that their demand to close down the food departments of department stores was out of the question, because a detailed report had shown that 'such a ban, in view of the importance of the food-departments for certain individual concerns ... would lead to [their] collapse, with incalculable consequences for the whole economy and the labour market'.[23]

The failure of the new regime to crush the 'department store pest' was seen by many previously loyal middle-class militants as a betrayal of the movement's ideals. And despite the party's ultimatum (via Hess) to its members to cease boycott actions, a number of semi-official boycotts broke out from time to time which attempted to claim the leadership's sanction by quoting Hess's lame apology (an addendum to his proclamation forbidding boycotts) that the National Socialist attitude to department stores was nevertheless 'unaltered'. Indeed many department stores prominently displayed the main text of Hess's proclamation in their shop-windows, while SA pickets on the door held placards quoting Hess's addendum to support their action!

As a sop to public opinion a law was promulgated in 1935 which forbade department stores to run refreshment rooms, food-departments and handicraft sections, and which limited the sale-season to three days in summer and winter. But 1935 marked the low-point of the department stores' economic performance during the Third Reich, and during the next three years their turnover increased by nearly 10 per cent per annum.

On Crystal-night (9 November 1938) some 29 Jewish department stores were burned to the ground and numerous others 'Aryanised'. Thereafter the stronger 'Aryan' department stores were seen as an ideal instrument for the needs of a 'rational' war-economy, and on 1 April the discriminatory taxes on such stores were abolished.

---

[22] Feder was apparently appointed to the post as a sweetener for the dismissal of Otto Wagener, who according to Schweitzer (op. cit.) was sent to a concentration camp for six weeks to cool his radical temperament!

[23] Winkler, op. cit., p.10.

The co-operatives

As with the department stores, the fate of the German co-operatives reflected the power struggle within the Nazi state in the aftermath of the take-over of power. However, unlike the department stores, the struggle reflected not so much a conflict of interest between a Mittelstand-politik and the demands of big business, as an internal party struggle for the spoils of power.

The German co-operatives were Nazified during the first phase of the Nazi seizure of power – the terroristic suppression of the left-wing parties and the trade unions by SA and SS units. In May, Robert Ley officially announced the total dissolution of the co-operatives, although he ordered this policy to be put into operation in a proper legal manner and 'preferably without loss' to savers. A month later, however, Göring ordered the Prussian police to prevent the Mittelstand Kampfbund from interfering with co-operative organis-ations, and it was announced that only the central government had the authority to determine their fate.

By September Ley seemed to have undergone a remarkable conversion. The anti-co-operative attitude of the party's militant rank and file was, he suggested, in danger of undermining the economic programme of the government; furthermore it had 'aggravated and embittered large sections of the German workers'.[24] In future, Ley announced, existing local co-operatives would be integrated into a new 'Reich's Co-operative Organisation', although their premises would be turned over to small traders in line with the Twenty-Five Point Party Programme. But in practice this rarely happened, and local co-operatives often continued to do business under their previous management as part of the Reich's Organisation.

The bitterness of the commercial Mittelstand at yet another betrayal of the movement's ideals was forcefully expressed by Karl Becker, the leader of NS Hago's education department in Aschaffenburg. In May 1934 Becker made a report in which he complained that 'the struggling Mittelstand, instead of seeing any improvement in their situation, feel it is getting worse. On the other hand, the co-operatives are putting out propaganda and adverts which can only be described as Jewish-Marxist in style.' And he

---

[24] *Völkischer Beobachter*, 19 September 1933.

continued: 'Those who once fought us to the bitter end, now do as they please. The old red bosses are still feathering their nests, and practise their trade under the protection of the party, to the cost of the whole Mittelstand.'[25]

In effect the co-operatives became the property of the NSDAP, and in July 1934 (after the Röhm affair) it was officially announced that:

1. No party organisation had any right to meddle in the business of the now Nazified co-operatives.
2. The Nazified co-operatives had the rights and opportunities pertaining to any other business with regards to advertising, gaining new members and conducting their business.[26]

In 1935 the whole co-operative system was overhauled and fitted into the structure of party controlled enterprises, after loss-making co-operatives had been dissolved.[27] And although quite a number of co-operatives were closed down by the authorities in the years that followed, it was almost invariably on grounds of 'national security', as the co-operatives became cells of political resistance to the Nazi regime.[28]

Agriculture

From a general reading of Nazi propaganda directed towards the farming community during the Kampfzeit, as well as from the early policy statements published by Darré's Agricultural Department, we can determine three fundamental principles which were supposed to guide the agricultural policies of the Third Reich:

1. State control and regulation of marketing and pricing to ensure maximum autarky in food production and an acceptable standard of living for the farming community.
2. The stabilisation of land ownership to prevent the expropriation

---

[25] Bericht über die Werbemassnahmen und Propaganda des Konsumvereins e GmbH für Aschaffenburg u. Umgebung, 5 March 1934. Sammlung Schumacher 242a.
[26] This policy was closely in line with the demands of the armed forces for an economy structured to the needs of war-planning.
[27] See Schweitzer, op. cit., pp. 121, 122.
[28] Winkler, op. cit., p.12.

of the farmer from his land, and to guarantee the principle of 'blood and soil' (*Blut und Boden*) doctrine.

3.   The redistribution of population in line with the ideological concepts of the völkisch movement which demanded a reversal of the drift from the countryside to the cities. At the same time agriculture was to be expanded through resettlement in the eastern regions as a first step in the conquering of *Lebensraum* for the German Volk.

In fact only the first principle of maximum autarky in food production was applied with any consistency under the Third Reich. State intervention led to a substantial decrease in grain imports from abroad, and a resultant increase and stabilisation of cereal prices in the home market. And although intervention was of benefit to almost all sections of the German farming community, it particularly favoured cereal producers and hence the Junker landlords, who had previously been subsidised by the Weimar republic's *Osthilfe* scheme.

The prices of nearly all farming commodities were fixed by the Reichsnährstand, and farming prices rose steeply during the first three years of the Third Reich. Thus for, instance:

	Price in October 1932	*Price in October 1935*
Potatoes	67	95
Butter	84	96

(1909-1913 = 100 in index)

Overall farm income rose from 4.2 billion RM in 1933 to 5.6 billion RM in 1937.[29]

Relatively speaking, however, farming did not fare as well as other sectors of the economy. In 1937 for example, farming income was 8.3 per cent of the national income, whereas in 1933 it had been 8.7 per cent. During the same four-year period the increase in farmers' income was 44 per cent but this compared with average wage increases of 49 per cent, and an increase in profits in commerce and industry of 88 per cent.[30]

[29] See David Schoenbaum, 'Class and Status in the Third Reich', DPhil thesis, Oxford 1964, pp. 263, 264.
[30] ibid., p.264.

Indeed, after a period of growth from 1933 until 1935, when the regulation of farming prices produced its most dramatic effect, income from farming tended to stagnate. Simultaneously the quality of agricultural life fell relative to that of industry; after 1934 the average shift worked in industry dropped to eight hours a day, while the farmer's day still averaged 10 to 12 hours.

In the case of agriculture, however, the shortcomings of Nazi policy were less a result of cynical opportunism vis-à-vis the programme so loudly proclaimed before 1933 than of a battle of priorities which was won by the proponents of rapid re-armament (even before the Four-Year Plan was announced in 1936). Hence there was a chronic lack of capital to invest in farming because all available credit was directed towards increasing industrial autarky and laying the foundations of a war-economy. Obviously autarky also demanded high output from the agricultural sector, but such increases as occurred were at the expense of the farmer and only rarely a result of increased capitalisation.[31]

Because of the lack of centralised investment, the total farm debt actually rose during the Third Reich as far as the small farmer was concerned. Josef Müller, writing six years after the take-over of power, observed that 'the crisis has been somewhat ameliorated since 1933, but the consequences for the farmer have been very limited indeed'. Müller estimated that the debts of small farms increased from an average of 569 RM in 1932 to 574 RM in 1935 – from 48 per cent to 49 per cent of their value. On the other hand, middle-sized farms managed to reduce their debt from an average of 44 per cent to 41 per cent, while large farms had reduced their debt from 68 per cent to 63 per cent.[32]

According to David Schoenbaum, 'to stay on the farm meant working longer hours for even less return ... the farmer ... was poor, coarse, dirty and overworked'.[33] The position was of course relative, but with booming armaments manufacture, and the corresponding rise in the demand for industrial labour power, the quality of life for

[31] The use of conscripted labour, via the Hitler Youth or other schemes (DAF) was not only a convenient way of disguising unemployment and furthering propaganda; it also provided cheap and desperately needed labour, especially at harvest time. Such schemes were highly unpopular among those so conscripted.

[32] Josef Müller, *Ein deutsches Bauerndorf in Umbruch der Zeit*, Wurzburg 1939, p. 28. Compare these figures with the statistics on the relationship between farm size and support for the NSDAP in Chapter 5.

[33] Schoenbaum, op. cit., p. 270.

the peasant farmer was patently inferior to that of the urban dweller. Nor was this lost on the Nazi regime. A Gestapo report early in 1935 noted 'a certain disappointment' among the rural population in the Lüneburg region, especially among the traditionally poorest members of the farming community. Together with artisans and small traders who depended upon the agricultural economy, the farmers considered the Nazi regime's policy 'not radical enough'.[34] And just before the outbreak of war, a District Farm Leader reported, 'I know many farmers who haven't bought themselves a new Sunday suit in years. In my district I know scarcely two who have radios, and they have sons or daughters who work in factories.'[35]

The promise to stabilise the ownership of farming land was carried out by the Nazi state – but only with regard to certain types of farm – and with consequences that were scarcely envisaged by its would-be beneficiaries.

On 15 May 1933 Darré published a law on the Farmer's Right of Inheritance (*Bäuerliche Erbhofrecht*) against considerable opposition from Hugenberg. On 29 September this initial law was superseded by the Reich Law of Inheritance (*Reichserbhofgesetz*), which, according to a Nazi propaganda broadside, was designed to give effect to the NSDAP's promise to make the farmer's ownership of his land 'an inalienable right'. In fact the law applied to little more than one third of all agricultural units, for it excluded very small farms as well as those over 125 hectares. Such farms could neither be sold nor mortgaged, and were to remain in the possession of the farmer and his male offspring in perpetuity. However, such a right enshrined only short-term benefits for a crisis-ridden economy; in the rearmament-led recovery that followed, the legal tie between the farmer and his land became 'a potential millstone'.[36] In fact as early as 1934, the previous Secretary of State in the Ministry of Economics, von Rohr, wrote to Hitler warning of the law's potential consequences: 'If the farmer must keep his farm, even when it cannot feed him; if the farmer's heir must take up farming, even if every other job offers him more, then the bond which unites the farmer to the farm becomes a

[34] See C. Krohn & D. Stegmann, op. cit., p.83.
[35] Müller, op. cit., p.83.
[36] As Schoenbaum suggests, 'for the moment the farm was attached to the farmer, for the future, however, the farmer to the land', op. cit., p.254.

terrible shackle.'[37] In this, at least, von Rohr displayed considerable vision.

Although the Nazi regime could at least claim to have carried out the letter of its promise to stabilise land ownership, it could not claim even a spurious propaganda victory on the question of agricultural expansion. Far from consolidating and strengthening the farming sector under the Third Reich, the Nazi leadership oversaw a massive shift in population from the land to the town. Between 1933 and 1938 the number of farm-workers decreased by 10.5 per cent in the Rheinland, by 9.9 per cent in Lower Saxony, by 17.6 per cent in Bavaria and by a massive 29.9 per cent in Hessen.[38] Most of these workers went to the expanding industrial towns in central and eastern Germany, whose demand for labour power grew rapidly because of the programme to expand the German chemical industry. Within five years the population of Halle more than doubled, from 98,000 in 1933 to 202,000 in 1938; while in Magdeburg it rose from 102,000 to 233,000 over the same period. Overall the agricultural population of the German Reich fell from 20.8 per cent in 1933 to 18 per cent of the total population in 1939.[39]

Nor did the much-vaunted programme for creating new agricultural settlements find any expression in practice during the Third Reich. In fact the figures clearly show that the Nazi regime (for all the efforts of the newsreels and the press) actually reclaimed less land and opened fewer agricultural settlements than had been the case during the Weimar Republic.[40]

	new settlements	*land area (ha)*
1930	7,441	79,833
1931	9,283	99,642
1932	8,877	101,926
1933	4,914	60,297
1934	4,827	72,969
1935	3,905	68,388
1936	3,308	60,358
1937	1,900	37,000

[37] See Broszat, op. cit., p.237.
[38] Schoenbaum, op. cit., p.283.
[39] ibid., p.286.
[40] Wirtschaft und Statistik 1929, 1932, 1937.

Again the reasons for this failure are not difficult to determine. During the first eighteen months of the new regime, Schmitt and von Blomberg (Minister for the Army) struck a number of deals with the Nazi leadership to prevent any large-scale nationalisation of the Junkers' eastern estates. At the same time the priority of the rearmament programme starved Darré's Reichsnährstand of the funds to buy out the eastern landowners and divide up their estates among small farmers.

This fact did not escape the notice of expectant Nazi militants in eastern Germany. The radical Gauleiter Erich Koch conducted a bitter rearguard action against what he termed 'the demands of the Reaction and counter-revolutionaries'; he was subsequently denounced as an 'absolute party-dictator on the Bolshevik model'. And on 24 May 1934 the high-ranking SA Fuhrer Krausser complained angrily to Darré that the Reichsnärhstand's handling of the resettlement issue was contrary to SA expectations, and warned that Chief of Staff Röhm would take measures to counter the 'anti-SA attitudes of the Reichsnährstand'.[41]

Unfortunately for the radicals, the measures taken only a month later were not taken by the SA but by Hitler and the SS. The Röhm purge was the last episode in the long-running conflict between the party radicals and the leadership; and although the battle had long been lost, the massacre of the Nazi militants marked the end of any attempt to press for the realisation of the 'old ideals' of the National Socialist movement in the Third Reich.

Conclusions

It has only been possible to review briefly the development of Nazi social and economic policy during the early years of the Third Reich, but it is quite apparent that the demands of the NSDAP's original Mittelstand following were largely ignored by the party leadership after 1933. In fact many of the quite frugal benefits gained by the middle classes came about not as a result of party initiatives, but as the by-products of policies initiated by the traditional power-groups of German society – the armed forces and heavy industry. Only the Law of Inheritance, as it related to the farming community, can be

[41] Bundes Archiv R43 II/207.

seen as an ideologically motivated act, designed to enshrine in law the 'old ideals' of National Socialism.

Other protective legislation, notably the 'Law for the Protection of the Small Trader', although offering some degree of protection to the commercial Mittelstand, was in effect a continuation of the social protectionism practised by the presidential cabinets under Weimar, and can hardly be thought of as a break with tradition inspired by ideology.

Heinrich Winkler has noted that the grievances of the commercial Mittelstand during the Third Reich are hardly distinguishable from the complaints voiced by small businessmen either in the Kaiser-Reich or the Weimar republic. Under earlier regimes, such grievances could at least be aired in public. Under the Third Reich, however, the conflict between the Mittelstand and other sectors of the community could only be conducted through an internal struggle within the party or state bureaucracy. Once the early battles had been lost, the taboo upon any expression of political conflict imposed by the threat of physical repression and the ideological myth of the harmonious Volk-community prevented any resurgence of Mittelstand demands. Moreover, compared with what was to follow as a result of the drastic rationalisation of the German economy set in motion by the Four-Year Plan (1936), the period from 1933 to 1936 was indeed a 'period of grace' for the traditional German middle classes.[42]

[42] Winkler, op. cit., p.15.

CHAPTER SEVEN

Nazi Political Ritual

In Chapter Six we outlined how the seizure of power in effect marked a deep cleft in the historical development of German fascism, as the demands of the NSDAP's original mass following were discarded and the Nazi state began to develop a politik favourable to big business and the traditional elites of German society. But, of course, it only *marked* this cleft, for the organisational links between the Nazi leadership, heavy industry and the conservative establishment had already been secured by the late summer of 1932.

So it is apparent that a major characteristic of Nazi ideology is precisely this rupture between the Mittelstand ideology of the party during the struggle for power and the praxis of the Nazi state. In turn, this 'rupture' raises a fundamental question with regard to Nazi ideology after 1933, for although anti-Marxism and anti-Semitism continued to play an over-riding role in the ideology of National Socialism, what was the fate of the NSDAP's Mittelstand *ideology*? Or, put another way, how did the Nazi leadership give expression to National Socialist ideology, given the increasing political contradiction between the Mittelstand and the Nazi state after 1933?

Certainly psychological and physical terror were vital to the process of ideological control in the Third Reich. But terror alone could not have guaranteed an acceptable level of social harmony in the Nazi state, especially in view of Hitler's decision to begin immediate preparations for war. There was of course control of the major organs of information through Goebbels' Propaganda Ministry, and press and radio pumped out a carefully orchestrated theme of racial solidarity and class co-operation. But the most original and possibly the most vital aspect of ideological control enforced by the Nazi state was through political ritual and celebration.

There have been surprisingly few attempts by social scientists to examine the political celebrations developed by National Socialism. In English, only H.T. Burden's book on the Nuremberg rallies deals with this general theme,[1] and it is necessary to look to the work of two German authors, Klaus Vondung and Hans-Jochen Gamm, to find any sort of systematic analysis of National Socialist ritual and its relationship to the wider aspects of the Nazi Weltanschauung.[2]

Burden's analysis of the Nuremberg rallies is limited by his failure to consider the Reichsparty-day within the context of the National Socialist Year (*Jahreslauf*), for although the Reichsparty-day captured the popular imagination, it was merely one event within a yearly calendar of political celebrations. More important, it is not possible to 'make sense' of the Reichsparty-day without some understanding of the symbolism and 'mythos' which it claimed to express, and in turn this requires an understanding of the so-called National Socialist Holy History. First, however, it is worth briefly reviewing the celebrations which made up this 'National Socialist Year'.

The celebrations of the National Socialist Year

National Socialism's political celebrations can be divided into two categories. On the one hand there were specifically Nazi festivals which had been celebrated by the party before 1933. Under the Third Reich these events, such as the Reichsparty-day, the Founding of the Party Programme (24 February), the Fuhrer's Birthday (20 April) and the Commemoration of 9 November, were raised to the status of 'Holy Days', and formed the major celebrations of the National Socialist Year. On the other hand, events which expressed non-Nazi cultural traditions in Germany (church or workers' festivals for instance), were taken over by the party's propaganda machine, emptied of their original significance, and transformed into public expressions of National Socialist ideology.

Remembrance Day on 16 March, traditionally a day of mourning for the dead of the First World War, was transformed on Hitler's

---

[1] H.T. Burden, *The Nuremberg Rallies 1923-1939*, London 1967.

[2] See Klaus Vondung, *Magie und Manipulation; ideologischer Kult und politische Religione des Nationalsozialismus*, Göttingen 1971; Hans Jochen Gamm, *Der braune Kult*, Hamburg 1962.

personal orders into 'a day to reflect upon the heroic sacrifices made by the German soldier'. Henceforth the swastika flag was no longer to be lowered to half-mast, but flown proudly 'at the top of the standard as a symbol of Germany's re-awakened faith and pride'.[3] May Day celebrations were also Nazified; all signs of a genuinely socialist tradition were obliterated, and instead massive military parades were held in Berlin to celebrate the new mood of 'national unity' and 'class harmony'. Goebbels wrote of 1 May: 'it must be a master-work of organisation and mass demonstration ... the whole people should unite itself in one will ... our wide experience of leading the masses comes into its own: no other movement understands how to direct the masses more successfully.'[4]

Other traditional celebration days, such as Easter, Whitsun, Mothers' Day, Harvest Thanksgiving and even Christmas suffered a similar fate, with party worthies announcing that the 'authentic' ceremonies of the Germanic tribes and ancient Teutonic folk-customs must be revived in view of the onslaught against 'traditional culture' by the spirit of Jewish-Marxist materialism.

However this is not the place to examine the various political celebrations of the National Socialist Year in detail. Indeed to do so would be tedious and repetitive, for the NSDAP leadership imposed the same (predictable) interpretation upon all these events, irrespective of their cultural origins. Instead we shall look at the two major festivals in the National Socialist calendar – the Ninth of November and the Reichsparty-day Celebrations – with a view to making sense of the Holy History and exposing the significance of political ritual for the Nazi regime.

The Ninth of November celebration

The event which Hitler and the party leadership celebrated each year on 9 November was the 1923 Munich Beer-Hall Putsch. Throughout the Kampfzeit Hitler met with his old guard in Munich to remember and honour the sixteen party members who had lost their lives as a result of this abortive coup.

After 1933, however, a radical reinterpretation of the coup became

[3] See *Völkischer Beobachter*, 13 March 1933.
[4] Joseph Goebbels, *Vom Kaiserhof zur Reichskanzlei*, Berlin 1934, pp. 304, 305 (28 April 1933).

necessary, for the party leadership could hardly allow the Fuhrer's name to be associated with an event that was generally thought of as a political blunder. Thus the defeat of 1923 was turned into the 'prerequisite for the victory of 1933'.

Naturally the mystification of the Munich coup did not take place overnight. Even during the Kampfzeit many aspects of the 'victorious' interpretation found their way into the annual ceremony which Hitler and his associates performed in Munich's Königsplatz. But on 9 November 1935 a ceremony took place in Munich which illustrates the extent to which the NSDAP had created a new historical myth to 'explain' the coup, complete with a style of ritual and symbolism which was reproduced in the other events which make up the National Socialist Year. It was the ceremony of the 'Resurrection of the Dead'.[5]

Late on the morning of 9 November 1935, Hitler and his entourage left the Bürgerbräukeller to march to the Feldherrnhalle (Soldiers' Hall), retracing the route used by the putschists some twelve years previously. At the head of the procession the standard bearer carried the 'Bloodflag' (*Blutfahne*), so called because it was the flag carried by the original conspirators and was 'stained with the blood of the sixteen martyrs'. Hitler had proclaimed an 'Order of Blood' which was bestowed upon the survivors of the putsch, and it was their privilege to march with Hitler and the Bloodflag at the head of the procession.

The route to the Feldherrnhalle was marked by 240 pylons, each with a plaque bearing the name of one of the Nazi movement's 'fallen heroes'. The 'hero's' name was read out solemnly as the head of the column marched past the pylon, whereupon the military band struck up the Horst Wessel song. When Hitler reached the Feldherrnhalle, the service of the resurrection of the sixteen 'blood-witnesses' (whose recently exhumed bodies were the centrepiece of the celebration) began. The *Völkischer Beobachter* described the scene:

The dead of the Ninth of November [do not lie] in dark graves and tombs but in a beautiful building, in a well-lit hall, under God's free

---

[5] One of Hitler's first acts on becoming Chancellor was to order the construction of a massive stone Temple of Honour in Munich's Königsplatz. Its construction lasted for two years, and the Celebration of 9 November 1935 was the event by which it was consecrated. See A.I. Brandt, *Meilensteine des Dritten Reiches*, Munich 1938.

heaven. In these brass sarcophagi beats the heart of our revolution ... We believe that these dead have found new life in us, and that they will live for ever. The belief that our flag is holy: the belief that the Creator has given us and them the strength for work and for victory, and the belief in our sacred mission to which these everlasting hours are dedicated, shows Germany her way forward. We know that out of the inner experience of our movement ... we have gained eternal life because of the struggle and the sacrifice of the fallen for Germany ...

How few marched off in the beginning? Today there are millions represented in the flags and standards who are witness to this celebration. How few had from the first a clear understanding of this German belief? Yet the way to victory was ever clear to our soldiers in those lonely quiet hours ...

We old and young National Socialists thank Adolf Hitler for this unforgettable day. We praise him and this holy symbol of the resurrection of Germany, for we have him and the flag of our struggle to thank. We go forward with open eyes and believing hearts under his direction.[6]

The centrepiece of the ceremony at the Feldherrnhalle was the admittance of the coffins into the sarcophagi, where the sixteen 'martyrs' were to lie as an 'Eternal Watch' for Germany. As the bodies were removed from the gun-carriages, Adolf Wagner called out the names of the fallen one by one, to be answered each time by the thousands of assembled Hitler Youth and party members with the response 'Here!' The *Völkischer Beobachter* explained the significance of the ritual:

Again and again the thousands roar 'Here!' ... the testament of these first Blood-witnesses is thus raised up to our entire Movement, while their spirit lives and works for Germany as its Eternal Watch ... Each of the dead thus greets the assembled thousands, who are themselves the reflection and the carriers of their will to victory.[7]

Then Hitler, flanked by his deputy and the comrades of the Blood-order, entered the temple and walked to the sarcophagi to 'greet his former true followers'. Having placed wreaths on each of the coffins, Hitler spoke to the assembly of the significance of the ceremony:

6 *Völkischer Beobachter*, 10 November 1935.
7 ibid.

These sixteen men, who twelve years ago gave their lives as a sacrifice for their people (Volk) and their Fuhrer, are today raised from the grave. Who does not feel the truth of this resurrection? Who does not see the glint of their eyes in the newly-raised-up Wehrmacht? And the Reich, which is itself built around this consecrated ground, is it not their kingdom? The kingdom of their 'will' and victory?[8]

Thus out of the events of 9 November 1923 the NSDAP fashioned the mythos of the Holy History, to which the 'martyrdom' of the sixteen was a 'witness'. However, the ideological significance of the Holy History only becomes fully clear when we examine the various symbols which 'revealed' its meaning.

The Bloodflag

The most powerful symbol of the Ninth of November 'revelation' was the Bloodflag, transformed into a 'witness' of the 'sacrificial blood' of the movement's martyrs. The Bloodflag was additionally portrayed as a manifestation of the 'historical inevitability' of National Socialism, for, as suggested, the shedding of the sacrificial blood was the prerequisite for the movement's victory.

Of course the Bloodflag was an obvious allegory of the Christian cross – a symbol of salvation achieved by the blood sacrifice of a martyr or hero.

Christ's death in Jerusalem	the putschists' death at the Feldherrnhalle
the staining of the cross with Christ's blood	the staining of the Bloodflag with the blood of the martyrs
the promise of salvation through Christ's sacrificial death	the promise of the National Socialist millennium because of the martyrs 'sacrificial death'
the thaumaturgical (healing) significance of Christ's cross	the thaumaturgical significance of the blood-flag
the crucifix as a symbol of Christ's resurrection and Man's salvation	the Nazi flag as a symbol of Germany's resurrection and the nation's salvation

[8] ibid.

The Bloodflag's power as a holy symbol was emphasised by the fact that it was only exhibited on 9 November and at Nuremberg on Reichsparty-day.

At Nuremberg the Bloodflag performed a special function in the political ritual developed by the NSDAP. It was carried in front of the Fuhrer during the flag-dedication ceremony, in which the banners and flags of the party formations were 'sanctified' by Hitler's touch and that of the original Bloodflag:

> The drums roll. The flags – so many are faded and tattered, soaked with the blood of fallen fighters and riddled with bullet holes. With his hand he presses the cloth of the Bloodflag against the new standards, and thereby they are consecrated with the blood of the sixteen, who as the first martyrs of the movement, gave their life-blood, and thereafter became immortal.[9]

But it was also claimed that the blood of the martyrs, like the blood of Christ, was a means of transfiguration. Thus the martyrs' blood, the symbol of their 'eternal life', passed into the blood of the new National Socialist man, to be recreated in the blood of his descendants (or in the earth) to allow for the recreation of the Volk. The choral oath in Böhme's Cantata for the Ninth of November makes this clear:

> He who has pledged, he who has taken the oath,
> Whether in death he passes away
> he continues to live in the earth.
> He who has recognised himself through struggle,
> he who burns within himself, whether death touches him,
> he continues to live in blood.[10]

So the Bloodflag, as the holiest relic of the National Socialist movement, projected its significance and power to all other party flags through the medium of the sacrificial blood, in the same way as the Christian crucifix derives its thaumaturgical significance from the original Cross of Golgotha. 'Place your hand proudly on the shaft of this flag' states Baumann, 'for from this one flag we derive all our strength.'[11] Simultaneously, the interpretation given to the death of

[9] Brandt, op. cit., p. 119.
[10] From Herbert Böhme, *Gesänge unter der Fahne*, Munich 1935, p. 49.
[11] Hans Baumann, 'Wir zünden das Feuer', in *Deutsche Reihe nr. 39*, Jena 1936, p. 50.

the sixteen conspirators by the party propaganda machine meant that the 'virtues' of absolute loyalty, unquestioning obedience and readiness to sacrifice life for 'Fuhrer and Volk' were equally imprinted in the flag symbol.

Indeed the Bloodflag, by symbolising the transformation of Germany which had brought about the Third Reich, provided an essential 'confirmation' for the entire structure of the Nazi mythos. It is not surprising, therefore, to discover that the flag or swastika emblem was rapidly embellished with other 'significant' concepts which related to the wider aspects of National Socialist doctrine.

The fact that the NSDAP had originally rejected the old nationalist colours so beloved of the other right-wing paramilitary formations in the immediate post-war era in favour of the swastika, was claimed as proof by the party ideologues that the movement represented a radical new social and political Weltanschuung, in opposition to both 'Reaction and Red terror'. The swastika was therefore presented as the deepest historical expression of the German Volk; as a symbol of profound religious significance for the early Teutonic tribes who were the first to give historical expression to the 'longing for a German homeland'.[12] The swastika or sun-wheel represented sun and light; the red backcloth blood and fire.[13] Möller's epic poem 'The Pledge', which accompanied the flag-dedication ceremony, gave expression to this 'most sacred' quality:

> We are sworn to our flag, for ever.
> Whoever dishonours the flag will be cursed.
> The flag is our creed, of God and Volk and land.
> Whoever wants to steal it, must first take our life and strength.[14]

---

[12] Many leaflets were circulated by the NSDAP and its secondary organisations which attempted to explain the 'mystical origins' of the swastika in German prehistory. In particular, Friedrich Rausch, *Das Hakenkreuz: sein Sinn and seine Bedeutung*, Munich 1935. Reusch equates the swastika with ancient German sun worship and suggests that it possessed great powers against the forces of darkness.

[13] But it is worth noting that during the early years of the Kampfzeit, the red backcloth of the flag was portrayed as the colour of socialism. Thus Gregor Strasser, at the 1923 Party-day, stated that 'the red colour represents the social attitude of our party'.

[14] Eberhard Wolfgang Möller, 'Die Verpflichtung', *Volksspieldienst nr. 5.*, Berlin 1935, pp. 15ff.

Just as the flag derived its 'sacred' character from the analogy of the Christian cross, so Hitler's image as the messianic Fuhrer was dependent upon analogy with Christ as the Messiah. Two distinct levels of interpretation operated here. On the lower level Hitler was presented as a cultural hero – the political saviour of his people and the leader of the *Volksgemeinschaft* (people's community). Robert Ley's creed, 'We believe only in Adolf Hitler on this earth', fits this notion perfectly.[15] But simultaneously Hitler is presented as a messianic Fuhrer, not only 'immortal' in his own right, but even (like Christ) capable of conferring immortality upon his followers:

> You walk among the Volk as a Saviour
> Because you are completely possessed by belief ...
> Now we need not fear, for you say to us:
> 'If you believe, then I have slain death,
> even when the body decays.'[16]

And at Nuremberg on Reichsparty-day, the call from the party ranks: 'The Fuhrer is Germany and Germany the Fuhrer', was answered by Hitler with the words: 'I am never without you, and you are never without me.'[17]

Thus the take-over of power and the establishment of the Third Reich (as the secular manifestation of National Socialism's 'will to power') provided the basis for the Nazis' reinterpretation of the events of 9 November 1923. The Munich coup was revealed as a turning point which heralded the coming of a New Age. Böhme wrote:

> The earth came to an end with your death
> But with your glory our life began.[18]

The Ninth of November was the manifestation of this 'new beginning', interpreted by the party ideologists as a metamorphosis of the human condition. The old world, it was claimed, was at an end, and with the coming of the Third Reich the true meaning of history would be revealed. The lives of those whose sacrifice was a precondition of victory, and those who now experience this victory, are transfigured in the symbol of the flag:

[15] See Gamm, op. cit., p. 72.
[16] Herbert Böhme, *Das deutsche Gebet*, Munich 1936, pp. 14ff.
[17] Brandt, op. cit., p. 118.
[18] Vondung, op. cit., p. 164.

Whoever follows the flag, lives,
And in him live those who died for the flag.[19]

We must now look in greater detail at the form of these political celebrations, and show how the structure of Nazi ritual was related to the content of the myth.

The community of the mass rally

The most obvious characteristic of the celebrations of the National Socialist Year and especially of the Reichsparty-day in Nuremberg was their monumentality: both in terms of the huge numbers of participants and in terms of the grandiose style of the architectural environment.

Hitler's obsession with creating monumental places of celebration for National Socialism was not merely a result of a frustrated architectural vocation. The following extract from *Mein Kampf* shows his understanding of the emotional mechanisms of mass parades. Describing a socialist rally in front of the Royal Palace in Berlin just after the end of the First World War, he writes:

> A sea of red flags, red scarves, and red flowers gave to this demonstration, in which an estimated 120,000 took part, an aspect that was gigantic from the purely external point of view. I myself could feel and understand how easily the man of the people succumbs to the suggestive magic of a spectacle so grandiose in effect.[20]

The Reichsparty-day was the great showpiece of the National Socialist Year, both during the Kampfzeit and during the early years of the Third Reich. But its 'function' should not be reduced to what Burden, for instance, calls 'a display (of) power with pomp and circumstance'.[21] Once again we need only turn to Hitler's explanation of the 'community of the mass rally' to understand what the NSDAP was attempting to achieve by this annual spectacular in Nuremberg.

---

[19] Böhme, *Gesänge unter der Fahne*, p. 44.
[20] Adolf Hitler, *Mein Kampf*, Munich 1925, vol. 2, p. 136.
[21] Burden, op. cit., p. 57.

The 'community' of the mass rally not only strengthens the individual, but binds together all, and helps create party spirit ... when a participant enters a mass gathering for the first time and suddenly has tens of thousands of men with the same views around him; when he, as one who is 'seeking' is swept along with the mighty effect of a suggestive ecstasy of three or four thousand others; when the visible success and agreement of thousands confirms the correctness of a teaching ... then he himself lies under the magical influence of mass suggestion ... The man who had entered such a gathering doubtful and hesitant, leaves it strengthened inside himself; he has become a member of the 'new community'.[22]

Therefore National Socialism's monumental celebration places were not only expressions of architectural megalomania. Far more important, they provided a carefully structured framework within which the feeling of 'community' could be created, and where the mechanism of mass suggestion could operate. The Zepplinfield in Nuremberg for instance could hold almost a quarter of a million people. At one end towered a massive construction of terraces some four hundred metres long, topped by a white stone column. This centrepiece was flanked by two further stone pillars on which 'eternal flames' burnt. A forest of flags and swastika banners on these three ramparts formed a spectacular backdrop to the speaker on the main-tribune.[23]

On the field below, the masses were gathered in detachments or columns; they were as much a feature of the architecture as the stone framework which enclosed them. Precisely because hundreds of thousands were gathered together on such occasions (and Hitler produced ever more fantastic plans for enlarging the 'community' of the rally) an architectural framework of massive proportions was necessary to contain them. Thus, on the one hand, great masses of party members and spectators could be *isolated* from the outside world within a painstakingly contrived National Socialist environment full of the sensory impressions of the Nazi *Lebenswelt*. On the other hand, the architectural surroundings were designed to concentrate the participants' attention upon the centrepiece of the Fuhrer-stand. On this massive column, placed slightly in front of the

[22] Karlheinz Schmeer, *Die Regie des öffentlichen Lebens im Dritten Reich*, Munich 1956, pp. 10ff.
[23] See, for instance, *Nürnberg 1935*, Berlin 1935, and *Parteitag der Arbeit*, Berlin 1937 (published by NSDAP) for details of the Reichsparty-day celebrations.

main platform, Hitler stood alone – above the masses – like a high priest on a temple wall. His 'message' – the word of the Fuhrer – was delivered from this vantage point and heard throughout the arena, thanks to a carefully prepared system of loudspeakers which were placed around the parade ground. The symbolism was deliberate; according to Wilhelm Lotz:

> Leadership is present everywhere, for in each meeting-point and parade-ground the place on which the Fuhrer stands is especially prominent architecturally ... Every individual participant sees in front of him the great colourful picture of the tribunes, with the powerful backdrop of the stone columns given dimension by the banners hanging between them. There hang the standards and the flags, and in the middle, projecting out into the field, is the place of the Fuhrer.[24]

So the masses were spatially overawed by Hitler's person; subjected to the symbolism of his absolute power; and forced to identify emotionally with the ideology of the Fuhrer-principle. Gerdy Troost, wife of Hitler's architectural mentor, wrote that:

> Before Nuremberg's parade complex was built Germany lacked a shrine for the whole nation [capable of strengthening] the bonds of community. [Previously] the Volk had been a formless mass without inner cohesion ... without an idea which it could experience in common. [But in the Nuremberg rally grounds] the community experience of the unity of Volk and Fuhrer was possible.[25]

It has often been noted that the visual and accoustic effects of the rallies were designed to conjure up 'religious emotions' in the minds of both participants and spectators. Henderson, the British ambassador, described Speer's so-called Cathedral of Light at Nuremberg as 'sacred and beautiful at the same time', while François-Poncet, the French ambassador, spoke of the 'mystical ecstasy, a sort of holy illusion' which overcame the spectators.[26] Goebbels himself frequently talked of the need to emulate the mysticism of the Roman Catholic church at the party rallies. In fact the entire paraphernalia of symbol, ritualised behaviour and mythos

---

[24] 'Das Reichsparteitagsgälende in Nürnberg', by Wilhelm Lotz, in A. Teut, *Architektur im Dritten Reich*, Frankfurt a M 1967, pp. 192-3.

[25] R. Taylor, *The Word in Stone*, California 1974, p. 30.

[26] Vondung, op. cit., p. 105.

at Nuremberg is exemplified in the following report of the nightly 'consecration hour' of the political leaders on Reichsparty-day 1937:

> The Zepplinfield lay in the shimmering light as we mounted the main-tribune. From the outside a sea of light streamed towards the walls, from which the flags of the movement shone out many kilometers-wide in the dark evening. The square of the Zepplinfield was divided into about twenty columns in which about 140,000 political leaders in lines of twelve were standing. On the tribunals, ripped from the darkness by spotlights, countless swastika flags were waving in the light evening breeze. The lights were pointing sharply upwards towards the pitch-black sky. The Zepplinfield was obviously too small. The tribunals could not grasp the enormous stream of people which wound around it unceasingly.
>
> The pupils of the *Ordensberg Vogelsang* approached ... their step is together, their deportment and direction exact. This selection of the party's new blood took its place in front of the main-tribune.
>
> A distant rumbling! The roaring comes closer and becomes louder! The Fuhrer! Reichsorganisations-leader Dr Ley announces him to the men who have entered. And then a great surprise. One of many! As Adolf Hitler enters the Zepplinfield, one hundred and fifty searchlights of the airforce are switched on. They have been stationed around the periphery of the square, and they cut out and build a canopy of light from the darkness over the whole field. For a moment there is a deathly hush. The surprise is just too great! Never before has something like this been seen – like a great and godly cathedral of light ...
>
> Blue-red stream the spotlights between whose ball of light the black cloth of the night hangs. 140,000 – there must be as many as that here – cannot tear themselves away from this sight. Are we dreaming or is it reality? Is such a thing possible; a cathedral of light?
>
> There is little time to dwell upon such thoughts, for already there is a new spectacle, possibly even more beautiful for those who experienced it. Dr Ley announces the march-in of the flag. At first you could not see anything, but then it dived out of the black night. Over there on the south side! In seven columns it pours into the space between the formations. You still could not see the men, you could not recognise the flagbearers; you could only make out a compelling red river, whose upper surface glistened gold and silver, and which approached like fiery lava. You could feel the power which lay in this slow approach, and receive a tiny impression of the sense of this holy symbol. 25,000 flags. That is 25,000 regional, local and factory detachments from the whole of the Reich assembled around the flags. These thousands of flag-bearers are ready to dedicate their lives to each of these colours. There is none down there for whom the flag is not the last command and the highest duty. The march ends. The 140,000 have dived under in this sea of glistening points which

resemble a thick entanglement – to penetrate it would mean death!

The song of the oath rises in the unending canopy of light. The Orden pupils sing it. It is like a great devotion, a prayer in which all of us have taken part in order to gain new stength. Yes, that's it! An hour of thanksgiving for the whole movement, protected against the darkness outside by a sea of light.[27]

The report is significant not only for the way in which the spatial aspect of the community of the mass rally is stressed – the searchlights 'cut out and build a canopy of light over the whole field' and the worshippers find themselves in 'a great and godly cathedral of light' – but also for its interpretation of the symbolic imagery of the parade. Thus the participants are 'protected against the *darkness outside* by a sea of light', while the glittering points of the flag standards 'resemble a thick entanglement, *to penetrate it would mean death!*'

In fact, if we separate the mechanisms of the celebrations (the sensory effects which were designed to stimulate the participants' emotions) from the question of ideological content and presentation (the mythos of the Holy History and its symbol world) we can see that there is a common denominator: namely, the plagiarisation and exploitation of traditional Christian imagery and its means of ritual consecration. The report, for instance, speaks of the rally as a 'great devotion ... a prayer ... an hour of thanksgiving', while even a brief look at the methods which the NSDAP used to 'consecrate' its holy objects shows how the party ransacked the various religious traditions of the German churches, and reproduced their ritual form in the political celebrations.

Just as the Bloodflag and much of Hitler's apparent 'charisma' were derived from analogy with the Christian concepts of the cross and the messiah, so the NSDAP used the style of Christian ritual to 'consecrate' the 'holy' symbols of National Socialism. In the speeches of the party leaders the suggestion that the flag is a 'sanctuary', the blood of the fallen is 'holy' and the Reich is 'eternal' are constantly repeated. Schumann even spoke of the 'Reich of the Holy Ghost' and said of Hitler that 'we need him like bread and wine'.[28] Even the relationship between the priest and his congregation, as well as the analogy of Hitler as Christ, is mirrored in the roles of the Caller and

[27] *Niederelbischen Tageblatt*, 12 September 1937.
[28] Gerhard Schumann, *Gedichte und Kantaten*, Munich 1940, pp. 44, 50.

the Chorus in Herybert Menzel's eulogy for the Day of National work:

> Caller: One for all, comrades. Who brought us this salvation?
> Chorus: Adolf Hitler the Fuhrer!
> Caller: One for all, comrades. Who has brought us honour again?
> Chorus: Adolf Hitler the Fuhrer!
> Caller: There is one who helps us. Who do we believe when he calls?
> Chorus: Adolf Hitler the Fuhrer![29]

So we have seen that National Socialism attempted to reproduce traditional forms of ritual in its own political celebrations, and that the 'power' of Nazi myth (and its symbols) was dependent upon analogy with Christian beliefs and traditions. However, it is interesting to note that National Socialism did not draw at random from various interpretations of Christian myth, but from one particular aspect – the millenarian tradition. Thus Hitler is not the Christ of the First Coming – the sacrificial lamb – who is sent to redeem through his own death; but the Christ of the Second Coming – the all-powerful saviour and final arbitrator, clothed in the imagery of resurrection, glory and light. The Volk, the Germanic nation, are the 'chosen people' who will experience the millennium of the Thousand Year Reich. And although it is not 'revealed' in the ritual itself, the Jew is the devil or Anti-Christ, whose power will be banished at this Second Coming.

The analogy with Christian myth should not be overdrawn, for it *was* mere analogy. But it is obvious that the National Socialist Weltanschauung of the Kampfzeit has undergone fundamental 'reinterpretation' and re-emerged as the myth of the Holy History under the Third Reich. So although the *structure* of the Nazi Weltanschauung is maintained (the binary opposition between the Volk-community and 'Jewishness'), the socio-economic criteria upon which this racial dichotomy was based before 1933 have been eradicated. The reasons for this become clear if we look back to our analysis of the Nazi Weltanschauung.

We have argued that the structure of the Nazi Weltanschauung was formed by linking together a number of diverse economic, social and political criteria into 'racial' categories. And although this racial

---

[29] See *Vorschläge der Reichspropagandaleitung zur Nationalsozialistischen Feiergestaltung*, 1/205, March 1936.

differentiation was itself an effect of manipulatory propaganda, it expressed (albeit perversely) *real* socio-economic conflicts and the desire of the Mittelstand to create a third way between socialism and monopoly capitalism. Simultaneously, however, Nazi propaganda had claimed that under the Third Reich the intense social and political conflict which had marked the Weimar era would give way to the utopia of the Volk-community – a period of class harmony between members of a racial brotherhood. But, in practice, class conflict, far from being overcome under the Third Reich, was *intensified*, though its *manifestation* was taboo.

Therefore it was the attempt to mystify the growing contradiction between classes, and to overlay the reality of intense political conflict with a veneer of images suggesting social harmony and class co-operation that led the Nazi leadership to place such reliance upon political celebration during the Third Reich. By exploiting certain aspects of Christian myth and symbolism, National Socialism was able to represent and reinforce the qualities of unity, obedience and a spirit of sacrifice through the mechanism of mass suggestion. Thus the ideological exploitation of real *class-based* conflict under Weimar – a conflict which provided the dynamic of the Nazi Weltanschauung – was replaced by a myth under the Third Reich which was constructed out of a series of powerful, but politically meaningless, symbols of harmony and salvation.

The logic of our analysis therefore suggests that political celebration constituted a fundamental means both of presenting 'ideology' and of legitimising National Socialist rule in the Nazi state. It cannot be considered simply as a peripheral phenomenon, as 'irrational' Fuhrer worship, but must be examined within the wider context of German fascism's historical development. Clearly we have only been able to sketch in a number of inter-relationships in a manner which has been somewhat schematic. Yet if the element of political calculation seems to be overstressed, we can look at the experience of the Thingspiel movement to demonstrate just how keen the Nazi leadership was to create a means of expressing the ideology of the Volk-community, and just how difficult this task proved to be.

The Thingspiel theatre movement

The so-called Thingspiel celebrations were theatrical events modelled on earlier lay productions, which made use of dramatic plot, key speakers and chorus. The Thingtheatres (Thingplätze) were invariably circular, based upon the design of the ancient Greek amphitheatre, and were variously believed to demonstrate the racial kinship of the German Volk to the ancient Greeks, and to recall the prehistoric German tribal meetings which took place in a forest clearing. According to Wolf Braumüller the Thingspiele were the 'outward embodiment of the National Socialist concept of community', for in the Thingtheatres the Volk's new experience of unity could be expressed in a form which their Teutonic fathers had used and which was still deeply rooted in the German character.[30]

Again the aspect of monumentality played a major role. The Dietrich Eckart stage in Berlin, for instance, held some 20,000 spectators, and the event by which it was consecrated, the *Frankenburger Würfelspiel*, had a cast of 1,200 players. The stage area of the Thingtheatre was almost always divided into three levels, corresponding to the three stages of the Passion Plays of the Middle Ages. These three levels denoted three levels of meaning. The lowest level, the arena, was the entrance field of the common people – the spectators. On the second level stood the worldly powers and sovereigns. On the highest level ruled the 'law':

> The highest level ... is embodied in seven judges, the power of true might, the voice of the people, and the expression of that which we Germans conceive of as the Fuhrer.[31]

The common people were the 'community of the celebration' acclaiming the Fuhrer, and they were integrated into the events by having the cast stream through the ranks of the spectators towards the stage, just as occurred at Nuremberg. Hence the Thingspiel was:

> theatre for the Volk as community ... [it] is at one with the mass of spectators ... at one with the actors ... who are no longer cut off by visible curtains dividing the dark auditorium from the brightly lit stage.[32]

[30] Wolf Braumüller, *Freilicht und Thingspiel: Ruckschau und Forderungen*, Berlin 1935.

[31] Ferdinand Junghans, 'Die theatergeschichtliche Stellung des Frankenburger Würfelspiels', in Möller, *Das Frankenburger Würfelspiel*, 2nd ed. Berlin 1936, p. 62.

[32] 'Jetz, wo Versammlungsraum und Schaubühne identisch werden', in J. Wulf, *Theater und Film im Dritten Reich*, Gutersloh 1964.

Goebbels' Propaganda Ministry went to great lengths to mould the Thingspiel movement to the direct needs of the party. In 1933 a separate organisation was founded to oversee its development, the Reichsbund der deutschen Freilicht and Volksschauspiele, and the Labour Service began to build the first of six hundred proposed circular outdoor theatres, which ideally included a natural substance in the building itself – a large ('sacred') stone or a small stream for instance. Naturally outdoor productions suffered from problems of weather and acoustics, not to mention their frequent physical isolation. Undaunted, Felix Emmel planned a German Festival House of massive proportions which included a flat roof, so that the 'eternal values of the Germanic race' could be celebrated without party dignatories having to suffer the discomforts of rain and cold.[33]

The state-controlled media also went to great lengths to eulogise the 'holy' nature of the Thingspiel. Thus the aim of the theatre was the 'education of the German through the medium of the mass meeting'; or 'it is the deepest meaning of the "idea" ... community experience through experienced community.'[34]

A special meeting of forty writers was called, who were urged by Goebbels to create 'feeling and belief', the 'soul of the movement' and 'mythical effect' in their work.[35] But the results were disappointing. Only a few works were suitable, because most of the proposed productions were short of plot and needed a choir to relate the story. It became apparent, even to the zealots in the party leadership, that tedious theatrical productions were an unsuitable medium for expressing the themes of the Nazi Weltanschauung. In 1937 Goebbels was forced to admit defeat. The plays and the building of the theatres were dropped from the level of 'Reichspriority'.

It was precisely because the Thingspiel movement attempted to intellectualise, or at least 'explain' the various aspects of Nazi ideology that it failed. The plays were utterly unconvincing. 'Feeling and belief' could not be expressed through dramatic interpretation

[33] Cf. *Theater aus deutschem Wesen*, Berlin 1937, pp. 92-6.

[34] J. Wulf, op. cit., p. 44.

[35] See Erich Trunz, 'Tatsachendichtung und Weihedichtung', in *Zeitschrift für deutsche Bildung* 11, 1935, p. 549.

without becoming laughable; they resisted 'logical' explanation. It seems, therefore, that the NSDAP's increasing flight into symbolic reductionism (itself a consequence of the need to mystify ideologically those socio-economic contradictions which could not be overcome politically) forced an increasing reliance upon forms of ideological presentation which persuaded by means of 'association' rather than explanation. The various aspects of Christian ritual, and especially the millenarian tradition, provided a model which was both *ideologically suitable* and *widely comprehensible*. Political celebration, with its capacity to create the community experience through cleverly organised sensory effects, was the means by which this 'conversion' or reinforcement took place. Removed from this particular environment the whole ideological facade of Nazism comes dangerously close to collapse.

'Flag, Fuhrer, Volk! Eternal Germany! Who can interpret their meaning?' asks the Nazi ideologist Ernst Berthold. It is:

> The Absolute! We sense it, therefore we believe it ... Let us take care that in the honouring of the flag, our youth is overcome by a reverential thrill, through which the ultimate and deepest meaning of the flag is revealed. Only then are the forces which form the soul and character of our movement revealed, which inspire the 'inner and outer behaviour' which corresponds to the Being of the Eternal Germany, which we all serve as followers of the Fuhrer ... for the deepest meaning of the flag is not to be understood ... in words, but from a sense of its divine meaning.[36]

Conclusions

During the Kampfzeit the NSDAP identified the twin threat to the Mittelstand – proletarianisation through socialism or economic extinction through the increasing concentration of capital – as the work of the Jew. Thus National Socialism promised an immediately achievable utopia which was free from the abuses of class struggle and parasitic capitalism, warning at the same time of the catastrophic consequences of defeat by the forces of 'Jewishness'. The reduction of social reality to the struggle between two mortally antagonistic racial forces therefore provided ample justification for the drastic physical repression of this 'racial enemy' (*Feind*) in the early months

---

[36] Ernst Berthold, *Heiliges Brauchtum um die Fahne des Reiches*, Leipzig 1936, p. 24.

of the take-over of power, since this was the essential condition for the achievement of the promised utopia.[37] At the same time an increasing flight into an ideology based upon the reification of symbols of unity and harmony (Flag, Fuhrer, Volk etc.) allowed the form of this utopia to remain vague enough to allow for the widest possible degree of social consensus.

The Nazi regime originally gathered mass support because of its promise to create a state free from the abuses of monopoly capital, high finance and the encroachment of 'modernity'. But the historical role of the Nazi state was to oversee an economic revolution in Germany which was the inevitable consequence of the rationalisation which accompanied rearmament. Thus the degree of flexibility and elasticity afforded by an ideological style which reduced socio-political conflicts and class contradictions to symbols of 'cohesion' (the Volk-community) and 'destruction' (Jewishness) was paramount.

[37] In this, of course, we see the element of political manipulation and expediency, for although 'Jewish socialist' elements, i.e. the organisations of the left-wing parties, were ruthlessly suppressed in the early months of the Nazi regime, the party leadership was far more circumspect in its campaign against 'Jewish capital'. See Chapter 6.

PART IV

Ideology and Genocide

CHAPTER EIGHT

The Interpretation of German Fascism

Before detailing our conclusions about the nature and the role of National Socialist ideology, it would be useful to look at how our initial findings relate to existing interpretations of German fascism. We cannot enter into a general debate about the qualities of these interpretations;[1] but the way in which the role of ideology is perceived by a particular interpretation of National Socialism does have an important bearing upon its internal consistency and indeed its historical validity.

Far too often, social scientists have consigned the ideology of National Socialism to the dustbin of history with little more than a few perfunctory remarks about its manipulative and pernicious nature, and with scant regard for its significance for the rise to power and the consolidation of the Nazi regime. Thus National Socialism has been viewed as 'non-ideological', in the sense that German fascism merely reflected the ideological characteristics of those economic and political forces which controlled its destiny. Or else it has been interpreted as a movement totally determined by the 'irrational' ideology of one man – Adolf Hitler – the absolute dictator of the Nazi party and the Third Reich.

Our examination, however, suggests that such interpretations not only fail to deal with the complex problem of assessing what ideological tendencies were at work within the NSDAP (and what was the role of 'external' forces in influencing the party's ideological direction); they also abdicate responsibility for the task of analysing *how* National Socialism was able to generate and sustain such a

---

[1] For discussion of interpretations of German fascism, see Reinhard Kühnl, *Faschismustheorien*, Reinbek bei Hamburg 1979.

significant level of popular support. We cannot blithely dismiss Nazi ideology as 'irrational'. Rather we must examine *why* such an 'irrational' ideology eventually became the expression of a *particular social consciousness* in Weimar society.

Ideology as a product of the Fuhrer

There is a tragic irony in the fact that so much of the post-war literature on German fascism has identified Adolf Hitler as the initiator, mentor and indeed the dynamic force of National Socialism; for such interpretations inevitably reinforce an image of Hitler which was created by the propaganda machine of the Nazi party itself. Hence a number of authors proceed from the assumption that Hitler alone determined the spirit and structure of German fascism.

According to Golo Mann, Hitler was the 'most gruesome human phenomenon of our century' who became dictator because 'it was his wish'.[2] Ernst Deuerlein claims that 'National Socialism was historically determined by one man'.[3] And Fabry asserts that 'a man emerged from the dark ... [and after] an unprecedented rise to the head of the kingdom, made this kingdom the mightiest in Europe'.[4]

Allied to such hypotheses are interpretations which view Hitler as the 'embodiment' of a 'national will'. Fabry, for instance, writes that 'Hitler did not come to power by force, through revolution' but that 'a great part of the German people called him'.[5] While Joachim Fest claims that Hitler was 'an all but exemplary combination of the Angst, protest and hope of his time' and speaks of a 'mysterious convergence of the meaningful individual and the social will'.[6]

These interpretations see history as the product of 'exceptional individuals' – a notion either explicit or implicit in the numerous studies of National Socialism which concentrate upon the career and psychic disorders of Adolf Hitler. Yet, even leaving aside the

[2] G. Mann in the Foreword to E. Calic, *Ohne Maske. Hitler – Breiting Geheimgespräche* 1931, Frankfurt a. M. 1968, pp. 5ff.

[3] E. Deuerlein, *Der Aufstieg der NSDAP in Augenzeugenberichten*, Düsseldorf 1968, p.13.

[4] W. Fabry, *Mutmassungen über Hitler*, Düsseldorf 1968; see Introduction.

[5] ibid.

[6] J.C. Fest, *Hitler*, Berlin 1973, pp. 21, 19.

question of methodology, how can such Fuhrer interpretations be justified *empirically*?

Hitler, it is claimed, was called by 'a great part of the German people'. But in the final free elections held in November 1932, the NSDAP polled only 33.1 per cent of the total vote. And even in the elections held in March 1933, which took place under a 'state of emergency' when the Nazis controlled most of the state's propaganda organs and let loose a wave of terror against their opponents, the party could only claim 43.9 per cent of the poll. In fact, as we have consistently suggested, Hitler was not the representation of a *nation* (as Nazi propaganda liked to claim) but rather the champion of a politik which represented particular *class interests*.

The obsession with the figure of the Fuhrer has in turn led a number of historians to conclude that an analysis of Hitler's own thinking can provide a key to the understanding of the National Socialist phenomenon. Ernst Nolte writes that 'in the Fuhrer movement only the Fuhrer can make binding statements. The representation of Hitler's thought ... is the centre of any attempt to determine the National Socialist epoch'.[7] Certainly an examination of Hitler's thought can provide us with a number of useful clues in interpreting the rise of fascism and the nature of the Nazi state, but such an approach has severe limitations. First, it ignores the complex relationship which we have uncovered between the ideology espoused by the party and the pressure upon party policy from big business. Thus in the final critical months of the Weimar republic, Hitler's secret 'guarantees' to the business community put him at odds with the ideology of the party whose 'will' he was supposed to express. Indeed it is often impossible to extricate Hitler's personal ideology from the mass of conflicting statements he made to various interest groups. Secondly, Hitler may have been the only individual in the party who could 'make binding statements', but it would be grossly naive to suppose that his pronouncements were always in line with his personal beliefs. Indeed we have alluded to just one such occasion, when Hitler was forced against his wishes to sanction the financial rescue of the Jewish Hertie group in 1933. Similarly the 'unalterable' Twenty-five Point Party Programme of 1919 was supposed to embody Hitler's political thinking – but it was either altered during the Kampfzeit (as in the 'reinterpretation' of Point Sixteen) or else

[7] E. Nolte, *Der Faschismus in seiner Epoche*, München 1963, p. 53.

simply ignored in many substantial details after the take-over of power.

However, the most fundamental shortcoming of the various Fuhrer hypotheses is that they deal with the issue of ideology in an historical vaccuum, thereby failing to identify any form of dialectic in the rise of National Socialism. Such interpretations cannot account for the catalogue of failure and frustration experienced by the NSDAP from 1919 until 1929. Conversely, the spectacular rise of the NSDAP after 1929 is not seen as a reaction on the part of *particular social formations* (and a particular social consciousness) to the *specific contradictions* of German society (which were sharpened by the depth of the economic crisis) – but as some sort of 'national' reaction to crisis which Hitler and his party embodied. So most Fuhrer hypotheses suffer from a lack of rigour in analysing how personality and ideology interact with social, economic, political and cultural forces.

This is not at all to suggest that Hitler's personal characteristics and indeed his private fantasies were *irrelevant* to the course of German fascism. Individual qualities and characteristics can be forces which determine history – but only, as Plechanow correctly points out, 'when, and in so far as social relationships permit them to be'![8] And only a careful examination of the interaction of material and ideological forces within a given historical situation can establish the degree to which the intervention of the individual affects the course of history. Plainly the great majority of Fuhrer hypotheses, which have been greeted with such jubilation by the media, fail totally in this respect. Moreover such interpretations have an insidious effect upon public opinion, for by identifying the unparalleled brutality and horror of German fascism with the obsessions of a single individual – 'a man who chose hell because his way to heaven was blocked'[9] – it is possible to ignore far more pertinent questions. Who, for instance, actively helped Hitler to power in 1933 (once the myth that he was elected has been demolished)? Who gained from the systematic internal repression of 'Jews and Communists' under the Third Reich? And who financed, planned and profited from the war of plunder and genocide unleashed by German fascism in 1939?

[8] G. Plechanow, *Uber die Rolle der Persönlichkeit in der Geschichte*, Stuttgart 1952, p.34.
[9] According to Toland and his publishers in 'Information about the Book' (J. Toland, *Adolf Hitler*) Bergisch Gladbach 1977.

Totalitarian theories

During the height of the Cold War in the 1950s, interpretations which viewed German fascism as an example of a totalitarian movement gained considerable academic credibility. Such theories hinge upon a distinction between the essential characteristics of 'democratic' and 'totalitarian' regimes, and concentrate upon a comparative analysis of the formal organisations of the state. As a result, Carl Friedrich finds that 'fascist and communist totalitarian dictatorships are, in their essential characteristics, the same'. This is because in both types of regime we find 'one ideology, a single party, which typically is led by one man, a terroristic police, a monopoly on communication, a monopoly of weapons and a centrally-directed economy'.[10]

We cannot take up the discussion of totalitarian theories here; but such theories promote a particular notion of fascist ideology, and it is important to outline their shortcomings. First, the totalitarian theorist's concept of ideology is totally 'static'. Thus the state may indeed espouse only one ideology, but the struggle within the party and state over the *interpretation* of ideology continues as part of the factional struggle for power. Totalitarian theories of National Socialism therefore fail to identify either the endemic struggle over ideology (and policy) which we have identified within the NSDAP, or, even more important, they ignore one of the major characteristics of Nazi ideology – namely the schism or rupture between the ideology of the mass party before 1933 and the praxis of the Nazi state. Thus the term, 'one ideology, a single party', as applied to National Socialism, fails to identify the continual factional struggles for control of the NSDAP's ideological and political direction (even though these struggles rarely spilled out into the open).

Secondly, if fascist and totalitarian dictatorships 'are in their essential characteristics the same', then we would expect some convergence of ideological principles. This, however, is not the case. Nazi doctrine, for instance, posits a *continual* national or racial struggle for existence, in which only the *strongest* elements will triumph at the expense of the weakest. Conversely Communist states claim to be working towards the stage of Communism (as such they

---

[10] C.J. Friedrich, *Totalitäre Diktatur*, Stuttgart 1958, p. 15; 'Das Wesen totalitärer Herrschaft', in *Der Politologe* 20 (1966) p. 43.

call themselves socialist states), in which the contradictions between classes are permanently dissolved and a society evolves in which political struggle becomes meaningless. Thus Communism is seen as a final stage of mankind, determined by an inevitable 'law of history', while the Nazi state was presented as necessarily temporal – a thousand-year Reich maintained only by constant racial struggle.[11]

Lastly, most totalitarian theories of German fascism contend that the Fuhrer maintains a formal monopoly on the political process, and by implication therefore, the Fuhrer has a primary influence upon decision-making. Bracher, for example, asserts that the Fuhrer alone 'builds the nucleus of the ruling system and its social, political and human structure'.[12] But such a statement seems to take little account of the struggle between the various factions within the Nazi state (the party administration, the military, the business community, the state bureaucracy and the SS) which determined the political options available. Hitler may, under certain circumstances, have been able to *choose* between a number of options, but he was unable to determine those options, and quite frequently his 'choice' was frustrated by the bitter competition between these forces. Equally there were vital occasions on which Hitler was *forced* to act, even against his will. Thus the decision to carry out the Röhm purge was a result of an ultimatum by the army who feared the competition of the SA as a paramilitary force. Hitler, although hostile to the political attitude of the SA radicals, nevertheless would have preferred to maintain the SA as an instrument of party authority and a counter-weight to the army.

Soviet historiography

If the Fuhrer interpretations, and to a lesser extent totalitarian theories can be criticised for lacking dialectical perspective by perpetuating an 'idealistic' view of National Socialism, then Soviet historiography must be taken to task for delivering an equally

[11] It must be stressed that only the ideological *principles* of fascism and Communism (Marxism) are being discussed here: this is not to suggest that the principles of Marxism have been put into practice under the Soviet system. Detailed discussion of such questions is quite outside the scope of this book.

[12] K.D. Bracher, *Die Auflösung der Weimarer Republik*, Stuttgart 1957, pp. 53, 54.

monocausal interpretation of German fascism by concentrating almost exclusively upon material factors.

The Seventh Congress of the Comintern concluded that fascism is 'the open terroristic dictatorship of the most reactionary, most chauvinistic and most imperialistic elements of finance capitalism ... fascism is the might of finance capital itself'.[13] And almost all Soviet-Marxist inspired interpretations of Nazism proceed from the assertion that fascist dictatorship and bourgeois democracy are 'two different forms of political superstructure built upon the same socio-economic structure – namely state monopoly capitalism'.[14]

Certainly the policies pursued by the Nazi party under the Third Reich met a number of the demands of monopoly capital. The destruction of the political organisations of the working class, and the trade union movement; obstruction of the promised corporate state; the militarisation of labour-power; forced rearmament; and the war of imperialist expansion, were all aspects of a Nazi politik which *in effect* guaranteed optimum conditions of reproduction for German monopoly capital. However, to proceed from these observations to the conclusion that German fascism was *the agent* of the monopoly bourgeoisie is to confuse a *structural contiguity* (i.e. an 'association of interest') with a *structural identity* (the notion that fascism was identical with monopoly capital).

The consequences of such interpretations (which follow from an oversimplification of Marx's concept of base and superstructure), work themselves out in a number of historically unverifiable assertions about the role of ideology in German fascism. Thus according to the standard GDR text, *Germany 1939-1945*, Hitler was 'the political spokesman of the real dictators of Germany – the men of coal, iron, steel, the chemical and electrical industries, as well as the big banks ... he was the tool, the figure and the creature of the German monopoly bourgeoisie'.[15] So it must be presumed that given the structural identity between Nazism and the monopoly bourgeoisie, either the ideology of National Socialism was that of the

[13] Protocols of the 7th Congress of the Comintern (1935) in W. Pieck, G. Dimitroff and P. Togliatti, *Die Offensive des Faschismus und die Aufgaben der Kommunisten im Kampf für die Volksfront gegen Krieg und Faschismus*, Berlin 1957, p. 87.

[14] D. Eichholtz and K. Gossweiler, 'Noch einmal, Politik und Wirtschaft 1933-1945', in *Das Argument* 47 (1968) p. 216.

[15] *Deutschland 1939-1945*, Berlin 1970, pp. 43ff.

'men of coal, iron, steel', etc., or else it was *historically irrelevant* to the course of German fascism, being at most a manipulation 'to divert attention from the class struggle'.

Such a functional interpretation of Nazi ideology cannot account for the historical evidence. It ignores the original Mittelstand basis of the NSDAP and the social, economic, political and cultural factors which account for the appeal of National Socialist ideology during the Kampfzeit. It ignores the schism between Nazism's original petit bourgeois social base and the policies of the Nazi state which favoured big business. And, most important of all, it ignores the evidence which suggests that the 'ideological' interests of the Nazi leadership in exterminating six million Jews took precedence over the objective demands of big business for their sorely needed labour power.[16] Nor is Gossweiler's account of Nazi genocide, which contrives to discover 'function' and 'disfunction' in the situation of German imperialism, a satisfactory solution to this theoretical dilemma. Gossweiler asserts that although monopoly capitalist elements 'needed labour power' to work the factories, they also 'needed' to exterminate all nuclei of opposition to their rule. Thus he concludes that the conflict of interest between labour power (function) and potential opposition (disfunction) 'disproves the notion that genocide was the 'triumph' of fascist ideology over the interests of the monopoly bourgeoisie'.[17]

National Socialism as a middle-class movement

Following largely from the work of Theodor Geiger, Seymour Lipset developed the notion that fascism represents 'the extremism of the centre'. This hypothesis stems from the fact that the Mittelstand was overproportionately represented in the Nazi party (before 1933), and our examination confirms that National Socialism gave strong

---

[16] Two studies by GDR historians which deal in some detail with the issue of Nazi anti-Semitism and avoid the simplistic reductionism which we are criticising here are Rudi Goguel's Introduction to *Kennzeichen J*, Berlin 1966 (a detailed history of the Nazi persecution of the Jews) and Kurt Pätzold, *Faschismus, Rassenwahn Judenverfolgung*, Berlin 1975.

[17] K. Gossweiler, R. Kühnl, R. Opitz, *Faschismus: Entstehung und Verhinderung, Texte zur Demokratisierung*, H4, Frankfurt a. M., pp. 20ff. Gossweiler does however add that: "this is not said as a complete explanation of the fascist persecution of the Jews.'

ideological expression to the 'dilemma' of the middle classes under Weimar.

Mittelstand theories concern themselves almost exclusively with an analysis of the sociological *origins* of Nazism. Lipset himself is aware of this limitation, and Geiger states that Mittelstand theory is in no way a total critique of National Socialism, 'but a single, if very important feature of the movement'.[18] Therefore Mittelstand theory does not attempt to analyse the conditions under which German fascism came to power, nor can it account for the rupture between the middle-class basis of Nazism during the Kampfzeit and the socio-economic policies of the Nazi state.

But Mittelstand theory does deal competently with the relationship between ideology and the socio-economic basis of the NSDAP before 1933, and most of our findings underline its general assumptions. Thus Geiger stresses that the NSDAP gathered support on the basis of its ideological appeal to the middle classes who were faced by the twin threats of socialism and capitalism: 'from the left the power of socialism had increased threateningly, from the right there was the psychological pressure (of economic extinction) from huge conglomerates.'[19] And it was the steadily deepening economic crisis at the end of the 1920s which intensified this process and created the psychological preconditions for petit bourgeois radicalism.

Lipset and Geiger have established an approach to the interpretation of National Socialism based upon the sociological analysis of National Socialism's mass basis. Wilhelm Reich and Erich Fromm have used the same evidence to develop a socio-psychological interpretation of German fascism. In effect they seek to identify the origins of Nazism in the disturbance of the human psyche, and their hypotheses are of particular relevance to any study of the role of National Socialist ideology.

Reich and Fromm attempt to discover the psychological preconditions for the 'irrationality' of Nazi ideology by integrating the psycho-analytical tradition of Freud with the political science of Marx. Indeed Reich outlines the task facing the social scientist in exemplary fashion:

---

[18] T. Geiger, *Arbeiten zur Soziologie*, Neuwied and Berlin 1962, p. 335.
[19] ibid., pp. 345-50.

> One is on the wrong tack when one attempts to explain Hitler's
> success solely on the basis of the demagogy of the National Socialists,
> the 'befogging of the masses', their 'deception', or to apply the vague
> hollow term Nazi psychosis ... For it is precisely a question of
> understanding why the masses proved to be accessible to deception,
> befogging and a psychotic situation.[20]

For Reich the ideology of every social formation has the function
not only of reflecting the economic process of society, but also, and
more significantly, of 'embedding this economic process in the *psychic
structures of the people who make up the society*'. Man is subject to the
conditions of his existence in a twofold way: directly through the
immediate influence of his economic and social position, and
indirectly by means of the ideological structure of society. Reich
believed that psycho-analysis had created the means by which the
material conditions of production could be analysed 'in the specific
process of creating the specific ideology in the mind'. Essentially,
then, Reich attempts to use psycho-analysis to detail the relationship
between the material structure of society and the ideological
superstructure.

In order to account for the 'irrational' attitudes of the German
middle classes in embracing National Socialism, Reich identifies an
historical situation in which such beliefs had a 'rational' social basis.
He argues that the psychic structure of man is formed in early
childhood, and that this psychic structure comes into increasing
conflict with material conditions; eventually a contradiction evolves
between the archaic psychic structure and new social relationships:
'ideology changes at a slower pace than the economic base, [and is]
far more conservative than the forces of technical production.'[21] And
because the psychic structure lags behind the social conditions from
which it derived, it eventually 'comes into conflict with new forms of
life'. Thus for Reich the contradiction between the psychic
consciousness of the German Mittelstand, which had its source in
the authoritarian Kaiser-Reich, and the rapid development of
material structures under Weimar, provided the preconditions for the
rise of National Socialism.

Fromm attempts a similar psycho-analytical technique, although

---

[20] W. Reich, *The Mass Psychology of Fascism*, Pelican Books 1975, pp. 69-70.
[21] ibid., p. 52.

he limits himself to the task of uncovering the 'human conditions' of the National Socialist epoch. He traces the lure of fascist demagogy for the Mittelstand to the beginnings of German capitalism and its peculiar development.[22] Most obviously, the psychic structure of the petite bourgeoisie was constructed within the framework of the Kaiser-Reich, and was shattered 'materially' by the hyper-inflation and the world economic crisis, and 'emotionally' by the lost war, the dissolution of the monarchy and the humiliation of the Treaty of Versailles.

Unfortunately the interpretations of Reich and Fromm remain little more than speculative, because they lack any form of comparative verification. Why did only certain strata at a certain historical juncture prove susceptible to fascist ideology? The psycho-analytical categories employed by Reich and Fromm are too vague and undefined to answer such questions, despite the useful subjective insights that they offer. For what serves as a model of individual behaviour (psycho-analysis) cannot serve as a model of collective social behaviour without substantial modifications which clearly define the areas of psychological, sociological, economic and political interaction. Equally, Reich and Fromm, by concentrating upon the formation of the Mittelstand's psyche in the Kaiser-Reich, fail to give sufficient consideration to the way in which National Socialism's ideology reflected the specific consciousness of the German Mittelstand in the 1920s and 1930s. We have argued that Nazi ideology during the Kampfzeit did reflect a specific Mittelstand consciousness by providing a Weltanschauung, which although 'befogging' and 'deceiving' the masses in terms of its explanation of the crisis, none the less addressed itself to the Mittelstand's political and economic dilemma. Thus the 'irrationality' of Nazi ideology lies *within* its structure, for it mystifies the origins of social conflict through the manipulation of ideological categories. The problem of interpretation, therefore, remains one of uncovering the specific social conditions which nurture such ideological 'irrationality'.

[22] E. Fromm, *Die Furcht vor der Freiheit*, Frankfurt a. M. 1966.

CHAPTER NINE

The Seeds of Genocide

Crisis and consciousness

As Kühnl suggests, 'it is specific social relationships, the experience of man in everyday life and work situations which forms consciousness, in its correct and its false elements'.[1] And because all the available evidence points to the fact that the economic crisis which engulfed Germany at the end of the 1920s was the *precondition* for the rise of National Socialism, we must look at the specific 'life and work' situation of the German Mittelstand under conditions of extreme crisis in order to understand how the recession created a climate which favoured an identification with Nazi racism. This requires some consideration of the general effects of economic crisis upon the petit bourgeois consciousness, as well as an analysis of the specific effects of crisis upon the German Mittelstand under Weimar.

When the crisis-stricken proletarian is unable to find work, his falling standard of living is generally seen as an effect of the *unavailability* of work (the factory stands idle – he is shut out from the means of production). Not so the small trader, who under similar conditions of capitalist crisis still retains control of his means of production. (Of course, his decline may be such that he is forced to sell his tools, his shop or land and join the lumpen proletariat.) In practice the petit bourgeois must extend his necessary labour time in an attempt to reproduce his old standard of living. The farmer and the artisan must produce more because of falling market prices; or the small trader must sell more as falling turnover and lower profit margins reduce net income. But under the most severe crisis conditions, not only does such 'extra labour' fail to make up the

[1] Kühnl, *Faschismustheorien*, p. 229.

shortfall in income (as lack of demand drives down market prices and turnover) – labour may even become *counter-productive*. Hence for the farmer, the market price of a fattened pig may drop *below* the price he originally paid for it, even before the cost of feed, etc. is taken into account. Or the artisan may find that the market price of his finished goods has fallen below the cost of his raw materials, regardless of the cost of manufacture. In practice, therefore, the small trader or producer risks furthering his decline by working harder, since production is permanently at a loss.

So for the petit bourgeois, severe or endemic economic crisis may *challenge* the entire notion that labour provides for the physical needs of his existence, and the small producer or trader may *objectively* find himself in a situation in which work actually appears to *destroy* the products of his labour. He is then in a 'life and work' situation which contradicts the entire 'rationality' of his existence. Yet at the same time the 'rationality' of capitalist development continues apace. Analysing the crisis of the German Mittelstand, Brecht suggests that:

> Because the economic process carried through a rationalisation which inflicted such terrible sacrifice upon these (middle) strata ... because they found themselves shut out of the economic system because of rationality ... they soon became totally anti-ratio, and in favour of the 'irrational'.[2]

In effect the petit bourgeois's social consciousness is ripped apart. 'Rationality' becomes irrational, and he seeks for the logic of this 'irrationality'.

If we take the example of the farming community in Schleswig-Holstein, we can see how this inter-relationship between capitalist crisis and petit bourgeois consciousness, between 'rationality' and 'irrationality', developed in practice. In the immediate post-war years, the small farmer was encouraged to capitalise his small-holding and modernise his work-practices. An early enthusiasm for political liberalism thus coincided with the stabilisation of the capitalist economy and the expansion of the livestock and fresh-food market after the dislocation of the war. By the mid-1920s, at the period of maximum economic growth,

---

[2] B. Brecht, *Schriften zur Politik und Gesellschaft*, Frankfurt a. M. 1968, p. 164.

increased production meant (providing that expansion had been judicious) increased profitability and major increases in the standard of living for the farmer and his family.

But the effect of the chronic agricultural crisis in northern Germany was to stand this capitalist 'rationality' on its head. As market prices collapsed, interest rates spiralled, and loans were arbitrarily withdrawn, those who had expanded most (and whose debt was therefore greatest) faced the greatest threat to their livelihood. And while it was indeed only the minority who were evicted from their farms and land, the threat of ruin and destitution hung over the entire farming community.

Nazi ideology struck at this point in the relationship between work-situation and consciousness. It carried conviction, not *because* it was an irrational ideology (or the farmers suddenly took leave of their senses) but because it was an ideology which *gave expression* to a concrete social situation which was *itself irrational*:

> Farmers!
> You are going to be expropriated!
> Taxes, usurious interest rates, debts to the banks, all sorts of financial burdens, middle-man profit taking and Stock Exchange dealing rob you of all that you have. You are forced to sell up ... You must watch, with anger and bitterness, as you are tricked out of the rewards of years of hard work ... You toil from morning till night, day in day out, week in week out, month by month; you toil and save, and yet it's more and more difficult to scrape a living ... Yes, you are slaves – no longer free farmers. Your property and your land is mortgaged. Every year, every month you go backwards! (**32**).

Of particular importance is the suggestion that the farmer is 'going backwards' and that he is being 'tricked' out of the rewards of his labour. Here the concept of 'conspiracy' is introduced, and this is plausible because, as we have already remarked, the mechanisms of crisis in the farming community were obscure and mysterious. A Silesian woman (one of many interviewed by Abel) expressed the 'logic' of a conspiracy like this:

> I searched and searched, but there was none that offered salvation from all this hopeless misery! If you went with open eyes through all this chaos, you could tell there was someone behind it all, trying to pull our fatherland into the abyss.[3]

[3] P. Merkl, *Political Violence under the Swastika*, Princeton 1975, Respondent no. 549.

The small farmer could not 'see' market forces or interest rates; the complexities of international politics and finance which initially determined such factors were largely incomprehensible; but he could identify the *agencies* which enforced the effects of such policies. And these were precisely the money-lender, the bank, the tax-office, the bailiff or the cattle dealer:

> In the meantime despair is deepening, the burden of debt gets greater and greater, the bailiffs and the Jews come more and more often to your door (**32**).

> Who's laughing? Certainly not the Mittelstand.
> The Jew's laughing. The banks belong to the Jews (**34**).

> It is a fact that the Jew never breeds cattle. He is never to be found working in the cow shed. But he dictates the price of cattle and food on the produce market (**42**).

> The farmer can no longer pay high taxes from what he earns from agricultural work. So the farmer is forced to take loans for which he must pay usurious rates of interest. He is plunged ever deeper into interest slavery, and finally loses house and home to the mainly Jewish providors of loan capital (**43**).

Here then is the substance of the 'racial explanation' advanced by National Socialism; for by concentrating upon what were in fact the *symptoms* of crisis (rather than the causes) and identifying these symptoms with a racial conspiracy against the German Volk, National Socialism was able to organise and manipulate the way in which the peasant-farmer responded to the dislocation of his 'community' and 'tradition'. So Nazi propaganda exploited a breakdown of consciousness, which was itself a result of the collapse of traditional norms and values. If the crisis could find no explanation in 'everyday' petit bourgeois consciousness, then radical or 'exceptional' explanations could expect a sympathetic hearing, especially when they gave expression to broad social and political demands or encompassed existing völkisch stereotypes. However, before proceeding to analyse the specific nature of Nazi racialism, we must deal with some of the general points which our analysis has raised.

If, as we have suggested, the crisis of capitalism at the end of the 1920s provided the key precondition for the rise of German fascism, then why did only the German petite bourgeoisie prove susceptible to the lure of such 'racial explanations' of the recession? Or put another way, why did the world economic slump not produce similar anti-Semitic or racial movements among the petite bourgeoisie of other countries?

We can offer a number of suggestions here, but we cannot pursue the question in depth without a far more detailed set of comparisons. First of all, a number of other European countries, Austria, Belgium, Hungary and Britain among them, did experience the growth of fascist movements whose ideology was largely inspired by anti-Semitism. Secondly, the NSDAP was able to build upon a comparatively strong anti-Semitic tradition in Germany – a tradition that was strong not only among the petit bourgeois völkisch intelligentsia, but also among the peasantry of Saxony and Hesse in the late nineteenth century. Thirdly, the depth of the economic crisis in Germany was greater than in any other western country, precisely because of the relative prosperity of Germany before the First World War, the weakness of German foreign policy after the war, and her reliance upon foreign credit to recapitalise her economy in the 1920s. Moreover, the effects of the recession fell disproportionately upon the German Mittelstand in view of their particularly archaic character, and their economic inefficiency vis-à-vis the modern, highly capitalised conglomerate companies which dominated the German economy (both politically and economically). Thus in Germany small businesses *lost* their percentage share of a *declining* market, in contrast to the USA where they increased their share of a similarly declining market. And this manifests itself in comparative figures showing the number of bankruptcies from 1928 to 1930 in Germany, France and the USA; for whereas these increased by 11 per cent in France and 19 per cent in the USA, they increased by 42 per cent in Germany. And lastly, it is worth stressing again that National Socialism (and its racial ideology) never received an endorsement from the German people in free elections. German fascism came to power not as a result of its popularity (although this was obviously a vital factor), but because of a crisis of hegemony at the level of the state, and (indirectly) because of the divisions within the German working class at this crucial time.

The nature of Nazi anti-Semitism

The stereotype of the Jew and 'Jewishness' linked the various 'negative images' of the Nazi Weltanschauung. And we have seen that Nazi propaganda presented and reinforced this stereotype in two ways. On the one hand, there was the constant psychological association of the Jew with the social evils of exploitation, profiteering, wilful destruction, etc. On the other hand, the Jews were identified as being the instigators of a 'system' which was undermining the 'natural cohesion' of German society, and subverting the economic independence of the Mittelstand. This two-pronged propaganda attack mirrors in many ways the two 'types' of anti-Semitism which evolved within the National Socialist movement.

During the early years, the NSDAP drew into its cadres a number of anti-Semitic sects whose origins can be traced back deep into the nineteenth century. Indeed many of the founding members of the DAP (NSDAP) were members of the rabidly anti-Semitic sect, the Thule Bund, while others either belonged to anti-Semitic völkisch organisations (notably the Deutsch Völkische Schutz und Trutz Bund, banned in 1920) or else were notorious Jew-baiters like Julius Streicher.[4] (It is important to note that such sects and individuals who entertain essentially paranoic fantasies about 'outsiders' are common to almost all societies, and that the way in which these fantasies are expressed is largely a matter of culture.) So there was a process of assimilation, probably complete by the mid-1920s, by which anti-Semites were drawn into the Nazi movement because of the NSDAP's image as the most radical and energetic of the various völkisch movements, and because of Hitler's reputation as the foremost leader of the struggle against the 'Jewish republic'.

Hitler himself appears to have been heavily influenced by the beliefs of pre-fascist anti-Semitic sects; but, more important, he also embodied a second 'type' of anti-Semitism – one which *consciously manipulated* anti-Semitism for political ends. Echoing Class's statements on the manipulative function of anti-Semitism, Hitler stated:

[4] For details, see Werner Maser, *Die Frühgeschichte der NSDAP*, Frankfurt a. M. and Bonn 1965, pp. 145ff.

You will see how little time we shall need in order to upset the ideas and criteria of the whole world simply and solely by attacking Judaism. It is beyond question the most important weapon in our propaganda arsenal.[5]

As we have seen, Hitler consciously tailored his anti-Semitism to the dictates of political expediency throughout the Kampfzeit and during the early years of the Third Reich.

The factors of 'belief' and 'manipulation' fed upon each other within the NSDAP during the 1920s. The sectarians peddled a coarse, pornographic anti-Semitism, which was refined and redefined by Hitler's undeniable genius (as a propagandist) and the NSDAP's propaganda department. And in turn this increasingly sophisticated anti-Semitism, which purported to discover the hand of the Jew in the collapse of traditional German culture and society, fed the paranoic fantasies of the sectarians.[6]

Clearly, however, it was the economic crisis and the 'breakdown of consciousness' that we have identified, which made it possible for the Nazi movement to gain 'converts' to its racial ideology from among sectors of German society who had previously been impervious to völkisch doctrine. Again two separate factors were at work in promoting this ideological consensus.

First of all, the vision of the Volk-community must be seen as an aspect of Nazi anti-Semitism, precisely because the Volk-community was the *antithesis* of Jewishness (*Judentum*). The Volk-community was a *racial community*, although of course its appeal was, in the first instance, political (that is, it promised a society free from the dislocation and conflict of class struggle). But increasingly Nazism paraded the social harmony of the Volk-community as the *only* alternative to the disintegration of Weimar society – a disintegration brought about by a satanic *Jewish* plot. Secondly, the Nazis' claim to have uncovered a Jewish racial conspiracy gave substance to the Mittelstand's fear of powerful but anonymous market forces: forces which were indeed driving them to ruin. The theory of a racial conspiracy also met their specific political demands for the

[5] Vol. 19 of the Proceedings of Nuremberg Trials, pp. 437-8.
[6] Moreover, it can be seen from even a cursory reading of the documents in Chapter 2 that anti-Semitism was in no way down-graded or softened as the NSDAP became a major political force – on the contrary, the denigration of the Jews became ever more vicious and threatening.

amelioration of capitalism and the destruction of proletarian socialism.

By identifying the Jew with the Stock Exchange, the profiteer, and to a lesser extent with the power of trusts and syndicates, the economic threats to Mittelstand existence were represented as symptoms of Jewish power, rather than as inevitable results of the laws of capital accumulation. Only an ideology which identified the 'excesses' of capitalism with the *perversion* of the capitalist system could be attractive to the petite bourgeoisie, given that their disillusionment with capitalism could not be expressed in the demand for its abolition. Of course proletarian socialism could be attacked in a far less circumspect manner, and the Nazis consistently distinguished themselves from their bourgeois opponents by the ferocity of their attack upon Marxism and by their promises to 'root out Communism' from the system. But again there was a tactical advantage to be gained by representing Marxism (and this meant the Social Democrats as well as the Communists) not as an ideology which gave expression to the *political* demands of the working class, but as a 'betrayal' of working-class interests by the Jews. Hence the myth of the Volk-community was also an attempt to reintegrate the worker into capitalist society, and to depoliticise the material contradiction between the worker and his employer.

It is therefore apparent that (at least within the bounds of its Kampfzeit ideology) Nazi anti-Semitism was only symptomatically *racist*: that is to say that the so-called 'Jewish question' for National Socialism was not *in the first place* determined by racial or religious considerations, but by politics. Certainly it was the individual Jew (or the Jewish community) who suffered discrimination, persecution and finally genocide at the hands of the Nazis. But as Sartre has remarked, 'it is the anti-Semite who determines who is a Jew', and when the Jew is identified because of some pre-conceived political characteristic, then it becomes necessary to sharply distinguish Nazi anti-Semitism from other forms of racism.[7]

Moreover, the determination of race because of 'political action'

---

[7] Here I am thinking of Apartheid, which is a 'doctrine' designed to *regulate* the relationship *between* races. Equally Nazi anti-Semitism must be distinguished from that of the Middle Ages, when the Jew was identified on the basis of religious conviction, and conversion to Christianity (through baptism) might save the individual Jew from the sword.

suggests why Nazi anti-Semitism was innately genocidal; for Nazi racism was not designed to order the relationship between races. It offered no rationale for the exploitation of Jewish labour power (although this was a *consequence* of Nazi racial policy). Nor did it underscore a social myth to account for the stratification of German society. Instead it gave 'logic' to the attempt to suppress physically the extreme internal class contradictions of German society. And precisely because Nazi anti-Semitism *disguised* the real causes of 'social disintegration' under Weimar, it could neither confront them nor overcome them. Thus anti-Semitism was vital to the political task of German fascism in creating a spurious unity among the Mittelstand. And it was vital to the eschatology which underpinned Nazism's ideological appeal during the final stages of its march to power. It must be stressed again that the Jew was 'Jewish' because of his actions, because of his 'destructive' nature:

> You can't change the Jew, any more than you can stop rust from destroying iron. You can only keep it at bay. The Jew has to destroy. But you don't have to put up with his destruction (**37**).

So the image of the Jew provided the motivating force for an ideology which delivered a complete explanation of social crisis. Nazi anti-Semitism was *explanation*; and because it was explanation it simultaneously offered *solution*. If the Jew was the source of destruction and disintegration, only his *negation* could usher in the age of harmony and prosperity promised by the Nazis:

> In Germany, in Austria, and in Russia – everywhere the same picture – everywhere destruction ...
> The NSDAP alone can show the way to salvation ...
> Without the removal of the Jews there can be no revival, no salvation!
> (**42**).

> The Jewish racial character has an effect upon the non-Jews similar to that of a rotten apple in a basket full of good apples ... The rotten apple cannot be made good. It must be removed so that the good apples are not spoiled. The Jew is 'chosen' to destroy; but the Christian is taught to root out the tree which produces rotten fruit (Appendix A).

Thus the Nazi Weltanschauung internalises a 'genocidal logic', for if the Jew is the dark, satanic force dragging the German Volk to destruction, then salvation cannot be achieved by the physical separation of the races: it can only come about by his *extermination*.[8]

I am suggesting that the seeds of racial genocide were sown during the Kampfzeit, and that the impulse to genocide was determined by contradictions which National Socialism internalised *at that stage* in its development. Such a hypothesis certainly raises new problems in any attempt to interpret the Final Solution, because until now orthodox interpretations have presumed that the policy of genocide developed at the end of a process of segregation – without any preconceived plan, and as other policy options (forced emigration for instance) were discarded.

Interestingly, Leo Kuper, in his study of the political use of genocide in the twentieth century, does offer this observation about the Nazi murder of the Jews:

> Looking back at the course of genocide, there is such a logical and systematic progression of stages that it gives the impression of having been planned from the beginning …

But, he adds,

> the order for the Final Solution was only given in about July 1941: the initial policy was to bring about a vast emigration of Jewry.[9]

We can now fundamentally question this assumption, for we have seen that the genocidal impulse of Nazi anti-Semitism was apparent even before the founding of the Third Reich. And the suggestion that the genocide of the Jews was consciously planned by the Nazi leadership even before the seizure of power is not mere speculation on my part. Indeed there is evidence to prove that as early as 1927 the Nazi leadership intended to carry out a systematic annihilation of the

[8] This is not to overstate the degree of anti-Semitism within the ideology of National Socialism, nor to overstate its appeal. Certainly many were drawn into the NSDAP simply because of its promises to destroy Marxism, to regenerate the nation, and to create a prosperous economy, without identifying positively with Nazi anti-Semitism. But, as we have suggested, within the National Socialist movement anti-Semitism was inextricably intertwined with all other social, political and economic aspects of its belief system. So any form of support for the NSDAP, whether finance from big business or electoral support from the Mittelstand, *in practice* reinforced the beliefs and the power of those within the party who saw the 'removal' of the Jews as the precondition for national salvation.

[9] L. Kuper, *Genocide*, Penguin Books 1981, p. 124.

Jews once they had attained power. In a leaflet *signed by the party leadership* and prepared for those taking part in the Nuremberg Rally of 1927, the SA, the SS and the Hitler Youth are warned not to provoke conflicts with their enemies during the festival. The leaflet continues:

> Never forget that our day of reckoning with the Jews will not come about as a result of some laughable single clash, but only when we have the power of the state in our hands to carry out a thorough annihilation (*Vernichtung*) of this international racial parasite (Appendix B).

The Final Solution may indeed have been ordered in 1941, made logistically possible by the annexation of vast depopulated territories in the east, where the process of extermination could be carried out. But there can be no doubt that the intention to annihilate the Jews physically was publicly stated well before the seizure of power; and the problem of interpreting the origins of that genocidal plan must clearly move into an analysis of Nazi anti-Semitism during the years when the NSDAP was struggling to gain power.

Appendix A

Leaflet produced for the Reichstag Election, September 14 1930.
Bayerisches Hauptstaatsarchiv (Rehse Sammlung, F11).

WHAT DO THE CHRISTIAN PRIESTS SAY TO THIS?

In the Protocols of the Elders of Zion is stated approximately as
follows: 'We must demand free marriage between Christians and
Jews. Israel can only profit by this even if it leads to impure blood.
Our sons and our daughters may then marry into the leading
families of Christians. We give money and get influence in return.
The Christian family has no influence upon us, but we can influence
it. That's one thing. The other is that we honour Jewish women and
instead practice our forbidden desires upon the women of our
enemies.

WE HAVE THE MONEY AND EVEN VIRTUE
HAS ITS PRICE!

A Jew should never make a daughter of his people (Volk) into a
whore. If he wishes to sin against the sixth commandment, there are
Christian girls enough. Why do you think that such pretty Christian
girls are employed in the shops? Those who don't make themselves
available get no work, and hence no bread! We mustn't begrudge
our young men their pleasure. Go into the big cities and you will see
that they are not slow in seeing the wisdom of all this. The worker
will have to be happy with our cast-off clothes. Make marriage into a
contract rather than a sacrament, and their wives and daughters will
be even more willing in our hands.'

This filthy depraved concept is not only set out in the Protocols of Zion, it is also written down in the Jewish law books and secret teachings. It is not only set down in writing, it lies in the very blood of the Jews and comes into practical effect daily in thousands of cases.

The Jewish racial character has an effect upon the non-Jews similar to that of a rotten apple in a basket full of good apples. The Jews do not become Christian, but the Christians become Jews. The rotten apple cannot be made good. It must be removed so that the good apples are not spoiled. The Jew is 'chosen' to destroy; but the Christian is taught to root out the tree which produces the rotten fruit.

It is not enough to be convinced of the baseness of an existing situation: it must be the highest duty in life to seek for and attain a better state of affairs.

Therefore read the *Völkischer Beobachter*, come to our meetings, fight with us and join the

NATIONAL SOCIALIST GERMAN WORKERS PARTY
VOTE LIST 9.

Appendix B

Leaflet produced by the Propaganda Department of the NSDAP, and printed in Munich, 1927. Bayerisches Hauptstaatsarchiv, (Rehse Sammlung, F8).

The paragraph stating that the Jews will be annihilated when the NSDAP comes to power is repeated word for word in a similar pamphlet produced for Nazi party members taking part in the 1929 Nuremberg Reichsparty-day Celebrations. This leaflet is also signed 'The Party Leadership' and was produced by the Propaganda Department of the NSDAP (Rehse Sammlung, F10).

SA- and SS-MEN!

Are you coming to the Reichsparty-day at Nuremberg on Saturday August 20?

Don't forget that from this moment on you are a representative of our movement in this old German town.

All eyes are on you; the spirit and character of our party will be judged by your behaviour ...

You have opportunities enough for living it up throughout the year. These two days however are service. Service to your movement and service to your people (Volk). That means that you avoid behaving like the Reichsbanner and Red Front people. You should not and must not bawl and shout as they do. You should not and must not get drunk as our opponents do. You should not and must not insult or even pester others as the Reichsbanner and Red Front men do. Rather you should and must win over others to our idea through your behaviour as National Socialists.

Party Comrade! SA and SS man; those of you who come to Nuremberg should not forget that Nuremberg's police are drawn from true-blooded German men, who are simply fulfilling their duty in maintaining public order. Our demonstration should not and must not degenerate into confusion or muddled disorder. On the contrary, it must be

A DEMONSTRATION OF GERMAN DISCIPLINE, GERMAN ORDER, and GERMAN STRUGGLE.

... Above all, avoid any type of affray. Don't forget that during these two days numerous paid agents will be seeking to draw you into some rash move ...

Never forget that our day of reckoning with the Jews will not come about as a result of some laughable single clash, but only when we have the power of the state in our hands to carry out a thorough annihilation (Vernichtung) of this international racial parasite.

... Party Comrade! SA and SS man! You look upon your Fuhrer with pride. See to it that he may look upon you with equal pride. Adolf Hitler wishes this Party-day, through your behaviour, to be a demonstration **of** overwhelming power, which, because of its inner order and discipline, will win over tens of thousands of Germans and lead them into your ranks, so that one day they will become fellow-fighters for that which we are all striving for, and for which so many have already died:

A FREE GERMANY OF SOCIAL JUSTICE INTERNALLY, OF POWER, STRENGTH AND BEAUTY EXTERNALLY.

The Party Leadership.

Bibliography

Archive sources

Bayerisches Hauptstaatsarchiv, München
  Archiv Rehse, Flugblatt Sammlung. F1-14, F42, F47.
  Plakate Sammlung.
Bundesarchiv, Koblenz
  R 43.
  Sammlung Schumacher.
Institut für Zeitgeschichte, München
  MA 743.
  MA 1226 (NSDAP Hauptarchiv).
Zentral Staatsarchiv der DDR, Potsdam
  Alldeutscher Verband, nos 45, 121, 123, 165, 204, 232, 357, 617.
  Nachlass Gebsattel.
  Nachlass Westarp.

Primary sources

(a) Published documents
Proceedings of the Trial of the Major War Criminals before the International Military Tribunal (Nuremberg Trials), vols I-XXII, Nuremberg 1947-9.
Documents in Evidence, vols XXIV-XLII, Nuremberg 1947-9.

(b) Newspapers/periodicals
Berliner Lokalanzeiger
Deutsche Reihe
Der Nationale Sozialist
Niederelbischen Tageblatt
Nordwestdeutsche Handwerks Zeitung
Reichsgesetzblatt
Der Stürmer
Völkischer Beobachter
Volksspieldienst
Wirtschaft und Statistik
Zeitschrift für deutsche Bildung

224 *Bibliography*

Secondary sources

E. Berthold, *Heiliges Brauchtum um die Fahne des Reiches*, Leipzig 1936.

Herbert Böhme, *Gesänge unter der Fahne*, München 1935.

K.D. Bracher, *Die Auflösung der Weimarer Republik*. Stuttgart, Düsseldorf, 2nd ed. 1957.

K.D. Bracher, W. Sauer, G. Schulz, *Die nationalsozialistische Machtergreifung*, Opladen 1960.

A. Brandt, *Meilensteine des Dritten Reiches*, München 1938.

B. Brecht, *Schriften zur Politik und Gesellschaft*, Frankfurt a. Main 1968.

M. Broszat, *Der Staat Hitlers*, München 1969.

A. Bullock, *Hitler, A Study in Tyranny*, London 1964.

H.T. Burden, *The Nuremberg Rallies 1923 – 1939*, New York & London 1967.

K. Burridge, *New Heaven, New Earth*, Oxford 1969.

E. Calic, *Hitler – Breiting Geheimgespräche, 1931*, Frankfurt a. Main 1968.

H.S. Chamberlain, *Die Grundlagen des XIX Jahrhunderts*, München 1932.

E. Czichon, *Wer verhalf Hitler zur Macht?*, Köln 1972.

E. Deuerlein, *Der Aufstieg der NSDAP in Augenzeugenberichten*, Düsseldorf 1968.

O. Dietrich, *With Hitler on the Road to Power*, London 1934.

D. Douglas, 'The Parent Cell, some computer notes on the composition of the first Nazi groups in Munich 1919 – 1921', *Central European History* X, no.1, 1977

D. Eichholtz & K. Gossweiler, 'Noch Einmal, Politik und Wirtschaft 1933 – 1945', *Das Argument* 47, 1968.

W. Fabry, *Mutmassungen über Hitler*, Düsseldorf 1968.

J.C. Fest, *Hitler*, Berlin 1973.

W. Fischer, *Deutsche Wirtschaftspolitik 1918 – 1945*, 3rd ed. Opladen 1968.

C.J. Friedrich, 'Das Wesen totalitärer Herrschaft', *Der Politologe* 20, 1966.

C.J. Friedrich, *Totalitäre Diktatur*, Stuttgart 1958.

E. Fromm, *Die Flucht vor der Freiheit*, Frankfurt a. Main 1966.

H. Gamm, *Der braune Kult*, Hamburg 1962.

T. Geiger, *Arbeiten zur Soziologie*, Neuwied, Berlin 1962.

J. Goebbels, *Vom Kaiserhof zur Reichskanzlei*, Berlin 1934.

K. Gossweiler, R, Kühnl, R. Opitz, *Faschismus: Entstehung und Verhinderung, Texte zur Demokratisierung*, Frankfurt a. Main 1972.

D. Guerin, *Fascism and Big Business*, New York 1939.

R. Heberle, *Landbevölkerung und Nationalsozialismus. Eine soziologische Untersuchung der politischen Willensbildung in Schleswig-Holstein 1918–1932*, Stuttgart 1963.

E. Helfferich, *Ein Leben*, Jever 1964.

A. Hitler, *Mein Kampf*, München 1925.

H.A. Jacobsen & W. Jochmann, *Ausgewählte Dokumente zur Geschichte des Nationalsozialismus*, Bielefeld 1963.

W. Jochmann, *Nationalsozialismus und Revolution. Dokumente*, Frankfurt a. Main 1963.

C. Krohn & D. Stegmann, 'Kleingewerbe und Nationalsozialismus in einer agrarisch-Mittelständischen Region', *Archiv für Sozialgeschichte* 17, 1977.

A. Kruck, *Geschichte des Alldeutschen Verbandes*, Wiesbaden 1954.

R. Kühnl, *Der deutsche Faschismus in Quellen und Dokumenten*, 3rd ed. Köln 1978.

R. Kühnl, *Die deutsche Revolution 1918/1919. Quellen und Dokumente*, Köln 1979.

R. Kühnl, *Faschismustheorien*, Reinbeck bei Hamburg 1979.

R. Kühnl, *Die nationalsozialistische Linke 1925 – 1930*, Meisenheim 1966.

L. Kuper, *Genocide*, Penguin Books 1981.

P. de Lagarde, *Deutsche Schriften*, Göttingen 1892.

J. Langbehn, *Rembrandt als Erzieher*, Leipzig 1900.

V. Lanternari, *The Religions of the Oppressed: a study of modern Messianic cults*, London 1963.

C. Loomis & J. Beegle, 'The spread of Nazism in rural areas', *American Sociological Review* 11, 1946.

G. Lukács, *Die Zerstörung der Vernunft*, Neuwied 1962.

K. Marx, *Early Texts of Karl Marx*, Oxford 1971.

K. Marx, *Economic and Philosophical manuscripts of 1844*, Moscow 1959.

K. Marx, *The Eighteenth Brumaire of Louis Bonaparte*, London 1926.

W. Maser, *Die Frühgeschichte der NSDAP*, Frankfurt a. Main 1965.

F. Meinecke, *Die deutsche Katastrophe*, 2nd ed. Wiesbaden 1946.

P. Merkl, *Political Violence under the Swastika*, Princeton 1975.

H. Mommsen et al., *Industrielles System und politische Entwicklung in der Weimarer Republik*, Düsseldorf 1974.

G. Mosse, *The Crisis of German Ideology*, London 1966.

W.E. Mühlmann et al., *Chiliasmus und Nativismus*, Berlin 1961.

J. Müller, *Ein deutsches Bauerndorf im Umbruch der Zeit*, Wurzburg 1939.

J. Noakes, *The Nazi Party in Lower Saxony 1921 – 1933*, Oxford 1971.

E. Nolte, *Der Faschismus in seiner Epoche*, München 1963.

E. Nolte, *Theorien über Faschismus*, Köln 1967.

D. Orlow, *A History of the Nazi Party 1919 – 1933*, Pittsburgh 1969.

K. Pätzold, *Faschismus, Rassenwahn, Judenverfolgung*, Berlin 1975.

J. Petzold, 'Class und Hitler. Über die Forderung der frühen Nazibewegung durch den Alldeutschen Verband und dessen Einfluss auf die nazistische Ideologie', *Jahrbuch der Geschichte*, Bd 21, 1980 (Akademie der Wissenschaft der DDR).

G. Plechanow, *Über die Rolle der Persönlichkeit in der Geschichte*, Stuttgart 1952.

G. Pridham, *Hitler's Rise to Power: the Nazi movement in Bavaria 1923 – 1933*, London 1973.

N. Poulantzas, *Fascism and Dictatorship*, London 1974.

F. Rausch, *Das Hakenkreuz, sein Sinn and seine Bedeutung*, München 1933.

W. Reich, *Die Massenpsychologie des Faschismus*, Köln 1972.

R. Saage, 'Zum Verhältnis von Nationalsozialismus und Industrie', *Aus Politik und Zeitgeschichte* 25, 1975.

J.P. Sartre, *Anti-Semite and Jew*, New York 1965 (trans.).

K. Schmeer, *Die Regie des Offentlichen Lebens im Dritten Reich*, München 1956.

D. Schoenbaum, *Class and Status in the Third Reich*, Phd Oxford 1964.

D. Schoenbaum, *Die braune Revolution*, Köln 1968.

Gerhard Schumann, *Gedichte und Kantaten*, München 1940.

A. Schweitzer, *Big Business in the Third Reich*, Bloomington 1964.

A. Schweitzer, *Die Nazifizierung des Mittelstandes*, Stuttgart 1970.

D. Stegmann, 'Zum Verhältnis von Grossindustrie und Nationalsozialismus 1930 – 1933', *Archiv für Sozialgeschichte* XIII, 1973.

G. Stoltenberg, *Die politische Stimmungen im Schleswig-Holsteinischen Landvolk, 1918 – 1933*, Düsseldorf 1962.

Y. Talmon, 'The pursuit of the Millennium', *Archives Européennes de Sociologie* 13, 1962.

R. Taylor, *The Word in Stone*, California 1974.

S. Taylor, *Germany 1918 – 1933: revolution, counter-revolution and the rise of Hitler*, London 1983.

S. Taylor, 'Symbol and ritual under National Socialism', *British Journal of Sociology* 32, no.4, 1981.

A. Teut, *Architektur im Dritten Reich*, Frankfurt a. Main 1967.

S.L. Thrupp (ed.), *Millenial Dreams in Action*, New York 1962.

H. Turner (jnr.), *Faschismus und Kapitalismus in Deutschland*, Göttingen 1972.

V. Turner, *The Forest of Symbols*, Ithaca 1967.

A. Tyrrel, *Führer befiehl … Selbstzeugnisse aus der Kampfzeit der NSDAP*, Düsseldorf 1969.

H. Uhlig, *Die Warenhäuser im Dritten Reich*, Köln 1956.

K. Vondung, *Magie und Manipulation: ideologischer Kult und politische Religione des Nationalsozialismus*, Göttingen 1971.

R. Waite, *The Vanguard of Nazism*, Cambridge Mass. 1952.

A. Weber, *Soziale Merkmale der NSDAP Wähler*, Diss. Freiburg 1969.

E. Weymar, *Das Selbstverständnis der Deutschen*, Stuttgart 1961.

H.A. Winkler, 'Der Entbehrliche Stand …', *Archiv für Sozialgeschichte* 17, 1977.

H.A. Winkler, *Mittelstand, Demokratie und Nationalsozialismus. Die politische Entwicklung von Handwerk und Kleinhandel in der Weimarer Republik*, Köln 1972.

P. Worsley, *The Trumpet Shall Sound*, Paladin 1970.

U. Wörtz, *Programmatik und Führerprinzip*, Phd Erlangen-Nürnberg 1966.

J. Wulf, *Theater und Film im Dritten Reich*, Gutersloh 1964.

Index

3 1543 50132 8225

320.533
T246p

DATE DUE

MY 8 '87			

Cressman Library
Cedar Crest College
Allentown, Pa. 18104